NOMEDA & GEDIMINAS URBONAS

DEVICES FOR ACTION

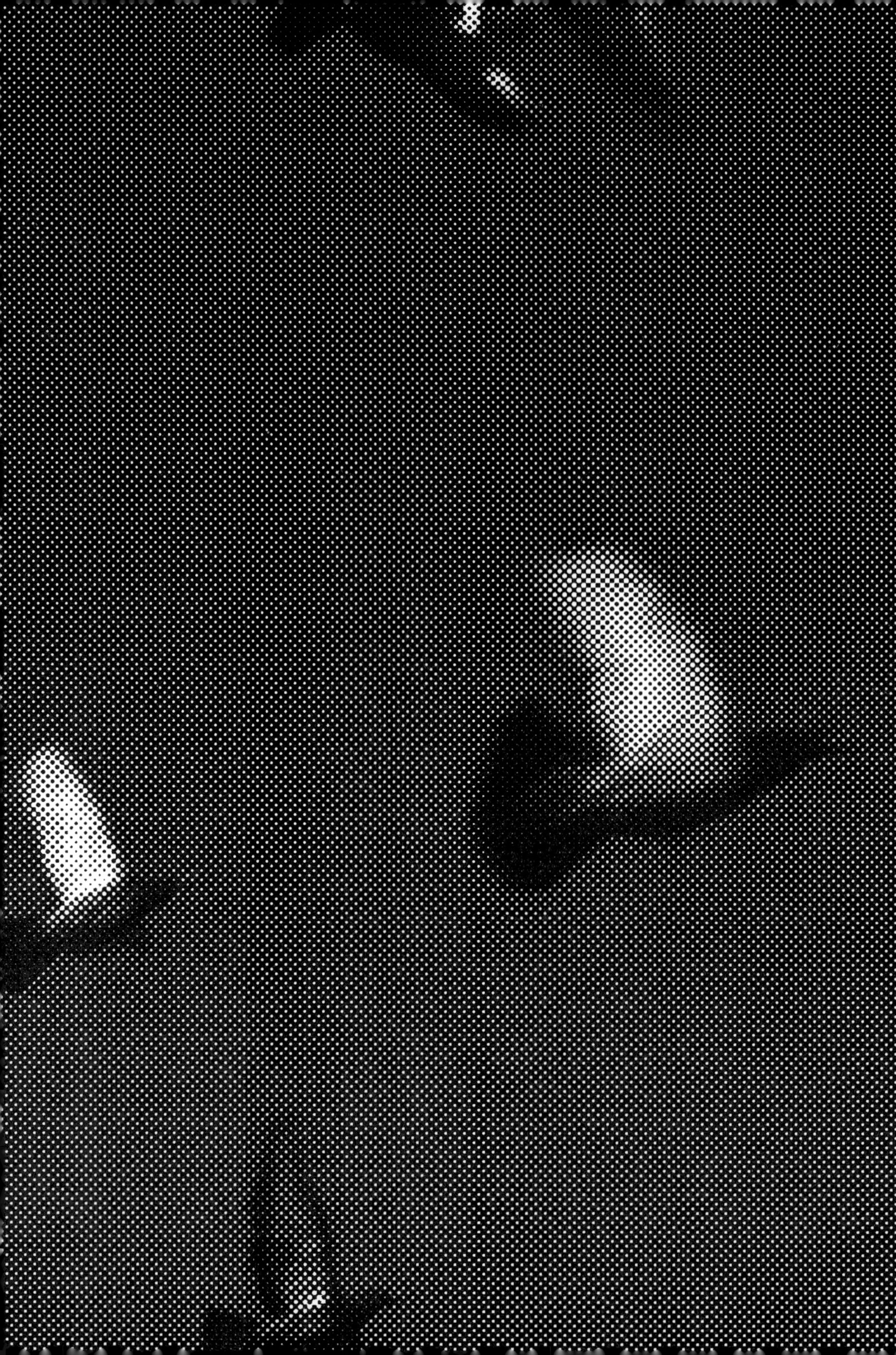

NOMEDA & GEDIMINAS URBONAS

DEVICES FOR ACTION

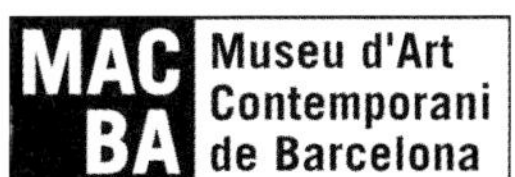

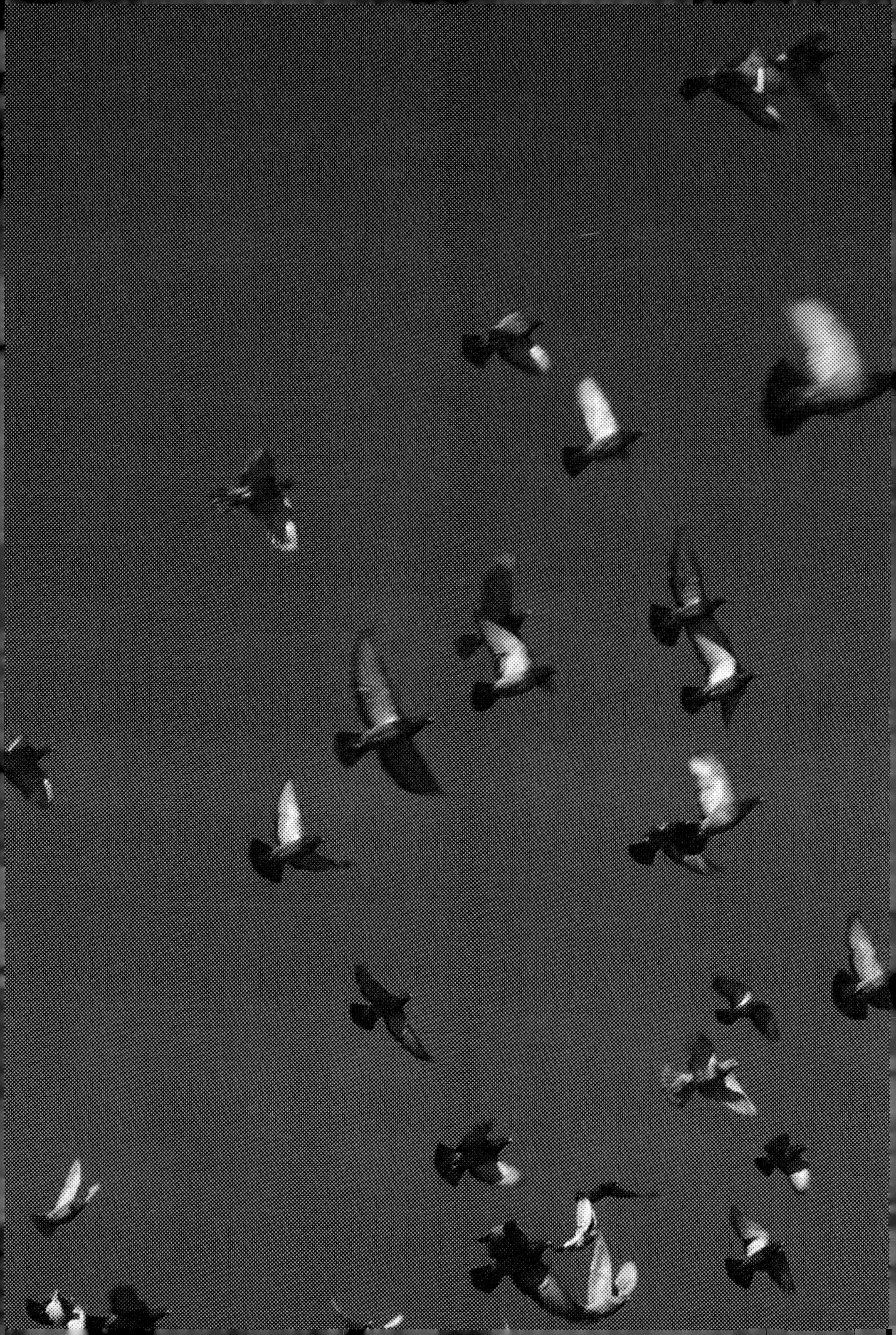

8   **DEVICES FOR ACTION**
Bartomeu Marí

14   **TRANSACTION** (2000-2004)

32   **RUTA REMAKE** (2002-2004)

50   **DRUZBA** (2003 - ongoing)

68   **PRO-TEST LAB** (2005 - ongoing)

86   **VILLA LITUANIA** (2007)

104   **AFTER LENIN, LITTLE FRANKFURT**
Lars Bang Larsen

116   Biography

123   List of works in the exhibition

DEVICES FOR ACTION

The work of Nomeda and Gediminas Urbonas

Bartomeu Marí

The northbound migrations the media have been reporting on an almost daily basis in recent years provide us with an emotional X-ray vision of the world and in particular of our environment. Let's think for a moment about the reasons that push emigrants to make those journeys and about the hopes placed in the change of location: we'll be able to perceive longings and fears that alternate like a growing organism's malable support. The emigrant's journey is no instalment in a science-fiction series, but in some way it's coloured by fictions linked to the mixture of desperation and fascination the other world exercises, however unknown this may be before starting out on the day's run. The dangers of the journey and of the unknown element that threatens the arrival do not manage to curb the impulse that renders the risk of the operation acceptable. In these conditions, the meanders that the thread of life follows beyond the frontier and the shock of the new landscape must be fully compensated for in the mind of the immigrant. And even like this, there are no spatial limits for the misery, poverty and violence of life, since this obeys neither geography nor latitudes.

Let's imagine for a moment what occurs when it's an entire population that suddenly *emigrates* without moving from the spot, because the political, economic, social and symbolic system that has ruled the country for various generations changes, so to speak, overnight. The geography and toponymy will not go on being the same for long. The human landscape will also begin to change. Where emigrants used to start out from, immigrants will begin to arrive. This occurred after 1991 in the Baltic Republic of Lithuania, when it gained independence from the Soviet Union, which had annexed the country in 1940 at the beginning of the Second World War. In the final decade of the last century the populations of the Baltic republics emigrated en masse to another country – or was it to another galaxy, perhaps? The rapid move of the system developed by the Soviet Union to liberalism was seen at the time as a panacea to all the oppression the society had suffered. The keyword was *privatisation.* Afterwards, other keywords would arrive: *European Union, NATO...* And in no time at all: *euro.*

The changeover of political and economic system from the Soviet to the liberal model cannot be represented in a two-dimensional image. The clichés and stereotypes the new values and ambitions of the population (freedom, well-being, abundance, progress) had been associated with have had effects of a very different kind: fascination, uneasiness, ambition, disillusionment, frustration or blind enthusiasm. More than one generation of citizens questions how and what to do. Little by little the epidermis of the cities renews itself, the physical framework of life in common is cleaned up and reconstructed, and the mechanisms by which society had organised itself are gradually altered. The blades of the past/present/future propeller start turning and accelerate to create a centrifugal effect that affects individuals in a very uneven way. A process of decomposition of the past and an emergence of the new has not occurred, but there has been a sudden replacement, instead. For most citizens, then, it has been difficult to assume their potential in a new legislation that grants them rights and responsibilities that were hitherto non-existent. Trauma and conflict with the present and with the past dominated the collective psyche while unknown social, professional and hierarchical relationships were being established.

Nomeda and Gediminas Urbonas have focused their work on grasping and making understandable the layers of meaning in which the psychological effects on society in this voyage-less emigration were lodged. Their methodology echoes the actual position of the figure of the artist within a system of increasingly commercialised exchanges and in opposition to the cross-border homogenisation of aesthetics and discourses.

In the mid-1990s the artists started Jutempus, a self-organised association which served as the basis for the planning of exhibitions and projects outside both the patronage of the government and the market. They have produced projects that involve an intense and painstaking investigation of the reality that surrounds them and of its genealogy, an exquisite visual formalisation that links up with the new popular cultures, and all this with eminently modern methods of presentation and staging. Their ethical position displaces them from the role of being mere producers of objects with aesthetic intent to that of actors who transfigure materials and forms in the service of knowledge and action. Knowledge, in fact, changes both the knowing subject and the known object. The aim of their artistic practice is thus to transform, to alter the poles in relation. Even today, a constant reformulation, according to the characteristics of the context of presentation, continues to nourish their work. Signs and graphics have always accompanied the displaying of the works in installations, and these have been presented in a format of complementary use, very different to ecstatic contemplation. The Urbonas begin their artistic programme where it is deemed that the aesthetic experience is a dimension of our behaviour. Their project as artists transcends the framework of the beautiful and explicitly enters into that of social and political activity, and this *graft* turns out to be effective as rarely before. Because in general any work of art maintains its quality as such in its potential for giving rise to thinking of a political kind. Only on rare occasions does it arrive at the embryo of an action; on most occasions it establishes itself as a commemorative referent or as a mere trace of one.

To view the works of Nomeda and Gediminas Urbonas is to go through an unconscious learning process, without schooling. In this process we obtain factual and symbolic information: about events and about intentions, about data and moral values framed in a given lapse of time. But the hypothesis which explains the Urbonas work as being representative of Lithuanian or ex-Soviet art of some kind has to be contradicted. In their case, working in and from a given social and cultural situation is not equivalent to transmitting signs of identity, as might not be the feelings shared by a given community which at all events defines itself more through relations of economic status than through racial, linguistic, historical or political attributes. Thus, this artistic practice is situated at the heart of a dilemma typical of the early 20th century, which modernism attempted to eradicate, or at least avoid: the association of nationalism with the folkloric expressions of local traditions as against the association of cosmopolitan values with the internationalism promoted by the modern movement. Soviet architecture in Stalin's time at the beginning of the 1930s provides a clear example of this. Identity is immaterial and irrational and does not let itself be contained in institutions or monuments: it lies in gestures and behaviour traits, not in logos or in slogans.

Nomeda and Gediminas Urbonas have devoted their attention to understanding and to rationalising the processes through which society lives a rapid series of changes and the very different facets of life that these affect: not only the political or legal order, not only work relations and information, the market and consumerism, but also moral codes and fears, responsibilities and the words everything is expressed with. Basically, their work has focused on the legibility of such a sudden substitution in the collective psychology of the different generations of a people who, due to the ongoing presence of an absolute police power, was not acquainted with any visible system of expression of discord and dissonance. The absence of mechanisms to limit the old order's capacity for imposing dictates continues in the new political order and tools do not exist for the rationalisation and contestation of the gestures and decisions that affect the practical and symbolic aspects of public life.

The technology the Urbonas use to do their work is very modest. It is practically invisible, but relies on the traditional media and on digital technology. The artists proceed from the format of the archive as an object that is converted into a tool for elucidating the relations between past and present. Careful consideration of gestures and behaviour organises the materials of the archive in such a way that the user can access contents with apparently simple interfaces, be clothing, manual gestures or public demonstrations. Up to a point the computer metaphor of the interface is appropriate to the Urbonas' work. On the one hand, the works are not about the formalist manipulation of any virgin material, a found object, but have to do instead with the ordering of sequences of information and arrangements of signs inspired by functional design. On the other, the activist intention in their works turns them into the instigators of a way of thinking directed towards countering the inertia of the practice of an administration which all too easily confuses the public with the private, and not only in the economic field, but above all on the terrain of values and beliefs. The archive does not obey the logic of collage, nor is it in itself a montage in space. It is in time, at all events: the time the materials contained in the archive refer to and to which the users are project themselves when using them. This is why it's also important to emphasise that the receiver of the work is not a mere spectator, but a user of the work whose benefit is practical, in mental terms, and therefore hermeneutic.

The presentations of projects like *Transaction* (2000-2004), *Ruta Remake* (2002-2004), *Druzba* (2003 – ongoing), *Pro-test Lab* (2005 – ongoing) or *Villa Lituania* (2007), brought together for the first time in an exhibition, reveal the combination of models and positions the Urbonas have organised their work with. In it they have undertaken a prospective investigation into the mechanisms of psychological internalisation by means of film, television and audio archives in order to elaborate these into the organisation of devices of access and use. By means of collaborations with psychiatrists, designers, musicians and other professionals the works become inclusive and participatory structures that have meaning only at the moment of their activation. These are structures which can remain infinitely open, and whose material elements do not prevent them from functioning like devices for action. These five projects respectively touch upon central areas of contemporary society's collective awareness and also provide opportunities to hyperbolically perceive the anaesthetising phenomena that the culturisation of capitalism had subtly introduced. From the aestheticisation of politics to the culturisation of the economy, the century has offered us, and goes on offering, relations counterposed between power and society, State and individual.

As a result of their involvement in the defence of an idea of public space and its material identity in the capital of Lithuania, since the beginning of 2007 the artists have found themselves subject to a civil lawsuit, accused of obstructing the interests of a developer. The social action triggered by the *Pro-test Lab* project paralysed the planned conversion of the Lietuva cinema in Vilnius into a consortium of offices, commercial spaces and apartments by proposing the conservation of the building as part of the historical heritage and denouncing the usurpation of the public space of the square in front of it. The same social action led to a revising of the laws of regional planning (or local city planning) and started the procedure of a new definition of the notion of public space based on the idea of public interest.

The works of Nomeda and Gediminas Urbonas insist on a figure, on a certain role for the artist within society which suffers profound and sudden changes: the artist as observer and analyst who seeks to understand the mechanism of change in order to alert, warn and make the society aware of the components of this change. And beyond that, the work leads to action and the expression of disagreement. Nomeda and Gediminas Urbonas have contributed to creating and enriching a public sphere in which dissent appears as an element necessary to coexistence. When politics seems to have been replaced by the activity and the inertia of political parties, art once again proposes occupying the spaces in which the essence of life in common is based.

TRANSACTION (2000-2004)

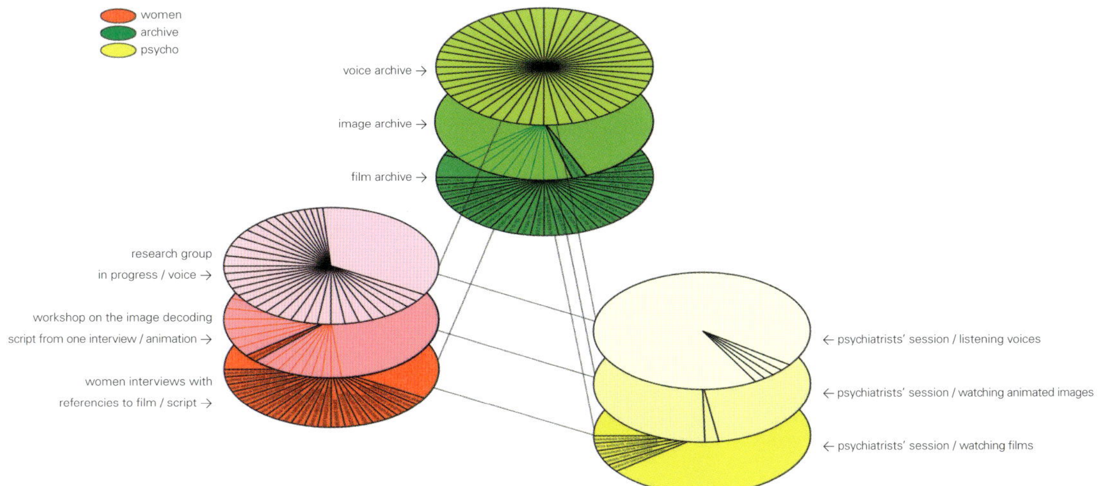

The *Transaction* project grows out of an interest in constructing a model that might describe the process of change in Lithuanian society. Based on the posing of everyday problems, *Transaction* utilises collective memory and situates it in relation to different media so as to deconstruct a script through which to reflect on the state of "transition". The project evolves as a work of construction in which existing narratives are subverted in order to be able to operate in a forward-looking scenario. *Transaction* is the visual prototype of a new cultural institution which links aesthetic experience to the therapeutic activity of psychology and which develops a new object, or objective, for artistic practice.

The strategies used in the research and presentation of the *Transaction* project – especially in relation to social networks, evolutive research and spatio-temporal architectonics – develop out of the artists' earlier projects: tvvv.plotas open-source television and the art projects presented within the framework of Jutempus. Both projects, located in the transitional spaces – one in virtual media space and the other in physical space – that emerged as a result of Lithuania's changing socio-political situation, were used to present initiatives and to analyse this context of transition in opposition to the cultural norms and contemporary art infrastructures that were being officially created at that time. Jutempus and tvvv.plotas share a preoccupation with the social dimension, since they were articulated as collective activities for creating new interest groups and communities, which connected up with each other through chat rooms and email and participated in discussions, seminars and interviews. The interviews and forums for debate, together with the recorded archives, are the main platform of dissemination used by *Transaction*. The projects presented in Jutempus and on tvvv.plotas had an undeniable political dimension, and focused in particular on political opinions that were non-existent in the conventional media and institutional world.

Transaction draws inspiration from an interview with Dr. Raimundas Milasiunas, Head of Psychiatry in Lithuania and Director of the Vilnius Mental Health Centre, in which he states that Lithuania is forever playing the victim's role.[1] Historically, the notion of the "victim" has been a recurrent one in the Lithuanian psyche and has been repeatedly referred to in different media. According to Dr. Milasiunas, Lithuanian society is facing the problem of coping with a new reality; individuals fluctuate between "what no longer is and what is still to come." This unfixed, unpredictable period of transition leads to a general feeling of unease.[2]

The title of *Transaction* alludes to transactional analysis (TA), a method applied in psychiatry, which postulates that life keeps to a "script" that has been developed and fixed in a series of operating rules during early childhood.[3] Psychiatrists treat their patients in order to "make their memories real" and to uncover this script, the aim being to accede to their "programmed beliefs" and to detect the origin of the problems that affect them.

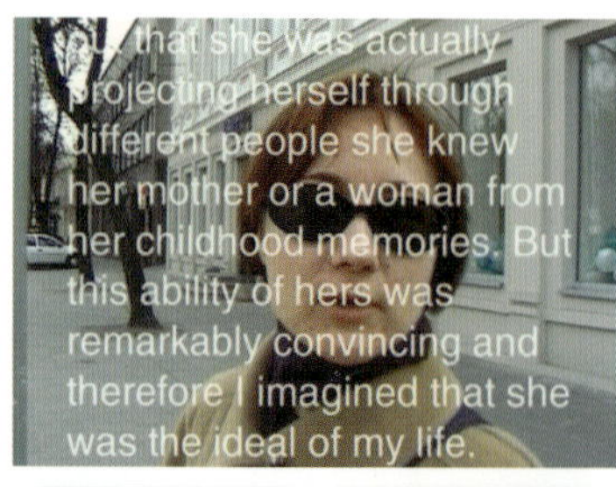

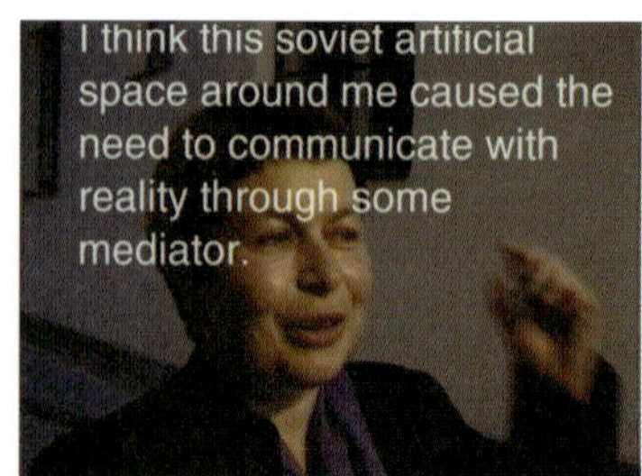

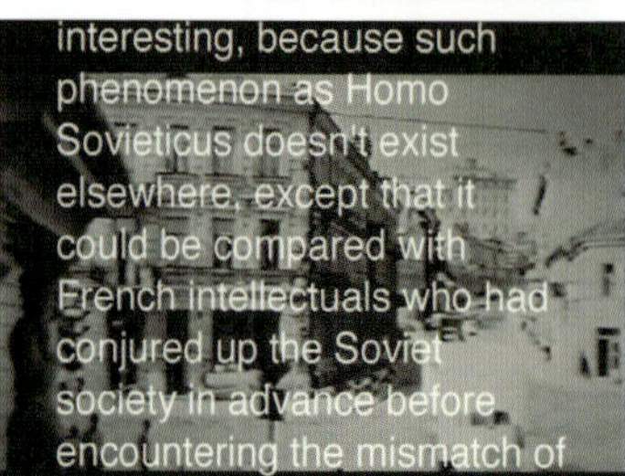

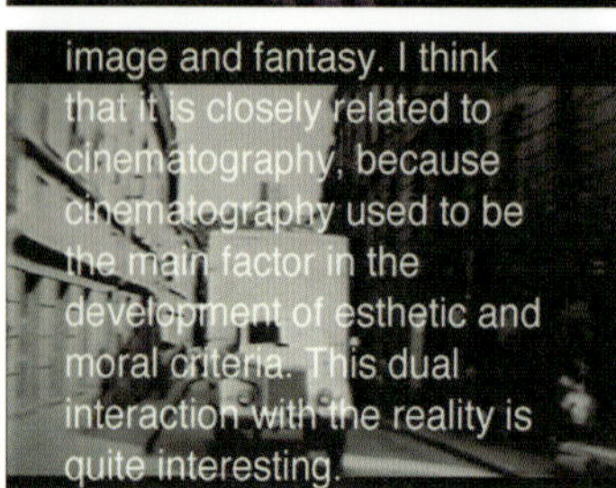

Women in the cinema

Zivile Pipinyte

I think that Lithuanian cinema used to be, and is, very misogynistic. It's by no means a coincidence that one of Zalakevicius's films is called *This World Belongs to Men*. Women play a supplementary role, more often than not often in the background. The first Lithuanian movie, *Maryte*, is about a heroine. It was made according to Soviet ideological standards, about the Soviet Saints – that's what I call this type of movie. In one way or another it displays, in condensed form, the attitude towards women we can find in all Lithuanian movies. Maryte is killed and Maryte sacrifices her life in the name of an abstract motherland and abstract ideals. And this is presented as the only true model, because she has separated herself from everything, from the family and all the other supposedly human values. Generally, in Lithuanian cinema a woman is valued when she is able to deny her own personal ambitions and she sacrifices her life in the name of her children, her husband, and so forth. A woman's life is not valued whenever her personal expression and identity are emphasised. A woman seeking to realise her personal desires is mostly presented as a negative character, an egoist and, most importantly, she ruins men's lives. The ideal woman in Lithuanian cinema is a mother, whose function is to give birth, bring up children, etc. And this is one of the most recurrent images in Lithuanian cinema, as far as I can remember.

On the other hand, there is the girl in the white polka dot dress as a metaphor of perpetual femininity. We can find a lot of Lithuanian movies in which the characters are naive little girls, taking their first steps towards adult life, coming up against the reality of the girl as perpetual victim. In the movie *The Last Day of the Holidays*, which is about initiation into adult life, a girl takes on the role of victim because she can't make independent decisions. And it's very interesting, it seems to me, that in Lithuanian cinema the girl is a model of the ideal woman: a girl who hasn't developed her own feelings or individual attitudes towards things. In other words, the world, which belongs to men, has to shape her according to its laws.

Lola Sutkaitiene

Cinema is generally men's work. The women being depicted at that time were the pictures they (men) saw. I don't know. I think that things are better than they used to be pictured. Those women are in fact able to seduce at a level men are incapable of. That's why I'm so fascinated with those women because they are able to seduce anyone, anytime – be it a Communist or a Fascist or a dissident. And to me that side of women seems one of the most beautiful, something that men don't have. Maybe men create movies about it because they can't manage to do that by themselves.

Dalia Marcinkeviciene

The first unreal and beautiful image of woman was in the movie *Herkus Mantas*, played by Eugenija Pleskyte, one of the two movies I'd seen. Being a child at the time,

We are often called "Homo sovieticus" in the West, labelled as antihuman and antidemocratic. But what are the values carried out by Western men longing for a patriarchal relationships?

In the context of TA, *transaction* is the flow of communication between individuals. The communication that is based on manipulation is called *a game*. Whenever someone plays, they step into one of the three roles programmed in the script: persecutor, rescuer or victim. The diagram used to analyse these games of communication is called *the drama triangle*.[4]

The idea of the drama triangle brings to the project a model of a three-way dialogue in a game format. In the framework of *Transition* the three agents which establish communication and are linked to each of the sides of the drama triangle are women, film and psychiatrists. The model allows no one agent a fixed role; it only traces a diagram of the circulation of the movement produced between them.

Transaction explores the role each one plays in the game, from the victim's position. It focuses in particular on the female scenarios that are socially constructed in relation to the history of misogyny in Lithuania, a country which according to film director Vytautas Zalakevicius has always been "a man's world."[5]

The absence of a female voice in cinema

A group of Lithuanian women academics and intellectuals speak about the cinema produced in the country during the Soviet occupation, in order to decode the habitual role of victim in these films.[6] The women refer to their personal experience of seeing those images and analyse them from a critical standpoint. What they identify in these memories is not the precise form of cinematic syntax but the communicative structures in which we are immersed.

Psychologist Ruta Baciulyte[7] refers to her interest in the absence of female voices and fills this void with a suggestion to meet Dr. Ausrine Marija Pavilioniene, founder of the Women's Studies Centre at Vilnius University. Pavilioniene starts the interview with a personal story in which she relates how her initial interest in English women's literature orientated her research towards the theory of language and feminism, and led her to try and understand the apparatus of repression. The doctor organised meetings with her colleagues to compile a series of interviews and texts that would later become the point of departure for thinking about programmed space. Her initiative had a snowballing effect: various meetings and activities were set up with women activists who, because of their personal experience and their tasks as such, had been able to free themselves of the script assigned to them. All this has created a network of individuals and institutions, disciplines and interdisciplinary experiences, narratives and references in the media, and female scenarios in Lithuanian history and contemporary society.

Zivile Pipinyte is a film critic who researches the script based on the ideology emitted by cinema. This notion is incorporated into the space of investigation and suggests references and trajectories for the characters in Lithuanian cinema. The mapping of the conceptual and mediated space that encapsulates *Transaction* articulates a theoretical visualisation – a model – of communication situated halfway between two realities.

Dr. Victorija Daujotyte bases her theoretical discourse on the idea – which is not without controversy – of the importance of women's experience in oral history (non-imported feminist theories). As an example she alludes to the Lithuanian writer Julija Zemaite,[8] who without knowing about theoretical feminism, managed to frequent New York feminist circles in her trips to the United States during the First World War. Language theory and feminist issues, artificial space and the concept of the victim, scripting techniques and ideology, types of char-

I thought that there were certainly no such women around me. At the beginning of the seventies I used to live in a small provincial town where I saw only fattish, worn-out Soviet women, so I thought that Eugenija Pleskyte had to be the woman who has never existed in Lithuania.

Zivile Pipinyte

Brigitte Bardot used to be every girl's ideal. At the beginning of the 1970s she was the ideal type of woman, a kind of child-woman. We had no opportunity to watch her movies. But there were Czech and Polish magazines full of photos. There was only one movie: *Babette Goes to War*. This shows that, although there was a lack of movies, the Iron Curtain didn't cut us off completely from the rest of the world. In 1968, while listening to The Voice of America, I discovered that the best-selling book was *One Hundred Years of Solitude*. I found it in a Russian translation and read it without leaving the house and going to school. In the morning I said to my mother "I'm going nowhere until I've finished it," so she left me alone. Those who say we were entirely isolated are wrong. Anyone could listen to The Voice of America. So we knew everything, including the movies. Before watching an old movie again I always want to encounter the vision I've created by reading articles about it. Then I realise it now seems totally different; something has changed. It already existed in my memory because I'd conjured it up and screened it in my dreams. But when I see it I'm disappointed because it seems too simple. It's possible to apply this principle to reality, because we used to recreate it for ourselves and to model the environment we lived in through our imagination, so that when all obstacles finally disappeared and everything became available, that new reality turned out to be alien because we anticipated something different. Such filters of reality are very interesting, because a phenomenon such as *homo sovieticus* doesn't exist elsewhere. We could be compared to those French intellectuals who'd conjured up an image of Soviet society and then came up against the mismatch of image and fantasy. I think that this is closely related to cinema, because cinema used to be the main tool in the development of a public aesthetic and of people's moral criteria. This dual interaction with reality is quite interesting.

Interviews With Women About Films, 2000

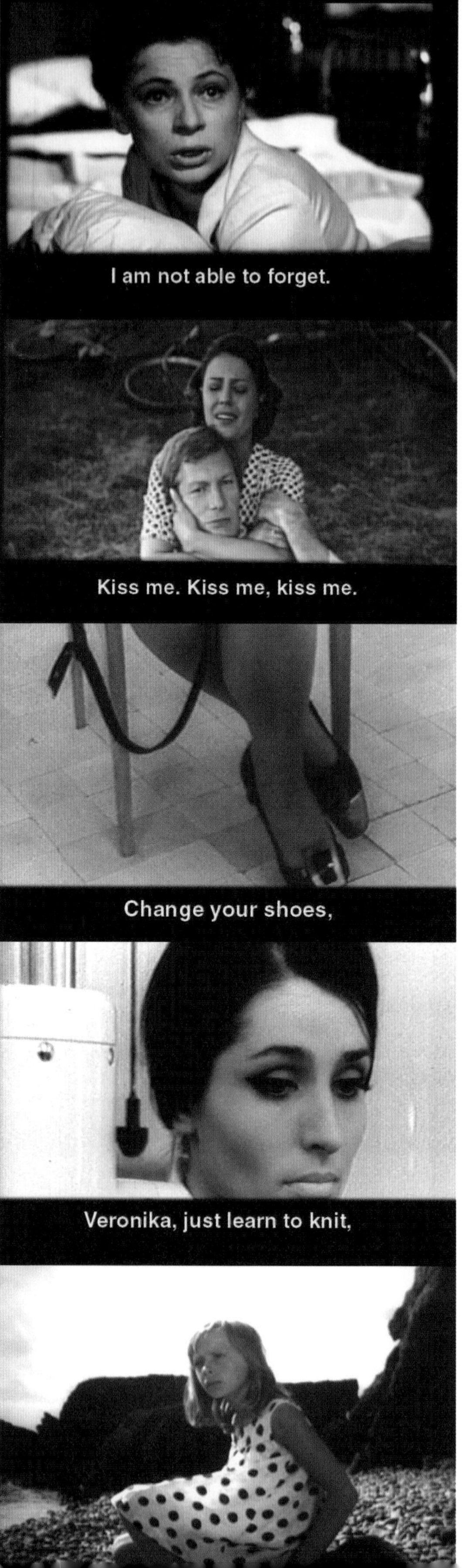

acter whether real or media-generated – all these nodes of the network are involved in transactional processes in which women exchange roles between themselves and other players in the game. The film archive presented in the installation reflects the wide range of issues and critical readings that mention women in the debate.

From past to present

Writers, linguists, experts in semiotics, musicologists, singers and activists join the *Transaction* project in order to investigate women's role in the construction of a "victim scenario". To do this, they try and find the body in the voice and isolate it in a kind of utopian pleasure; they decode the dichotomy between sound and voice, expression and language, *being* and *becoming*. Through media memories they make their way from past to present. The resulting voice archive reveals a social construction with metaphysical qualities, with samples ranging from speeches and storytelling to recitals and songs.

Two of the participants, psychologist Ruta Baciulyte and musicologist and semiotician Ruta Gostautiene, suggested a couple of methods for retrieving the voices. These methods proceed from two simultaneous perspectives. The first evolves from the construction of social and behavioural patterns typical of the mental state of the period of transition. The second channels the discussion on the timbre of the voice in the direction of writing and then on to weaving, in which the concept of a soundscape finally evolves towards a kind of language-garden.

Lithuanian patriarchal tradition has delimited a space for the repression of women's voices, which understands weave forms as writing and song as narration. Ideology first used women's voices as a representation of the motherland and later as an embodiment of commercial consumption. Even today the voice is of vital importance for the articulation of female identity in contemporary society; it is a voice orientated towards reclaiming meanings wrested by patriarchal society and liberal ideology.

The voice archive is understood as a sound project that shapes a psycho-geographical space consisting of samples. The voices of the participants suggest a norm and a logic for a notation of sounds that works as a platform and connects the threads of the voice archive up with lines – and routes – of information. From this it is possible to elucidate the norm that relates voice to language.

The film archive

In order to complement the interviews and discussions about the role of women in the cinema, *Transaction* presents an archive of more than fifty Lithuanian films, mostly dramas, made between 1947 and 1997. With the collaboration of the women interviewees, the *Transaction* archive salvages copies of postwar Lithuanian films which are difficult, if not impossible, to find today. The archive is more singular than exhaustive and constitutes a reflection of the references cited by the interviewees. The public can establish an equally personal, or evolutive, relationship and generate different superimposed layers of script and voice.

Drama is the form of narrative most cultivated in Lithuanian cinema, in which women, reflecting their everyday status, live in a man's world. The films reveal the depersonalised, oppressed role of women in Lithuanian film – as is stated in the interviews – and as such produce a "victim script".

Most of these films were produced under the aegis of Soviet ideology. Lenin's slogan about cinema – "the most important of all the arts" – was followed by Stalin's dictum that "Cinema is illusion, although it imposes its own laws on life."[9] Having lived in a mass culture dominated by a single ideology that programmed the space of *homo sovieticus*, it is difficult to grasp, from a contemporary perspective, what constitutes an authentic cultural experience or condition.

Transaction deals with Aesopian language[10] as a way of speaking and disguising a communication that abounds in allegories, metaphors and double meanings, and leads to a point of no return, often making it impossible to grasp the sense of what someone wishes to communicate. *Transaction* seeks to retrace and open up this insidious mechanism of communication in order to obtain a reaction of our previous identity in a kind of echo of the distorted communication between "image" and "being". By rewinding the tapes, *Transaction* returns to reality and defines the present through meaningful moments of the past.

Session in the hospital

Psychotherapy room, Vilnius Mental Health Centre, 2000.
Ruta Baciulyte: psychotherapist, assistant to the Head of the Mental Health Centre, Vilnius.
Raimundas Milasiunas: Chief Psychiatrist of Lithuania, Head of the Mental Health Centre, Vilnius.
Raimundas Alekna: psychiatrist, Minister of Health.
Dainius Puras: psychiatrist, Dean of the Medical Faculty, Vilnius University.
Eugenijus Sarovas: psychiatrist, Head of the Mental Crisis Centre, Vilnius.

All are members of the Transactional Analysis Association, Lithuania.

R M: Are these male scenarios? I wonder why they think so? All of them stare with such frenzied eyes. Dehumanised. If we can say that these are male scenarios and women are dehumanised, then men are probably humanised. But there are also plenty of male victims.

E S: If we take a closer look, the fear of castration is not solved at all and therefore women should not be here. In fact, if she is present, then she should not have a woman's form.

R M: It is she who de-castrates herself.

E S: That's it.

R M: She's taking back what she doesn't have.

E S: Then men are very brave, when there is no threat. Actually, these are homo-social movies, there's no eroticism as such.

R M: Those women are trying to take back what they don't have, i.e. de-castrate themselves. A sign of equality may be constructed between them and men.

E S: Yes, they are sexless.

R M: That's right. In these movies men have gender, whereas women are sexless.

R B: Then, the question is: are men sexy in these movies?

R M: Well, no, but it is not discussed here. So this is the stage when sex as a term doesn't exist yet.

R B: I think that here men and women are sexless, they don't possess self-identification, because sexuality is born within an interaction. Therefore, without mutual interaction there is no sexuality.

R M: If we speak about relationships, we should speak about relationships between objects, not between genders. I don't remember this film well enough, but in the episode a bull is mounting a cow, it's not people doing it. It means that animals have a soul and certain relations between sexes.

R B: Don't forget that sex didn't exist in the Soviet Union.

R M: No, sex didn't exist, and heroes in films were not interested in sexual matters.

R B: Sexuality was only a prerogative of animals.

R M: The world of instincts. This is fantastic.

R B: Everything in the Soviet era was communicated by using Aesopian allegory, in a very symbolic, indirect way.

D P: Maybe this is a daring comparison, but if we compare the woman with a national symbol, then an impression emerges that she didn't find it unpleasant. Maybe it's not fair to compare the life of the people and the nation. The discussion is still in progress, even life at the political borderline: who can prove that we had a tough time? Even though we experienced suppression, when we were subordinated, tortured physically and spiritually. People still talk about those days as the golden age of Lithuania and take today to be bad because there is no longer an apparatus where we used to be locked and whipped. We were released and given the freedom to do anything. And everyone is angry and unhappy. And everyone returns to the same situation as in the movie, where it turns out to be good, as nothing depends on us, someone else can be blamed. A certain black humour laced with cynicism has developed – as a protection.

R M: Movies aside, speaking about apposite issues – why do we keep recalling the Soviet past and saying how good it used to be then? Here it's appropriate to use a phrase about childish omnipotence: if today I'm not satisfied with what I have, I return to my past – consciously or unconsciously. And there I find I was powerless, I couldn't control that past. Every so often in the spirit of childishness, which we all have, I travel to that Soviet

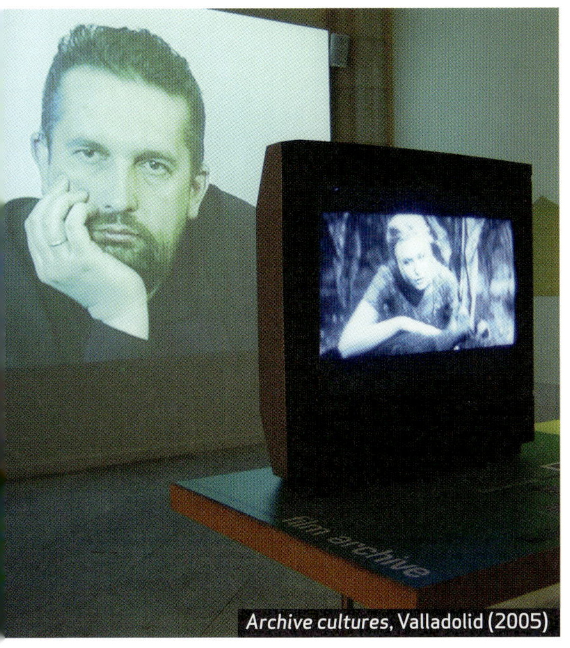

Archive cultures, Valladolid (2005)

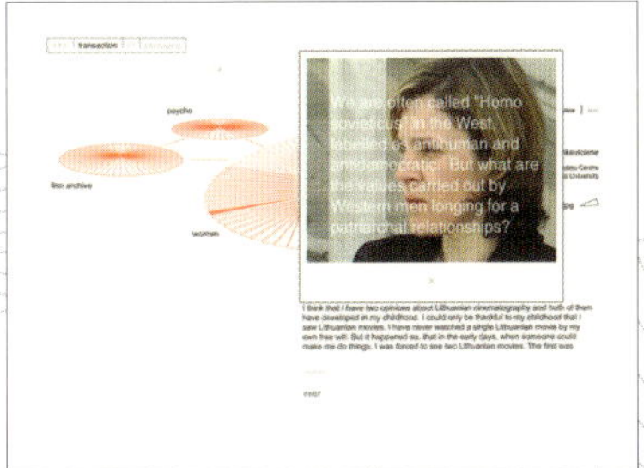

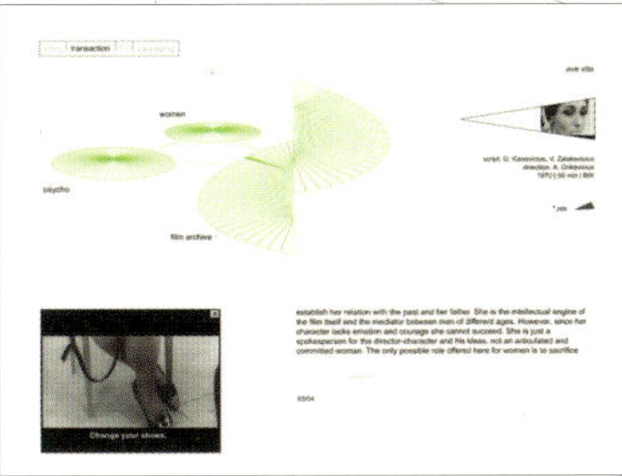

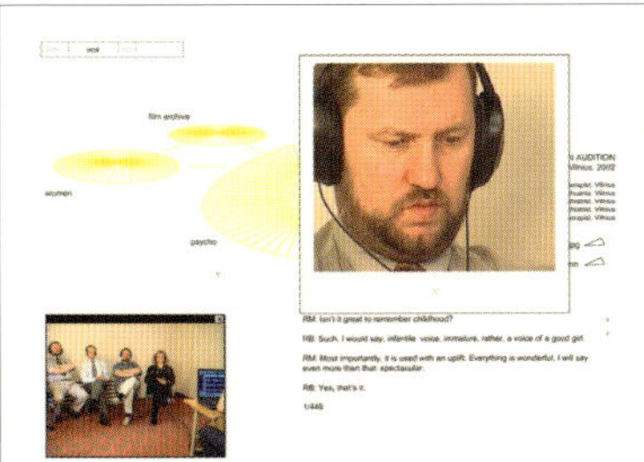

Session with the psychiatrists[11]

Although historical experience demonstrates that psychiatry has been useful in the ideological isolation and organising of voices, the *Transaction* project suggests that this science may be the means of connection between individuals and the collective realm-society.[12]

The psychiatrists viewed a number of sequences from the film archive relating to the previous debate the women had had and they analysed and discussed the role of women in the film excerpts. By defining the function of women in Lithuanian cinema, they went from playing the role of "rescuers" to that of "persecutors" in the drama triangle. There is a game linked to the project that begins by positioning the camera and asking the viewer to choose between the roles of "rescuer" or "persecutor" in relation to the field of psychiatry.

The debate between individuals and institutions, feminists and psychiatrists, furnishes a paradigm for the analysis of a script based on the invisible territory of the transference; in this way it becomes a kind of "revelation" of forgotten memories and voices. *Transaction* offers the audience a mediating space, a library of signs that can be consulted in a dynamic and spontaneous way.

The drama triangle

The web archive of the *Transaction* project is built around notions of the script, staging and representation, rooted in subconscious or repressed constructions. Its interactive functions enable the spectator to archive the material – in a virtual space that reflects the architecture of the drama triangle – with unpredictable elements and a notion of play based on transactional analysis. The structure of the drama triangle is expressed in a scenario in the shape of a spiral staircase which offers a direct route at every step and links to virtual spaces in which characters negotiate their prescribed roles. Here, the interface amplifies the norm, the framework and the technologies that come into play. The model of the drama triangle allows us to analyse the links between scripts and the interaction between the different game characters. The user's movement through the spaces helps elaborate the fabric of the information and the

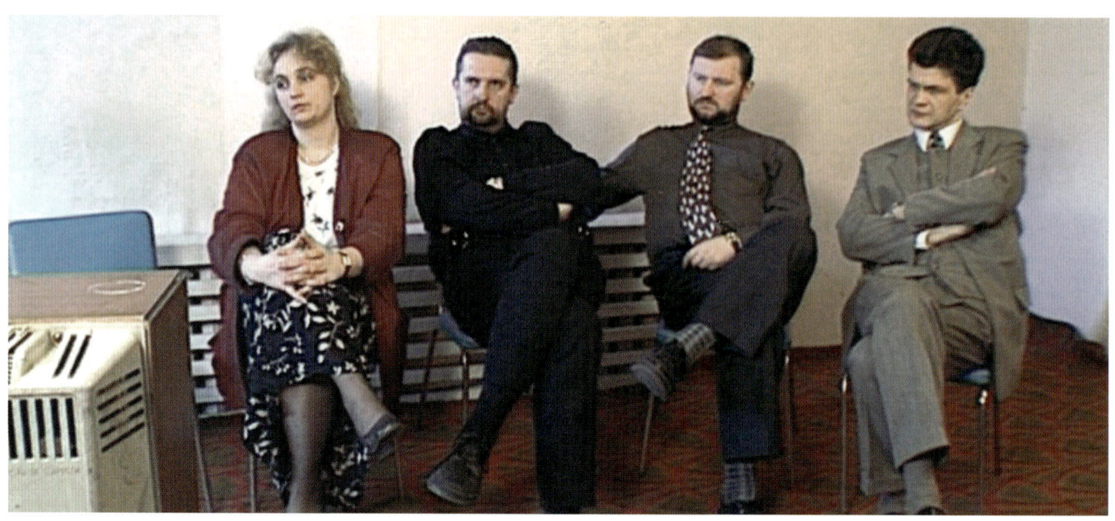

period, to the time of Brezhnev's rule, and diminished freedom, when everything used to be restrained. I cast my mind back to those times and control them, watch the movie and giggle. In those days I couldn't do this, I could only watch, glued to the screen. And now I can giggle a little, with omnipotence, and take control of everything. This gives me satisfaction. Then I can romantically say, "Those were the days, and how good they used to be." And this often leads to arguments and discussions.

D P: It used to be good, because you were chaperoned. Constraint or compulsion is often exercised along with guardianship. In the film she says: "He's a nice guy, he's not hitting me very hard." This was similar to our situation – they didn't suppress us that much, they were quite good. They saved some of us – didn't deport us – maybe we shouldn't be too angry with them.

E S: Lithuanians have a fear of taking responsibility for their own actions. They are dependent. It is easier to consider oneself incapable of being self-reliant, than say, "I am managing this world." This responsibility is an aspect of maturity. The tendency to favour the past will remain as long as there is no responsibility: "We used to feel safer back then..."

R B: How does one meet the expectations of society? Because by saying I want to meet expectations, it means I want to get an award in the broad sense. Now, I don't know why I deserve an award. Before, it used to be clear – now it's not.

R M: Yes, to get an award and avoid punishment.

E S: In a society, everyone is confused when suppression is actualised in daily reality. Reality not only required you to meet parental expectations, it threatened you with deadly punishment.

R B: Let's not forget that Lithuania (with Latvia and Estonia) was considered to be the Soviet Union's "West". We were given a little more liberty than elsewhere. People who lived here were torn between two ideologies: on the one hand, they were forced to assume the Russian-Soviet ideology; on the other hand, they felt somewhat Western and that made the whole situation very complicated. Now we liberated ourselves and we may feel totally independent, Western people, but we are not. There is no ideology nowadays. There is no paternal image, which is difficult to endure. There is also disillusionment about the fact that we are not Westerners, that we aren't developed well enough as a country and nation.

D P: There may also be different kinds of "new ideology". We have suffered from ideologies so much that I'm sick of all ideologies, so that I can say such things as: I spit on ideologies, I'm anti-ideological! I spit on concepts of the state, the citizen. This attitude is perfectly illustrated by what we watch on TV. What it screens is a mockery of everything and is generated from an attitude, which is itself an ideology of preaching that nothing is a "big deal" and that I'm not a citizen of this state. This is the absence of any ideology and at this point the advent of a vacuum.

Psychiatrists' Session, 2000

standard of the work. The positions of subject and object – their syntax – are developed in the procedural dynamics of the transactions.

The spatial construction of the architectural model contains the interviews with the group of women, the film archive and voice archive, plus the psychiatrists' sessions. The interrelations between the different roles evolve in three phases: first the transaction, then the transmutation and finally the *vox*. The archive operates within the script and, conjointly with the latter, like an itinerary through a diagram, follows the shape and outline of a victim scenario.

Itinerancy

Designed as a work in progress that can be installed in different physical and psycho-geographical settings and operate in an evolutive manner, the *Transaction* project has been exhibited in some fifteen institutions over a six-year period.

Each installation has been specifically designed for the location and in relation to the institutional architecture in which it is housed. Some aspects of the project, and of the archives, have been emphasised in different centres in order to reflect local concerns, burning issues at the time of the installation, and the rapid changes in the social situation of Lithuania, including the status of the work and the progress made in artistic research (in that relatively short period of time).

The transformation and adaptation of the work over time is a demonstration of the "networking" strategies that the artists use in their research and likewise reflect the state of their research into new issues, which are gradually incorporated in *Transaction*.

Witte de With, Rotterdam (2000)
Transaction unfolds spatially (and in the exhibition architecture) and takes the form of an enormous box – and interface – that extends through the space of three rooms on the second floor. The box shape was chosen as an interface because it alludes to the archive container and to the meta-language (and the

organisation) utilised by Soviet institutional psychiatry for locking people up. Paradoxically, the box now possesses a new economic meaning – a symbol of consumerism – suspended between product packaging and housing.

In the Witte de With a room was created for the archive of female voices collected by Lithuanian women intellectuals and presented on two monitors with a textual conclusion printed on the sides of the cardboard boxes. The public was invited to compile its own narrative from the archive of personal notes and references printed on the pages hanging from the cardboard structure, which was also able to take on the function of shelving or a table. In the adjacent room two synchronised slide projections were also presented, evocative frame-stills taken from the filming and sequences from the documentary and fiction films that had been cited in the interviews: a monitor, on which scenes from different films were seen, was sited to one side of the big screen with the projection of the session in which the psychiatrists analysed and commented on them. The three sides of the T-shaped space articulate the three-way dialogue of the drama triangle.

haus.0 Künstlerhaus, Stuttgart (2000)
Within the framework of haus.0, the *Transaction* project incorporated the methodology of the institution, participated in it and contributed towards communicating with this political, social and gendered space.

In this instance, the project focused on the articulation of a philosophy of the archive (programme plug-ins) and media resources (production) in relation to artistic practice. The installation formed part of a binary system: its physical presence, on the one hand, and the archive and the conceptual material generated by the collaborators on the project, on the other. Also presented was the archive of Lithuanian cinema with the films cited during the debate on cinema recorded in the installation video, in order to offer the Stuttgart public – and the institution – ample access to Lithuanian culture. The archive was offered as a donation to the Künstlerhaus collection, which has generated the possibility of undertaking educational and comparative studies, and programmes that may be presented in other spaces in future.

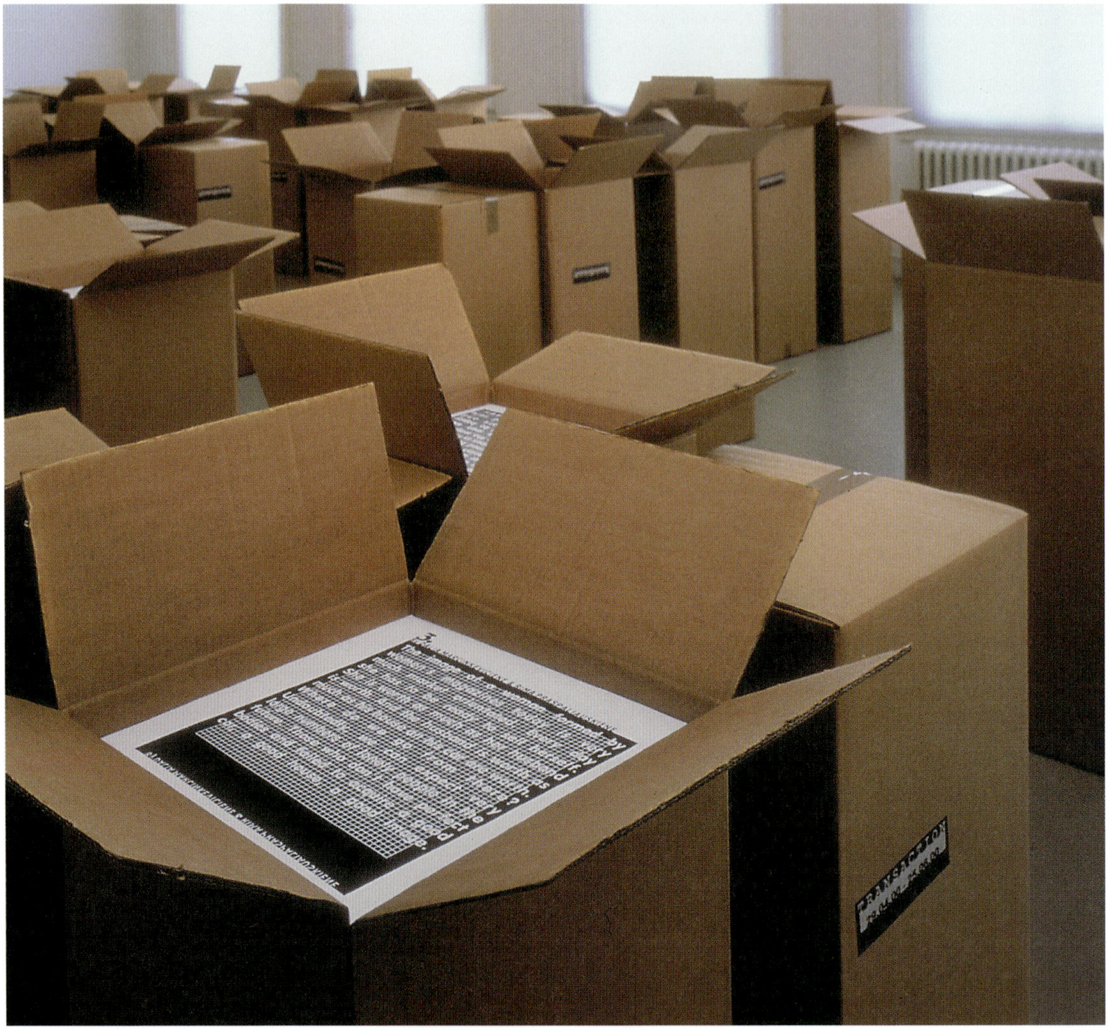

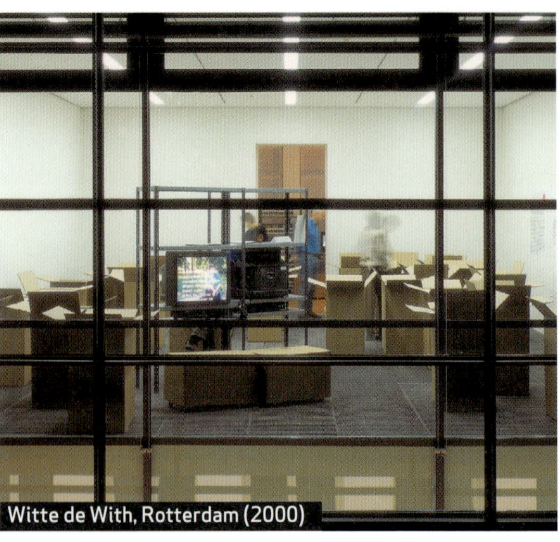

Witte de With, Rotterdam (2000)

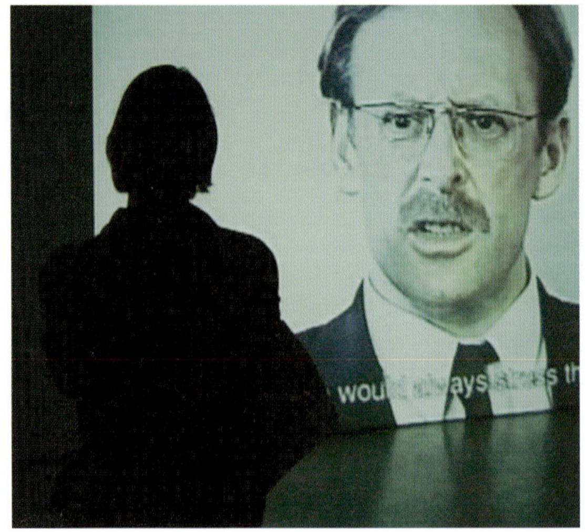

Transaction is an ongoing project in which nation and identity, history and the future are orientated via gendered spatial narratives. It is clear that the three points of the transactional process migrate around the "void" of the current discourses that identify Lithuania since 1989. *Transaction* unites the notions of past and future, conveys a given position with regard to the role of the artist and reflects a set of unequivocally Lithuanian issues relating to East/West discourse from a new strategic position.

Although the basis of the communication is articulated through references to national cinema and memory, it is not dealt with from a nostalgic point of view. In fact, cinema provides a rich interface with the present – comprehensible for the public – and the female interviewees articulate a critical analysis on the role of women in the cinema, the social attitudes that these are obliged to confront and the intervention of Soviet propaganda in their creation.

IASPIS, Stockholm (2001)

At IASPIS, *Transaction* continued to construct a spatial narrative and a platform for analysis on the basis of the cinematic memories present in the archive and in the screening of key sequences from cult movies. The transactional analysis grew out of the installation, the projection material and the activities of the public in the space. The basis of the spatial design and the articulation of the drama triangle were conceived as a result of a debate and a single visual motif. Polka dots, present in the dresses of the young women in the film clips, became a symbol of the innocent girl (female victim) in Lithuanian film. The cotton print also served as a model for the architecture of the exhibition, in which holes were made (and printed on the walls) to create the effect of a camera obscura. And this generated panoptic sightlines, a position similar to that of institutional psychiatry within the work and within Soviet society. The polka dots and holes facilitate the visual transaction and are a way of navigating between the spaces of the project as well as programming them.[13]

Ludwig Museum, Budapest (2002)

At the Ludwig Contemporary Art Museum in Budapest, *Transaction* invited the public to intervene in

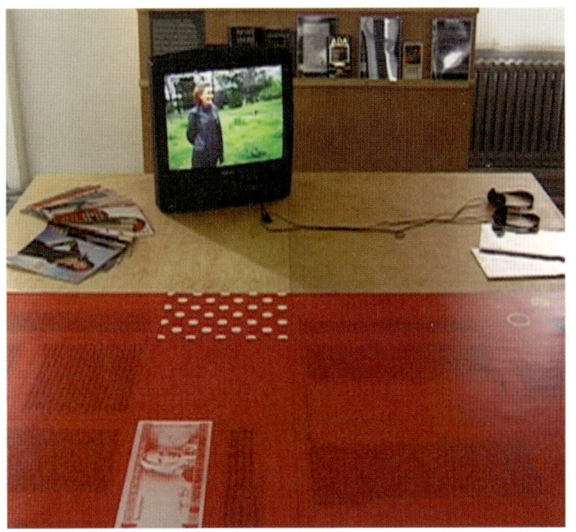

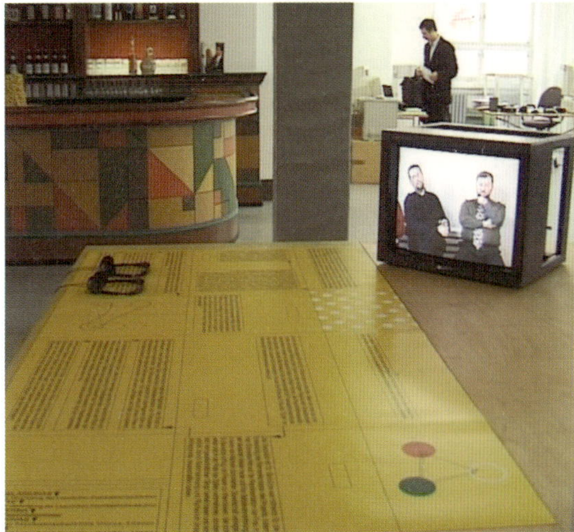

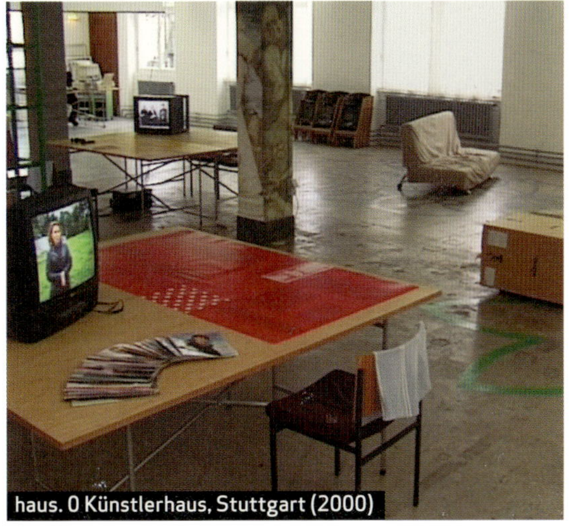
haus. 0 Künstlerhaus, Stuttgart (2000)

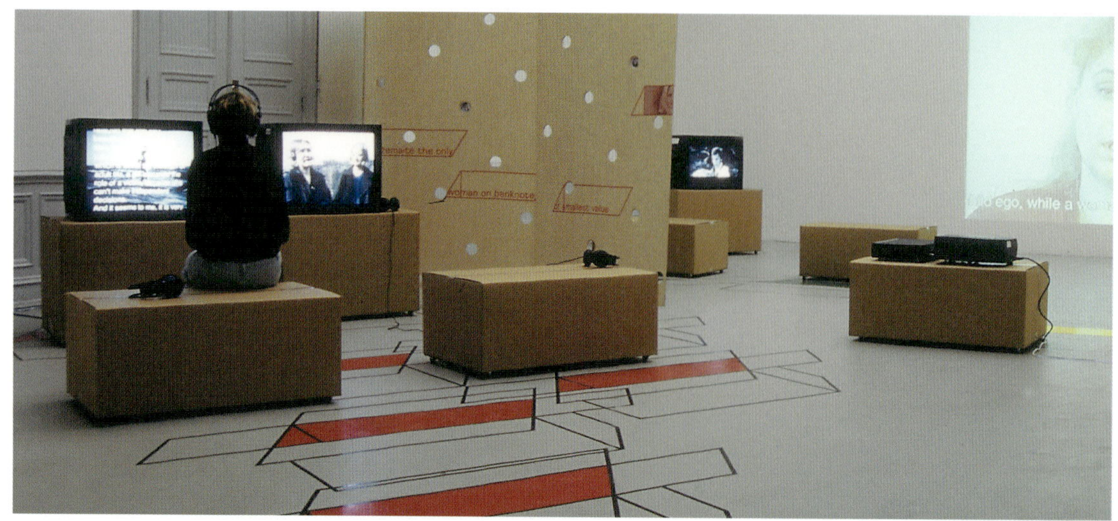

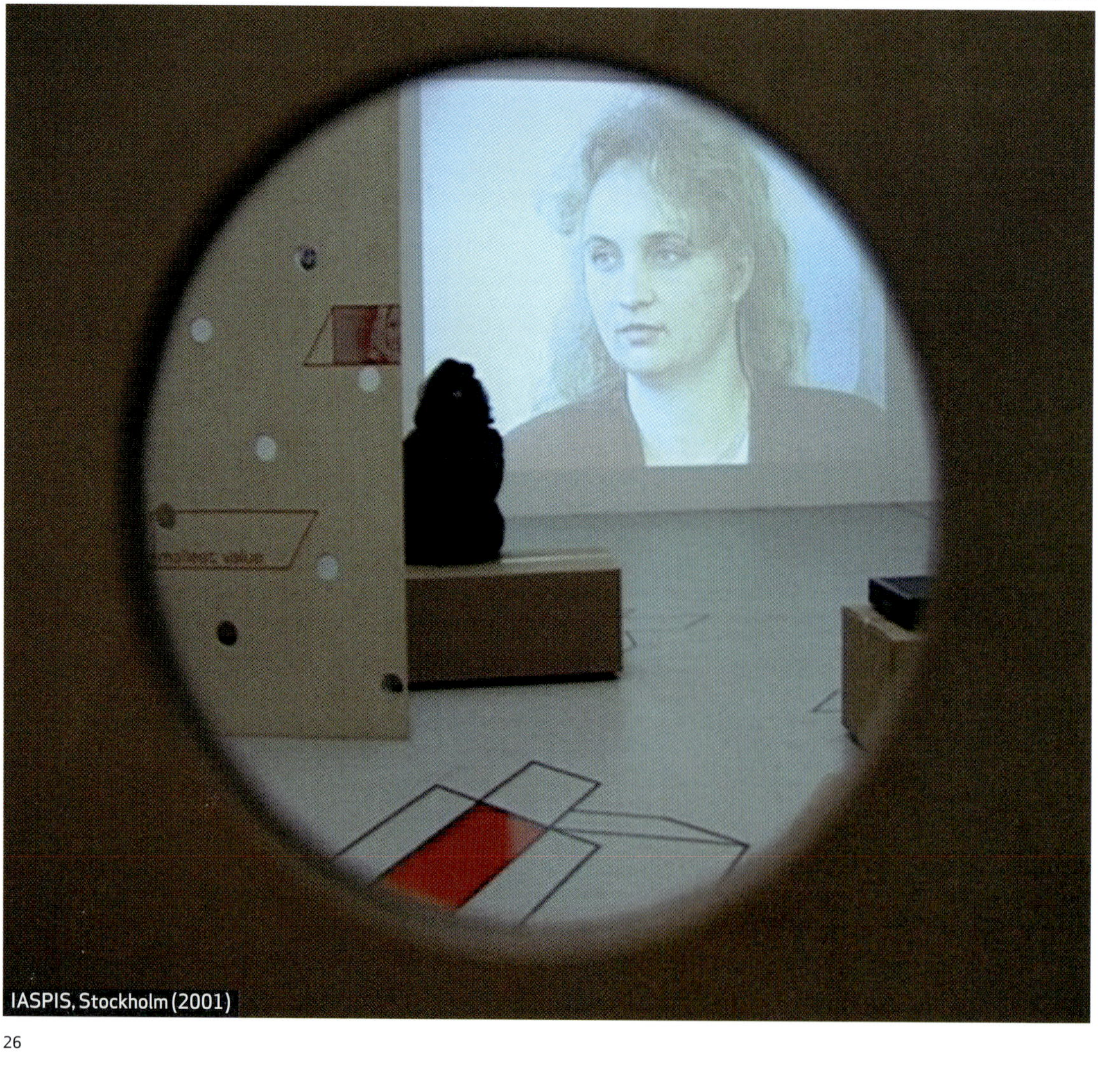

IASPIS, Stockholm (2001)

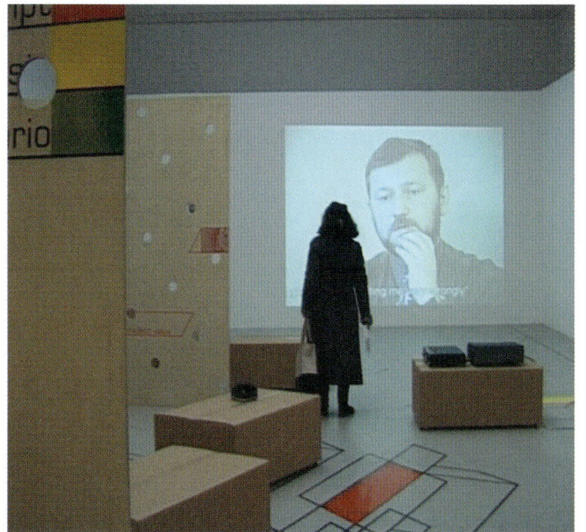

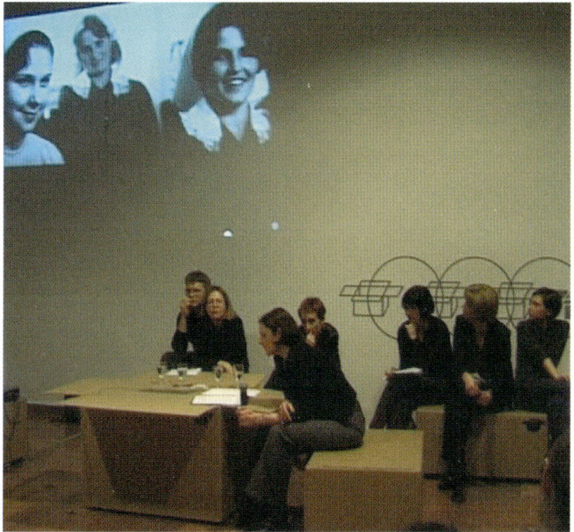

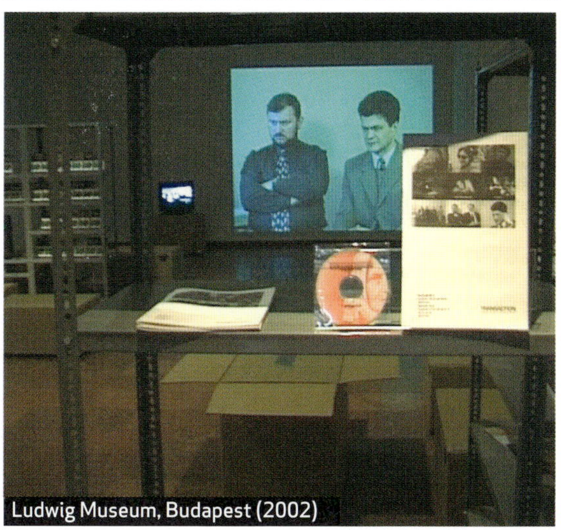
Ludwig Museum, Budapest (2002)

the interactive research methodology of the project and to participate in the drama triangle. During the course of the exhibition a seminar was held in which Lithuanian and Hungarian theoreticians analysed women's social roles, their images in the world of art and media, and other themes relating to sexuality and identity. The discussion focused on the role the media had played in social construction and the creation of artificial models on the basis of Socialist and Soviet Communist ideology. The recording of the symposium became a central point of the installation, with which the spectators interacted as if they were participating in a (therapeutic) psychoanalytical process.

The *Transaction* installation at the Ludwig Museum demonstrated the ability of the new research methodologies to include new materials as well as to relaunch the project by means of active comparison with the host culture. The *Transaction* project in Budapest was characterised by its capacity to generate an exchange with Hungarian culture. Hungarian films were shown along with the Lithuanian ones presented in the archive, and Hungarian books and periodicals were displayed alongside Lithuanian publications in the centre's research library. Moreover, the participants in the seminar (three from each country) offered vivid comparisons of their respective situations and drew historical parallels.

On the wall a diagram of overlapping boxes was drawn, which turned into a unique model for the *Transaction* seminar in Budapest. The talk evolved in a similar way: the participants were grouped by themes, they sat on cardboard boxes and the time of each communication was limited to fifteen minutes. On their computer screen each speaker saw a box with visual material, in such a way that the spectators were able to simultaneously view the illustrations of the theme and a set of images in continuous projection: a visual commentary elaborated with photos, film clips and magazine covers. During the seminar there was no moderator; everyone relied on the free circulation of ideas and, after giving their presentations, each participant would simply introduce the next speaker.

documenta 11, Kassel (2002)
As part of documenta 11, *Transaction* presented a special performance, a session of djembé, in which two

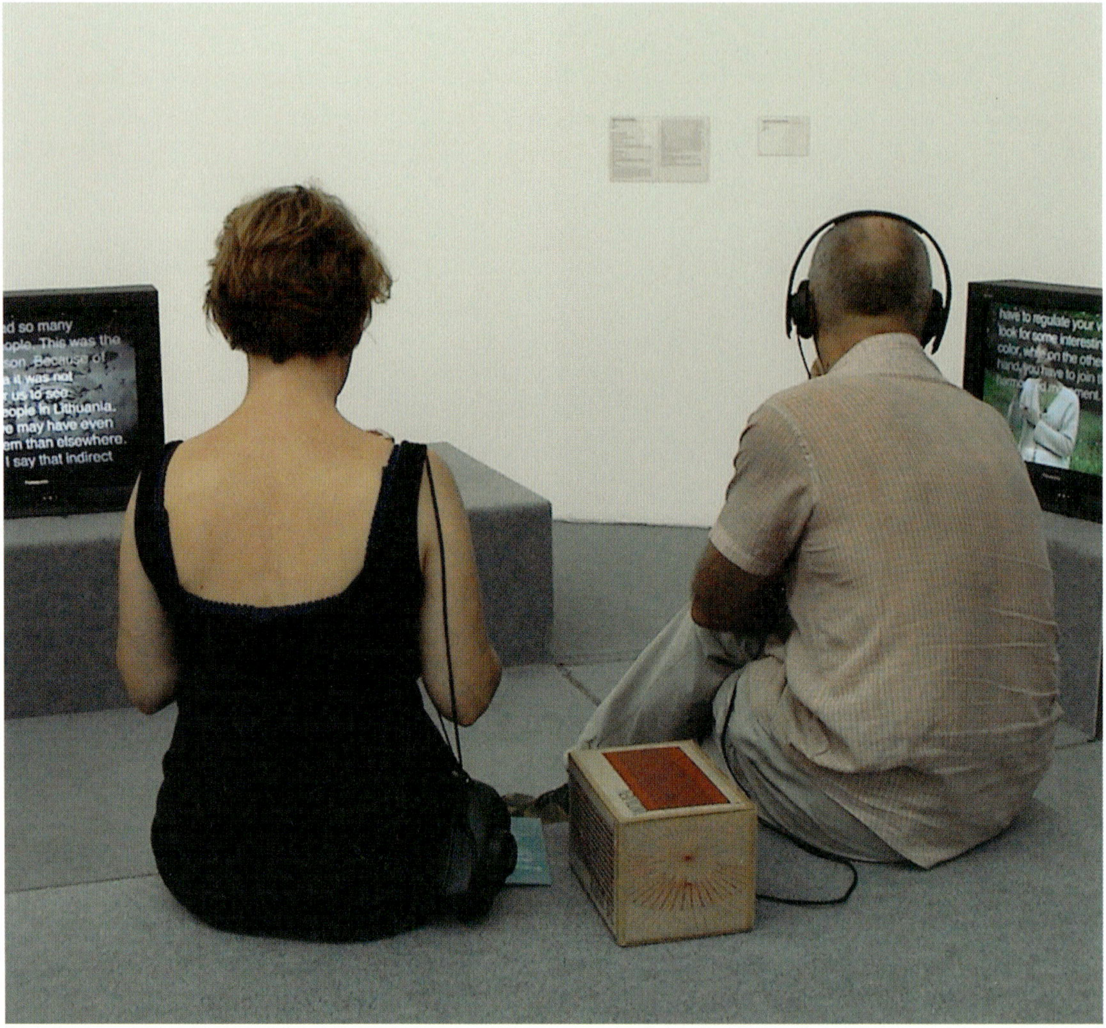

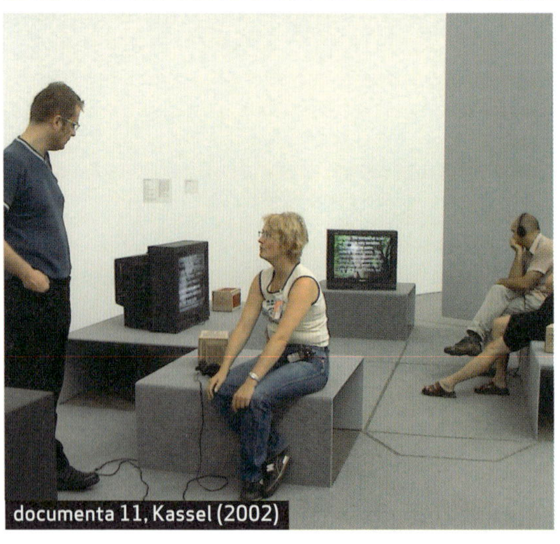

documenta 11, Kassel (2002)

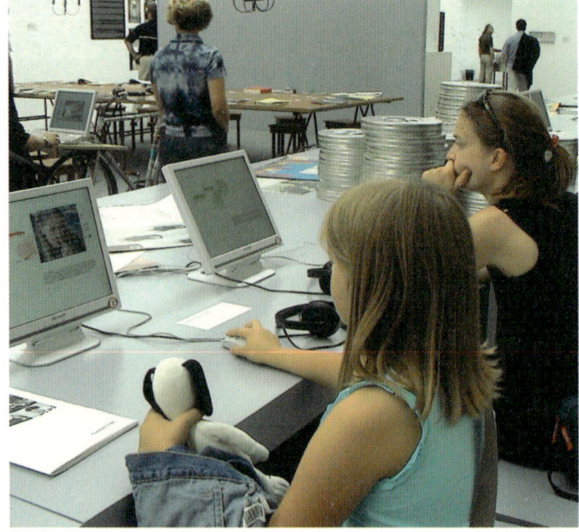

young musicians, Linas Rimsa and Linas Paulauskis, interpreted the archive in their own way. The session was inspired by the utopian vision developed by Lithuanian researcher Kazys Pakstas[14] during the 1930s, in which he proposed relocating Lithuania in Africa, away from the meddling of Germany and Russia. Although this idea obviously never became reality it serves as a reference for the sound piece by the Lithuanians composers. The composer Linas Rimsa proposes this poetical schema by reactivating the voice archive through a creative performance in which the djembe performers interacted with it via one of his compositions, which combines voice and drums. The computer keyboard is used as an instrument to navigate through the video samples of the voice archive. By introducing the logic of navigation, the composers invite the audience to join in the session.

NOTES

1. Interview with Dr. Raimundas Milasiunas: "Between socialism and capitalism: in a changing society man feels ill at ease", *Veidas*, (5 February 1998).

2. According to Raimundas Milasiunas, "the role of victim has fallen to some of us in childhood, since we have always had to adapt to others and have never had the possibility of choosing. Later, when having to confront the difficulties of life, we start to behave as victims, because the values that are most important to us have disappeared. Those who opt for the role of victim in childhood can only be at rest in prison or in the morgue. These are dangerous games. There are relatively innocent ones like 'Hit me, too', in which the opponents provoke one another until someone gets hit. Those on the receiving end justify their decision by the conviction of 'being a victim' and so they feel satisfied. In this way they confirm their feeling of being hated, alienated and humiliated. Unlike sporting competitions, in which everyone knows the rules and submits to the control of a referee, these games are characterised by the fact that only one person knows what he wants, and the others don't. These games begin in our bedrooms, homes and shops and end in Parliament. If we live without understanding this, we simply go on repeating stereotypes in order to justify our opinion of the environment, the world and ourselves. Lithuanians like being hit." Ibid.

3. Eric Berne: *The Games People Play*. New York: Grove Press, 1964.

4. The drama triangle is a psychological and social model of human interaction in transactional analysis (TA) first described by Stephen Karpman.

5. *A Man's World* is the title of a series of short stories written by the playwright and director Vytautas Zalakevicius in 1966. The title is not fortuitous, since a masculine energy is evident in his plot lines.

6. In spring 2000 artists Nomeda and Gediminas Urbonas conducted over thirty video interviews with female intellectuals on the possibility of investigating women's histories and role models.

7. Psychologist Ruta Baciulyte is the librarian of the Transactional Analysis Association and assistant to the Head of the Vilnius Mental Health Centre.

8. Julija Zemaite (1843-1928) is a Lithuanian writer, the only woman whose image appeared on a banknote – for one *litas* (0.29 euros), the lowest denomination in Lithuanian paper currency.

9. Dmitri Volkogonov: *Stalin: Triumph and Tragedy*. New York: Grove Weidenfeld, 1991.

10. Aesopian language is a form of communication that conveys an innocent meaning to outsiders but holds a concealed meaning to informed members of a conspiracy or underground movement.

11. From 2000 to 2002 various sessions were organised with members of the Transactional Analysis Association, all of which took place at the Vilnius Mental Health Centre.

12. In the Soviet Union, psychiatry was used for punitive ends. The authorities utilised psychiatric hospitals as prisons in which they could isolate political prisoners from the rest of society, discredit their ideas and destroy them physically and mentally; as such they were considered a form of torture. The official explanation was that "nobody in his right mind would go against Communism and the Soviet government."

13. Norman Klein: *Scripted Spaces: The Chase and the Labyrinth*. Exhibition and workshop in haus.0 Künstlerhaus, Stuttgart, from 25 June to 25 July 1999.

14. Kazys Pakstas (1893-1960) was a well-known Lithuanian geopolitician. Geographer, traveller and public figure, he was known under various designations: minister of propaganda without ministerial rank, the marcher of free Europe, Ulysses, the Lithuanian nomad, a patriotic tornado, the nation's herald, the national apostle, the Lithuanian Cicero, and compared to Lincoln and Von Humboldt. He had a personality not unlike Columbus, forever in search of new spaces. He was a unique character, since he took direct action to protect Lithuania and Central Europe from various threats, without using purely rhetorical means. Among other initiatives, he tried to found a union of Central-European Christian Democrats, as well as a "reserve" homeland called Dausuva, and a Baltic-Scandinavian Confederation. He wanted to relocate Lithuania in Africa because he foresaw the future destiny of his country.

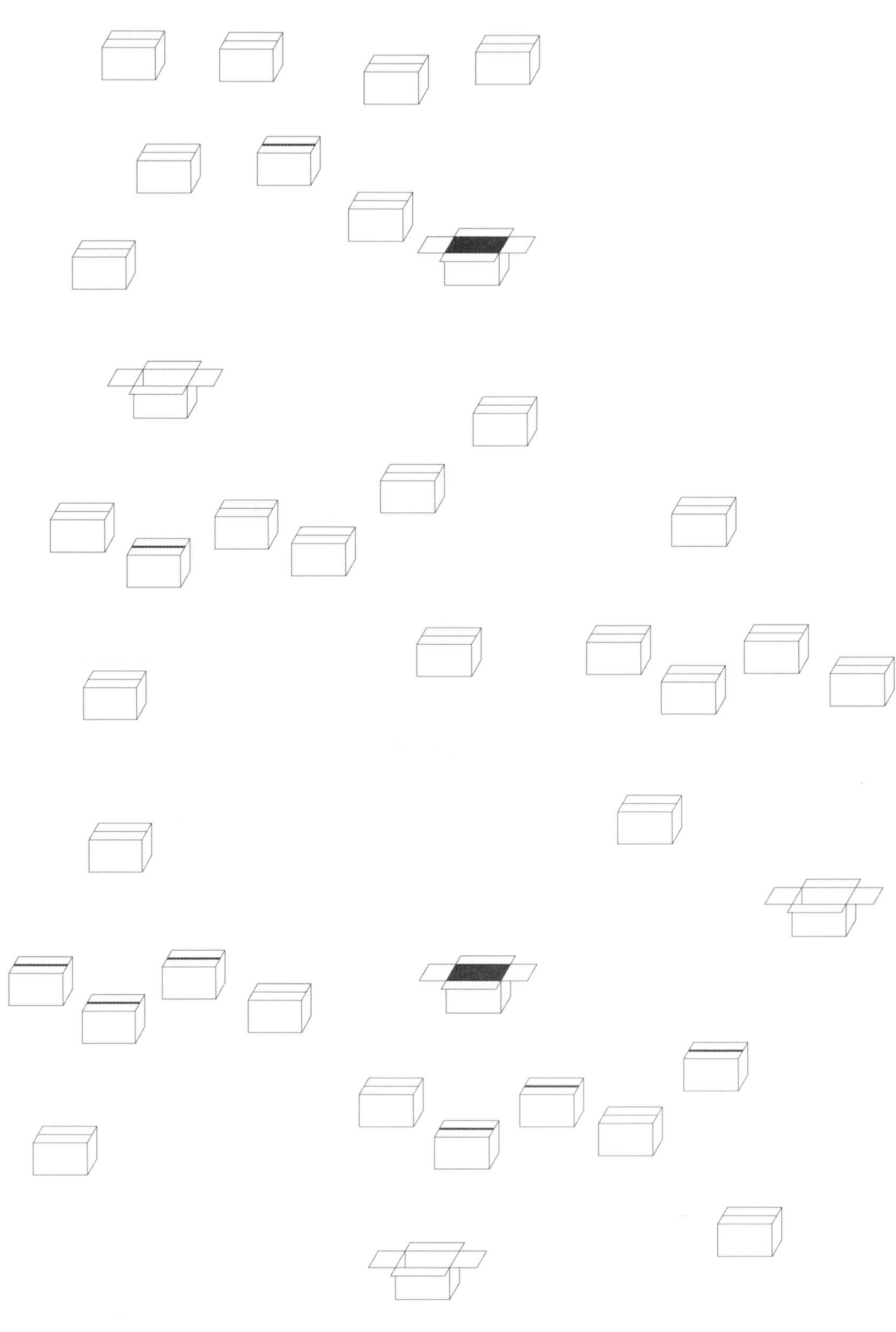

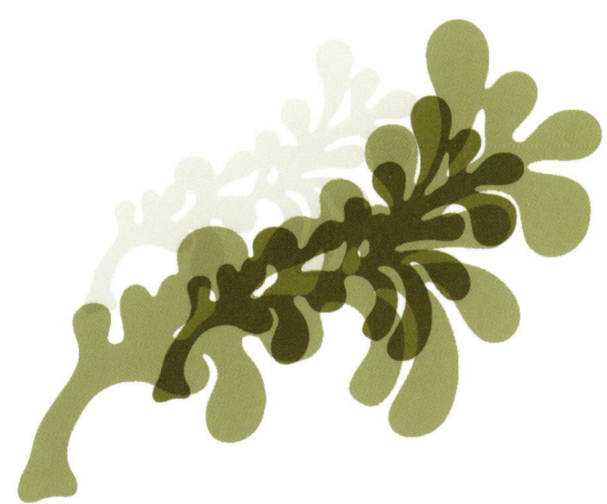

Precedents

Ruta Remake is a project that by its very nature cultivated and developed nodes of meaning. The different levels of the project were incorporated by the artists within the context of the symposium *Shifting Boundaries* at the Royal Academy of Art in Stockholm. This text is a revised and shortened version of the lecture that was given.

Ruta Remake began in 2002 as a corollary of the *Transaction* project, in collaboration with the haus.0 programme at the Künstlerhaus in Stuttgart.

Transaction analysed the notion of the "victim" (as it operates in the psychological method of transactional analysis) in relation to the role of women in cinema and Lithuanian cultural tradition. The project focuses on a traumatic period of change: the move from one system (the Soviet) to another, and structures a triangular dialogue between a collective of women, a group of psychiatrists and an archive of films specially chosen to elucidate this phenomenon and to understand and deconstruct the role of victim. According to one of the participants in the project, the musicologist Ruta Gostautiene, one of the possible interpretations of the concept of victimhood is "the absence of a female voice or voices."

The notion of the "lack of a female voice" became *Ruta Remake*'s starting point and was the driving force for constructing a new analysis and project that might turn this lack into a virtue.

Layers

The work as a whole investigates new modalities of production. Through group work, it intervenes in different areas of communication, and utilises a networking methodology that generates different strata, each of which adds new meanings, associations and experiences.

The interviews recorded on video are an important part of the project, since they situate the investigation in the production of oral history. The references of the interviewees enabled the artists to locate the main sources of communication, which were brought together to create an archive, which was called the *voice archive*.

The voice archive consists of a series of recordings of voice samples and personal memories, and has evolved in line with the technology required for recording and storing the voice. With time, a type of logic typical of machines has developed, which has turned out to be essential for the project.

The contemporary media interface provides a useful tool for navigating through the archive and exploring the recorded voice as a territory situated halfway between the body and language, as a social and metaphysical construction. In fact, the logic of the interface refers to concepts relating to patterning and mixing. The design used as a pattern intervenes in all the phases and levels of the development of the project, and becomes a multidisciplinary paradigm that is revealed in various

The inner voice

Rasa Kalinauskaite

I started to think about the way I feel the voice.
I clearly remember the first time I heard my own
voice recorded. I found it very strange, because it was
a stranger's voice, a stranger's voice on tape. Because
it had a low timbre many people would say it was a
strange voice, I couldn't stand it for quite a long time.
It's curious, but I later realised that I no longer heard
that strangeness – I started to record that voice.

I remember a saying by the German philosopher Gadamer
about how poetry is read: the inner voice that is active
during silent reading is totally different to the one you hear
when reading aloud. It seems to me that my experience,
when I slowly became accustomed to the sound of my own
recorded voice and how it sounds when it is heard by other
people, is the same as Gadamer's description. Perhaps the
recognition of the difference between your inner voice, the
one which is solely yours – that has an audience of one
– and the one which is heard by others, is at the root of
socialisation. That voice becomes an expression of human
socialisation, the distance, which you have to manage. Of
course, you lose your inner voice to a certain extent as you
no longer hear its strangeness. And in the recorded voices,
especially, if you listen to some old recordings you hear
the socialisation as a kind of time buzz, background noise,
because, after all, voices of different epochs and voices of
different people are marked by time.

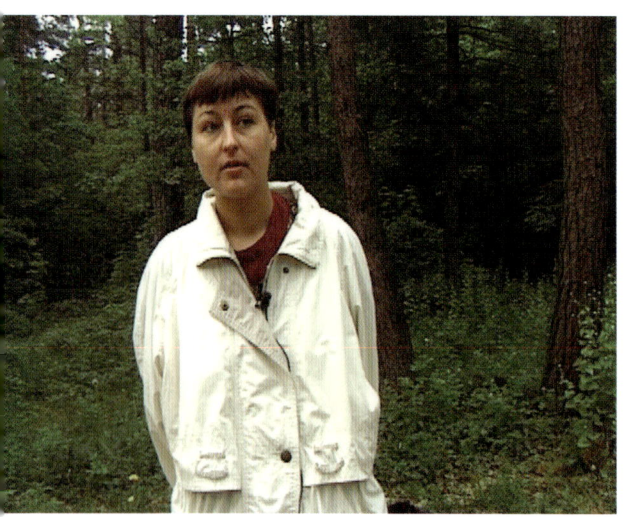

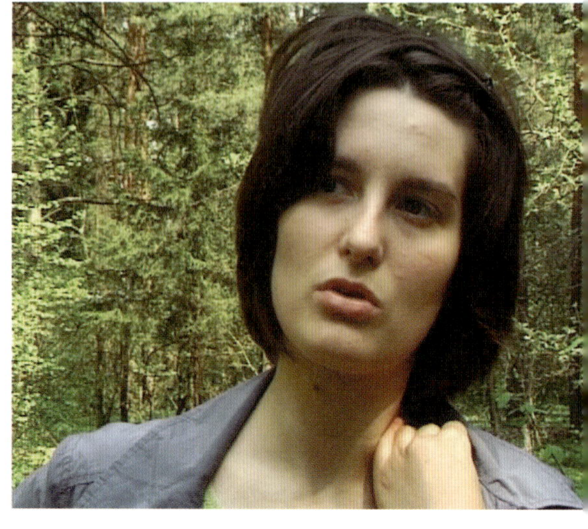

Veronika Janatjeva

That voice is so natural, so elemental, that it seems to
exist outside of consciousness. That metaphysical *I*,
my voice, isn't the one I use when I speak internally,
it doesn't have any characteristics of voice, and it is
perhaps pure thought. But it can exist as a voice – I
heard it once in my life, when I gave birth to my child.
It was the only time that I plainly heard my voice, not
embellished, not transformed in any way. That was a
truly feminine voice, it was so ugly, but so natural.

Viktorija Daujotyte

When a woman performs in public, especially to a kind
of intellectual public, she often starts talking in a
strange voice. She speaks like a woman but her voice
reflects certain, shall we say, typically masculine
tendencies, and she uses masculine content. By
assuming these masculine characteristics, a woman's
voice loses its subtle and organic qualities, which
possess her spiritual nature, and I'd say her primary
qualities. The masculine content, which is not the
product of her thinking, does not stir up, reveal,
or give sound to such inner intentions. It seems
that you hear an external voice, not an inner voice.
Perhaps we hope, or we want to think, that the real
voice of woman should be revealed in sound, timbre,
intonation, even as a rhythm of speaking, which is
deeply supported and inspired by an inner voice, and
an inner speech. Voice is a corpus, it is very closely
related to a body, and it is corporeal. But it is not only

is still slightly important for
pop music of that time. We
remember many of such
works, which address
mother staying somewhere
far away. Other women's
heroes appear. I would
single out two such types,
generalized and having
their own unique subclasses.
One of them is woman angel

areas: the score, graphics, identity and the clothes collection. The mix refers to contemporary forms of sound recording and production, and as a further element in this production, it incorporates an invitation to the public to interact with the archive in real time.

Interviews with Lithuanian women

Shared memories

The project began with a series of interviews with Lithuanian women who work with the voice in different fields. A group of writers, linguists, semioticians, musicologists, singers and activists analyse the voice in relation to the personal memories suggested by the voices recorded and retransmitted by radio and television. In keeping with the philosophy of transactional analysis of the *Transaction* project, the participants in *Ruta Remake* investigated the role of the female voice in the construction of a "victim scenario". Through shared memories they compile material and make their way from past to present.[1]

Oral tradition

The interviews register the participants' opinions through the voice, and record their memories and references. The *habitus* of oral history is registered in the interviews, since voices and memories are transmitted by word of mouth and from generation to generation. The most common form of transmission is storytelling and the reciting of epic poetry – what is known as the oral tradition of a people. History is fundamental to the accounting of women's stories, since generally speaking these "have never been written down, but have remained fixed in the models established by gardening and needlework."[2]

Between speech and writing

The absence of female voices in written history is a social aphasia – a collective loss of discursive function. According to the Russian sociolinguist Roman Jakobson, for whom aphasia and the acquisition of language are mirror images, two basic patterns or mechanisms might be established in relation to disorders of contiguity or similitude. Jakobson identified these disorders in great works of poetry and in the fundamental aspects of language: metonymy and metaphor. The individual use of language is described as a selection of metaphoric (poetic) or paradigmatic units and their combination in a metonymic order (prose).

The French philosopher Jacques Derrida also developed a theory of the voice and language, proposing that in Western metaphysics meaning derives from utterance, that is to say, the word. In his theory, speech is privileged over writing because it guarantees the presence of the subject – the one who speaks. A text is authentic when it refers to the existence of the subject implied by the voice. The feminist and literary theorist Hélène Cixous claims that "women writers are the extension/prolongation of speech," when describing the relationship between women, writing, and speaking. In her essay "The Medusa's Laugh" (1975), Cixous extends the concept of female writing by claiming its proximity to voice and stating that this type of writing should take place in an *intermediary* space, an abstract space that does not cleave to opposing terms:

> "In female writing the text established a strong relationship between voice and maternal voice. Women create a privileged relationship with a voice because they lack a defence mechanism. No woman would call on as many defences against her own libido as a man. Men eliminate the mother, while women do not, or almost never do. Therefore, a woman's writing and language are very powerful, as if her mother were speaking through her."[3]

a body. It is already transformed into something else that can probably be related with spiritual things. Because in speech, in a voice's timbre, intonations, you can hear something that we don't consider to be merely voice physics. Therein, in the space beyond voice physics, voice *metaphysics* start emerging.

Audrone Zukauskaite

Another well-known example of this is the love affair between Narcissus and the nymph Echo. We know that Narcissus becomes fascinated with his own image, while the nymph Echo becomes fascinated with Narcissus and his masculine voice. Her problem is that she cannot say anything about herself; in other words, there is no self-reference, and she can only repeat someone's echo. Supposing Narcissus is a modern subject, who observes himself and in this way constitutes himself, then we may assume that the nymph Echo is a post-modern subject, who exists only in the form of an echo, repeating the other person's voice, and that she can have no other constitution. Now, let's consider why feminist strategies exist, striving to recreate a specific woman's voice. I think this mechanism seems suspicious because from the beginning a mechanism of repression has been operating, that woman's voice has never been represented. It was either identified with specific masculine speech, integrated with patriarchal structures, so to speak, or it was considered a silence, a secret, something mysterious which cannot be put into words. And it is proposed to compensate for this lack by recreating a specific woman's speech. We might ask whether this emancipatory mechanism is reiterating a mechanism of patriarchal domination.

I always find the women's features that are aggrandised by feminists suspicious. Theirs is an emotional, very private, sisterly and patronising manner of speaking. That sincerity is some kind of patriarchal construct. I don't think we need to use compensatory mechanisms. Maybe we should try looking into a specific feminine subject situation, a certain metonymy and ask whether the feminine subject metonymically represents the entire situation of contemporary subject. As Zizek says: "Is not woman more human than man?" In that sense can we ask whether Echo is such a post-modern heroine. Does she represent the contemporary subject? In other words, the subject, which exists only by repeating the voice of the other and is unable to say anything for itself. Isn't the contemporary subject, plainly put, the echo of the voice of the other?

Rasa Kalinauskaite

I work for the radio nowadays and I construct voices by myself. I record them creating a montage, and the main voice, performed by me, is interrupted by several pauses. It seems to me that if we consider the voice as a construct of the modern epoch, it is the voice without pauses. These days people avoid pauses, they fear pauses. Because a voice without pauses is information and the more information it imparts, the more it is supposedly valuable. I think, however, our reaction to the voice principally resists such castration: the most valuable elements are sighs, natural inhalations, exhalations, and some kind of bodily physiology – everything included in pauses. During the sound editing – especially if it's done by someone else, not by me – these pauses are most often removed. You can observe how bits of voice – in this case the tape – are physically cut out. There's a voice which is actually no longer there.

Viktorija Daujotyte

Generally, after all, we will return to the point at which everything starts. How much freedom does a human being have? It's not how much freedom is given, as it is never given enough, but rather it is as much freedom as the human being is able to bear inside.

The more a woman is free, free to think, free to project the world in one way or another, the more she is free to speak. And the more she is free to speak, the more her voice acquires freedom to express herself. And in that sense we may think that this voice is a metonym of a human being, which in the voice a human is very naked… Humanity is naked in the voice.

Interviews With Women About Voice, 2002

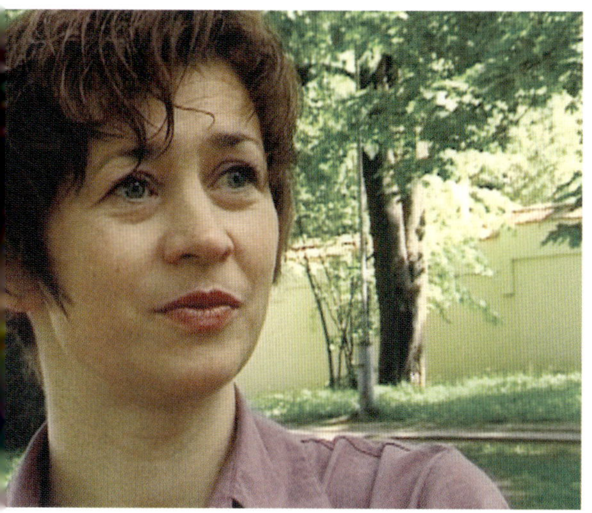

The pleasure of hearing

For psychoanalyst Guy Rosolato the association between the musical and the maternal is established before the subject is born, when the foetus is immersed in the sounds, rhythms and voices of the mother's body. Lacan also typifies the desire to hear as one of the four main sexual drives, and argues that sounds, music and rhythm function as fetishes due to a feeling of plenitude, provoking in the subject the evocation of a past plethoric moment.

Rosolato also argues that the pleasure produced by musical harmony corresponds to the subject's nostalgia for its original fusion with the mother, and that music continually activates the imaginary scenario of separation and reunion between subject and mother. Although the voice involves an oscillation between two poles, body and language, for Rosolato this movement is what leads to the pleasure of hearing.

This complex interaction between body and language provides *Ruta Remake* with a point of departure from which to build the next stratum: the voice archive.

Voice archive

Female archetypes

The voice archive consists of a compilation of audio samples of female voices drawn from the Lithuanian media.[4] This collection of samples, which ranges from speeches to narrations and songs, enables one to reflect on social constructions as well as metaphysical questions. Some prototypical characters appear time and again in the media. For example:

The mother: a worn-out, perpetually tired mother, obliged to shoulder great responsibility and to take care of family and social tasks. She is often (although not always) used as a metaphor for the motherland: Russia or Lithuania. In film and/or song, the maternal voice provides a refuge and evokes the repressive security of home and the homeland, which is governed by a script with patriarchal values, often of religious origin.

The innocent girl: in many films she wears a polka-dot dress and is erected as a symbol of eternal innocence or adolescence. She is often killed or suffers a tragedy, which immortalises her in the pantheon of so-called "Soviet martyrs". This infantilism was promoted by the patronising administrative system and encouraged in the collective imagination, in film as well as in other manifestations such as choral groups.

The siren: she is a fascinating creature, blonde or brunette, although she is never the leading actress. She is a supporting character, who exists on the fringes of the film's main events in which the lead intervenes – always a man. The siren seduces and disturbs the man, who is responsible for the world and the development of society. The image and the voice of the siren get in the way of those who pursue lofty ideals, which necessarily renders their struggle all the harder for them.

The witch: the witch or hysteric is an infrequent role in film or traditional song, possibly due to its critical potential. Her characteristic insanity may provide her with a potentially anarchist position from which to question the authoritarian regime. Paradoxically, this type of character is often depicted as an artist, composer, musician, actress or writer, with a tragic life that prevents her from ascending to the rank of Soviet martyr.

Library of samples

These characters, and their voices, reappear in messages recorded on radio and television. Actors, announcers and public spokespersons (recorded in stadiums, stations and markets) are embodied in women writers and poetesses, folk singers and opera divas, and equally as

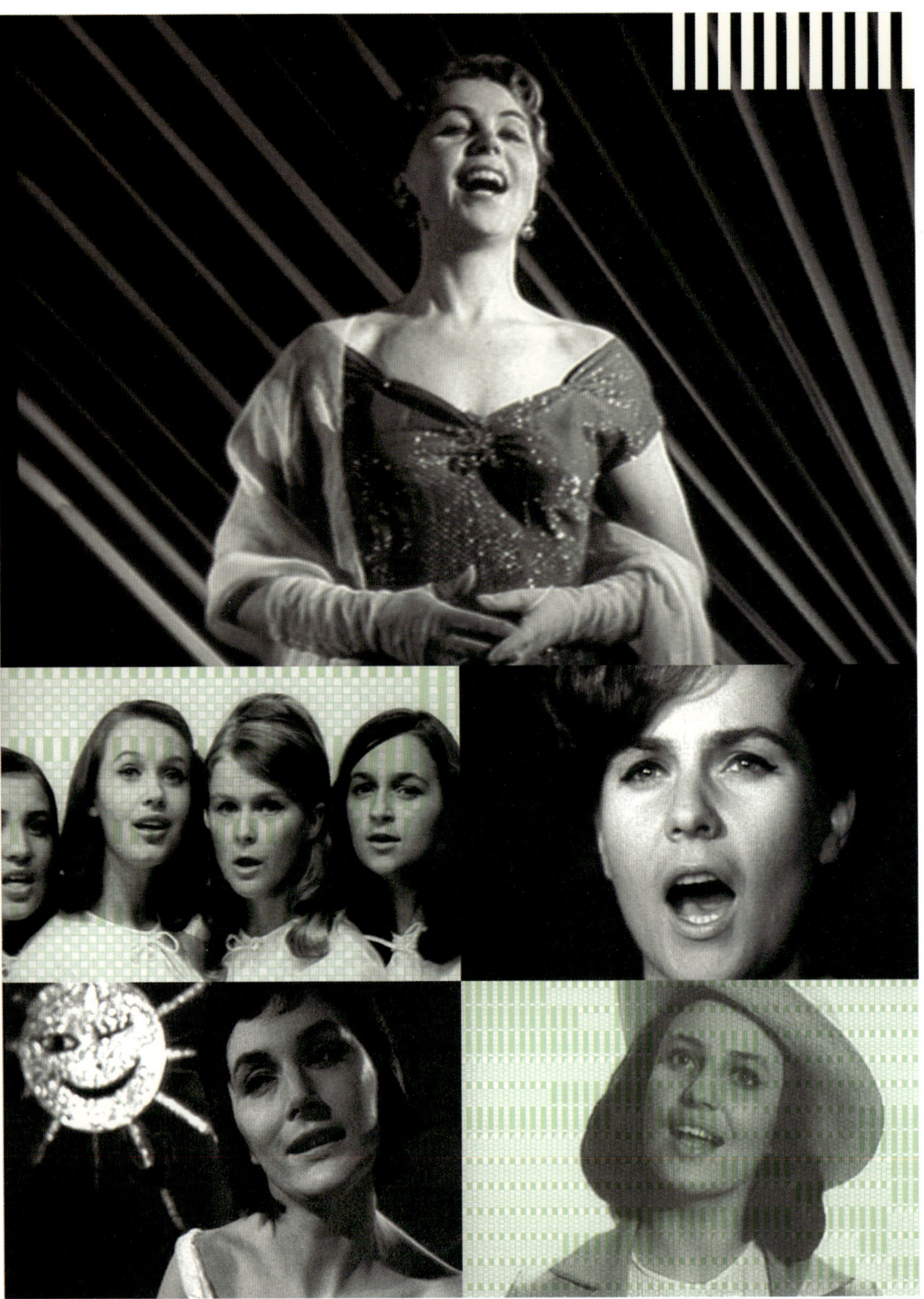

or more important, the pop voices of Soviet *estrada*, the only legitimate genre of popular music.

According to feminist theories, the woman's voice is opposed to dominant power and ideology: within the context of *Ruta Remake* this means Soviet power and ideology (as the samples are taken from that era). The contradiction within this theory is that the voices often express themselves in the name of power and ideology. This dialectical articulation is apparent in the songs and voices that the Soviet state promulgated.

Ruta Remake confronts a similar dialectical contradiction: how to make the voice archive function without repeating historical conditions and positions. To redefine the voices in a strategic, up-to-date and politically conscious way, the project developed specific technical and theoretical interfaces and strategies in order to establish the conditions that would provide for a new deployment of the voices in the future.

A tour through the voice machines

Ruta Remake exploits contemporary industrial science's passion for developing ever more realistic synthesizers and "voice-activated machines" (which shows the interest the voice arouses). According to Giorgio Agamben, each moment is pregnant with potentialities (*abstract* possibilities) that offer an alternative to reality (*practical* possibilities). These potentialities are present but not yet fully active or acknowledged. Reactivating this future potential, associated with the concepts of utopia and technological development, is essential for the politics of hope and is connected to notions of utopia or technological development. Utopian theories are generally considered as being emancipatory and imbued with great visionary potential.[5]

Since Antiquity there have been numerous attempts to imitate human speech and to build voice machines: from the golden mouth of the Oracle to Schlemmer's experiments for the Bauhaus theatre, by way of the "talking heads" of the Middle Ages. They were probably only fancies resulting from the fascination for automata and mechanical toys, although in the 18th century Wolfgang von Kempelen's talking machine

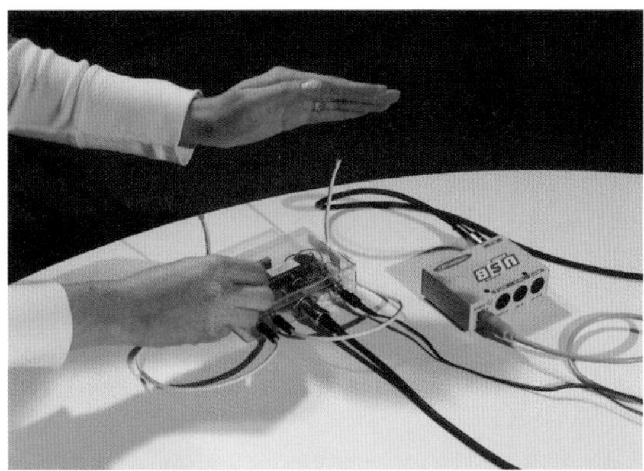

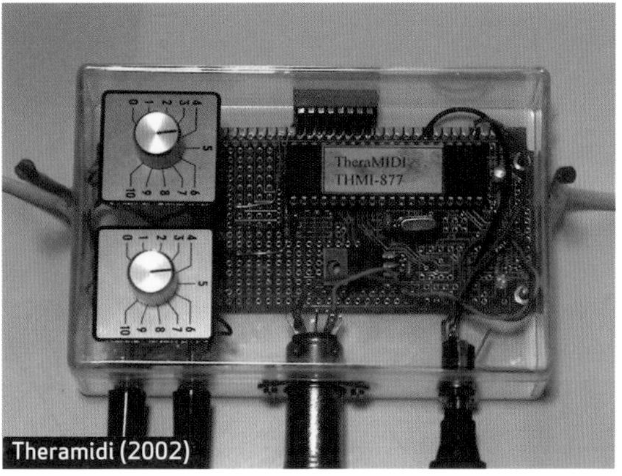

Theramidi (2002)

amounted to a real advance in experimental and mechanical phonetics.

An interest in these kinds of artefacts led the project to the theories of Lev Sergeivitch Termen (Léon Theremin) on the etherphone and the invention of the Thereminvox or Theremin. The Thereminvox is unique in that it requires no physical contact in order to produce music and was, in fact, the first musical instrument conceived without any need for touch. The instrumental box, with two radio antennae around which the performer moves his or her hands, generates sounds similar to the human voice.

These advances, which extend from the invention of voice machines to other visionary attempts, such as those in the field of the EVL electronic voice applied by Friedrich Jürgenson and Konstantin Raudive's speech synthesisers, provide a stimulating point of departure for undertaking research based on the actual logic of machines.

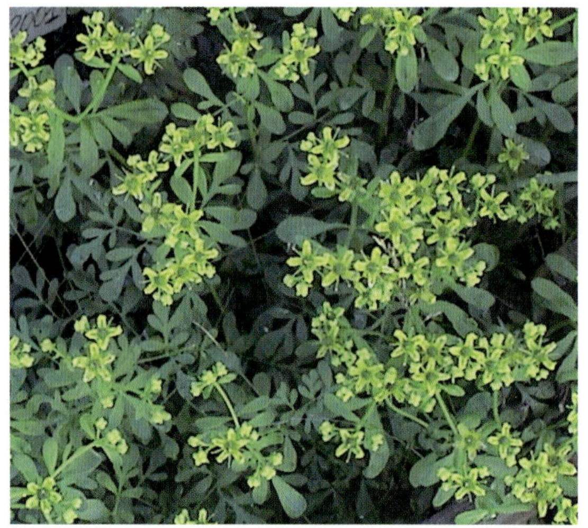

The new media interface

The voice, or *vox*, of the *Ruta Remake* project is produced by using a Theramidi, a digital version of the Thereminvox. It functions with the help of MIDI (Musical Instrument Digital Interface) technology, which creates each musical note and enables the Theramidi and the computer to exchange data and to "communicate" with one another. The Theramidi device is designed so that the user's hand intervenes in the groups of acoustic samples that utilise two light-sensitive sensors linked through a MIDI interface. The movement of the hand upon the light casts shadows, which register the output of data and represent it by following the logic of an inverted film. The hands make the light emerge and mould it; in this way, the hand becomes both an instrument of identification and of notation. Thus, the public dramatises the voice archive in real time and gives rise to a dialogue that ends up as a sound landscape.

The movement of the spectators' hands in space – and their shadow play or virtual puppetry – is a natural consequence of the disembodied attributes of the human voice, suspended between body and language. Just as voices, as ethereal as they might seem, can produce causes and effects, so the shadows interact with the archive to create music and reactivate the scenarios of the film archive.

Apart from the logic typical of the machine connecting the voice archive to the representation of shadows, it

is also necessary to create a translation interface to transform movement into sound. For this reason a *score* is introduced into the project.

A bitter-tasting plant

A pattern or model was developed for *Ruta Remake* in the shape of a modality – or, more abstractly, a set of rules – with which voices or parts of a voice were generated. The pattern was used to structure the interface. The word *Ruta* became a term of reference on three levels: it was simultaneously the title, the name of two of the women interviewed, and the scientific denomination of a plant (rue).

These two participants, psychologist Ruta Baciulyte and musicologist/semiotician Ruta Gostautiene, suggested two methods for reactivating the female voices. The first method has to do with the construction of social and behavioural models that constitute the present mental state of the transition period. The second channels the discussion about the timbre of the voice in the direction of writing and then of weaving.

Ruta

Ruta Baciulyte and Ruta Gostautiene also suggested a specific model called *ruta*, to do with a perennial plant (rue) with a strong, pungent odour and a bitter taste, which is also known as "herb of grace". In Lithuania the word has different meanings coming from the world of gardening, homeopathy and common language, and is a symbol of virginity and femininity – despite its well-known efficacy in inducing abortions.

The weave

Ruta plays an essential role as a word in sound terms, and as a theme in ancient polyphonic folk songs known as *sutartines*.[6] *Sutartines*, compositions based on complex harmonies, were sung by groups of two, three or four women. The layering of two independent melodies is closely linked to the process of weaving or needlework. In weaving, the woof threads seem to sink beneath the surface, to rise back up to it and then to be hidden from view. Likewise, the musical structure of the *sutartines* is woven together in the melody, sung by different voices, and this generates their characteristic polytonality.

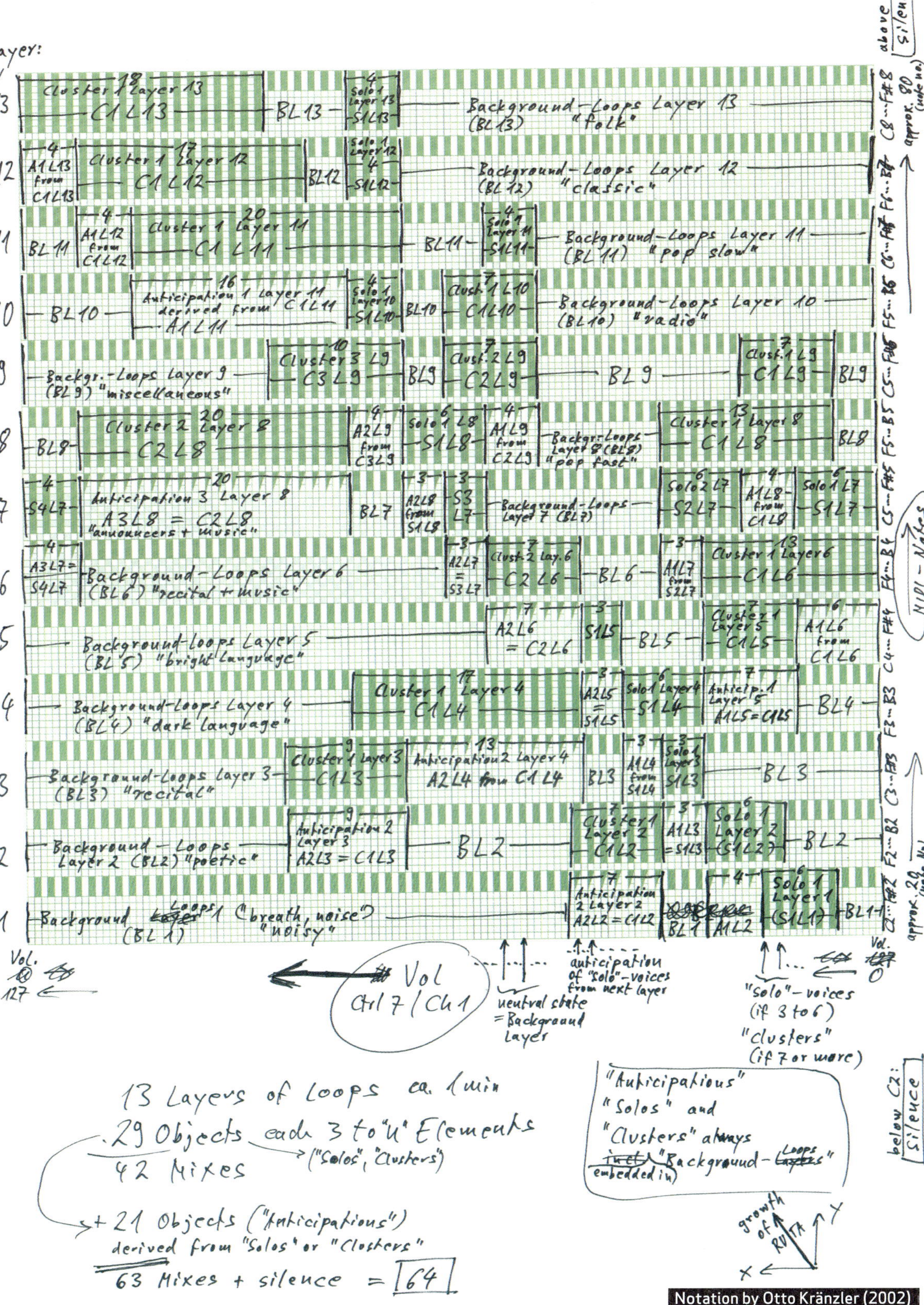

Notation by Otto Kränzler (2002)

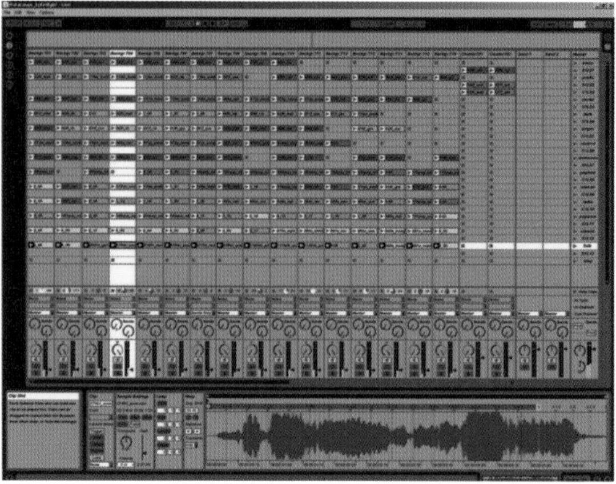

The sign system

The voice archive forms a psycho-geographical terrain consisting of samples. *Ruta* creates a system for the notation of sounds, a shuttle for composing the threads of the voice archive, as routes and lines of information, united by designs and prints that reveal relationships between voice and language

The sound artist Otto Kränzler joined the project in order to perform the *Ruta* design and translate it into this language. Kränzler created a conceptual and technological system for interweaving voice samples into mixes controlled by the Ableton Live music programme. The *Ruta* mixes are conceptually related to John Cage's *Rozart Mix* (for magnetic tape and tape recorders), in which Cage used the logic of the *I Ching* as a long-range organisational device.

Since the weave design involved the image of a plant, 63 sound mixes were selected and arranged so that a movement of the plant would produce what is perceived as an audible process of growth. By means of a dense layering of sounds in thirteen categories, the semantic content is suppressed or cancelled out, thus intensifying the phonetic and onomatopoeic quality. When traversing the "empty" parts of the model, a background texture is perceived.[7]

The theme of "growth" is addressed as a way of condensing and loosening the fabric of sound. In the word *Ruta* we hear echoes of the French *route* (road), the English *root*, and also the German *rute* (rod), another reference to the weaving process. These conceptual associations turn into part of the programme, especially the suggested method of interweaving.

The essential difference with regard to the reproduction of a musical composition is that in this instance the public can interact with the programme in order to intervene personally in the growth of the plant. On the basis of the creation of a sculpture in the air by means of a gesture, the spectator manipulates the medium that emits the sounds.

Remake

As the word *remake* suggests, the work attempts to subvert an existing narrative in order to produce another scenario. It creates a mechanism and a space in which the spectators can perform, play, compose, rewrite and remake the script of the female voices and experiences.

The film sequences of a weaving factory led to the discovery of the ruta pattern in the headscarf the women workers wore. This headscarf, a sort of chador, was a basic part of the uniform in Soviet factories and prisons. The suppression celebrated by the plant is weakened by the digital strategy of the design of *Ruta*, which is generated in the fabric of the curtain.

The role of the curtain

The cloth curtain blocks the natural light from the gallery windows, or indirect light from under the doors, and creates the necessary conditions (darkness) for

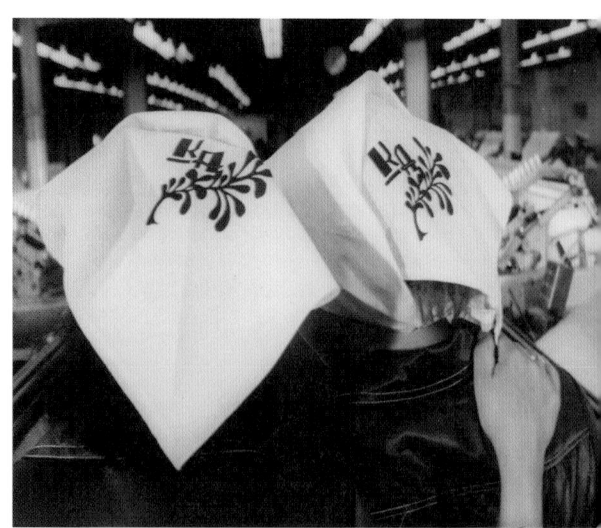

the Theramidi's play of shadows. The curtain assumes a vigilant role towards the machines and the mechanics of the installation, and also towards the space of feminist deconstruction. Its position as an obstacle and framing device situates it as a portal between reality and the world on the other side of the screen.

Symbolically, the curtain occupies the place of the chador – an element of sexual repressive – because by absorbing sound and light, it silences the voice of the woman. However, it also presents the characters of the weaving factory in a positive way and with a new design. And this design is the transactional device that enables the female voices to be remixed.

Fashion

The point of departure for the fashion collection was a discussion with the Lithuanian fashion designer Sandra Straukaite about restrictions on wearing the burka and chador in public in France and Germany. It also proceeds from a Russian media phantasm, the "White Ruta" group, a battalion of snipers from the Baltic, supposedly consisting of women, who played a subversive role in the aftermath of the guerrilla war in Chechnya. Analysing the political norms of East and West, the artists developed the design of a camouflage fabric printed with rues: a reinterpretation of the headscarf discovered in the film sequence in the textile factory.

It began with a limited edition of headscarves, and ended up becoming a collection of unisex clothing made of linen distributed through the *Ruta Remake* online shop.

NOTES
1. Participants: Marija Ausrine Pavilioniene, philologist; Solveiga Daugirdaite, literary critic; Viktorija Daujotyte, philologist; Egle Laumenskaite, sociologist; Laima Kreivyte, art critic; Margarita Jankauskaite, art historian; Rasa Kalinauskaite, journalist; Ruta Gostautiene, musicologist; Veronika Janatjeva, musicologist; Zita Kelmickaite, musicologist; Karina Firkaviciute, musicologist; Audrone Zukauskaite, philosopher; Daiva Sabaseviciene, theatre critic; Daiva Budraityte, musicologist; Daiva Raciunaite, musicologist.
2. Viktorija Daujotyte: "Parasyta moteru" [The History of Lithuanian Women Writers], *Alma littera*, Vilnius, 2001.
3. Hélène Cixous: "Le Rire de la Méduse", *L'Arc*, no. 61 (1975)
4. The compilation is based on references made by Lithuanian women intellectuals and producers during the interviews.
5. Giorgio Agamben: *Il linguaggio e la morte: Un seminario sul luogo della negatività*. Turin: Giulio Einuadi, 1982. English translation: Giorgio Agamben, Karen Pinkus and Michael Hardt: *Language and Death: The Place of Negativity (Theory and History of Literature)*. Minneapolis: University of Minnesota Press, 2006.
6. The word *sutartines* derives from the verb *sutarti*: to be in agreement or to concur with another person. Dr. Daiva Seskauskaite: "Rutos Vaizdinys sutartinese", *Liaudies Kultura*, no. 5 (2000), pp. 49-51.
7. The musicians and producers Jens Neumaier and Maik Alemany from the Maik Maier studios in Barcelona perform this version at the MACBA.

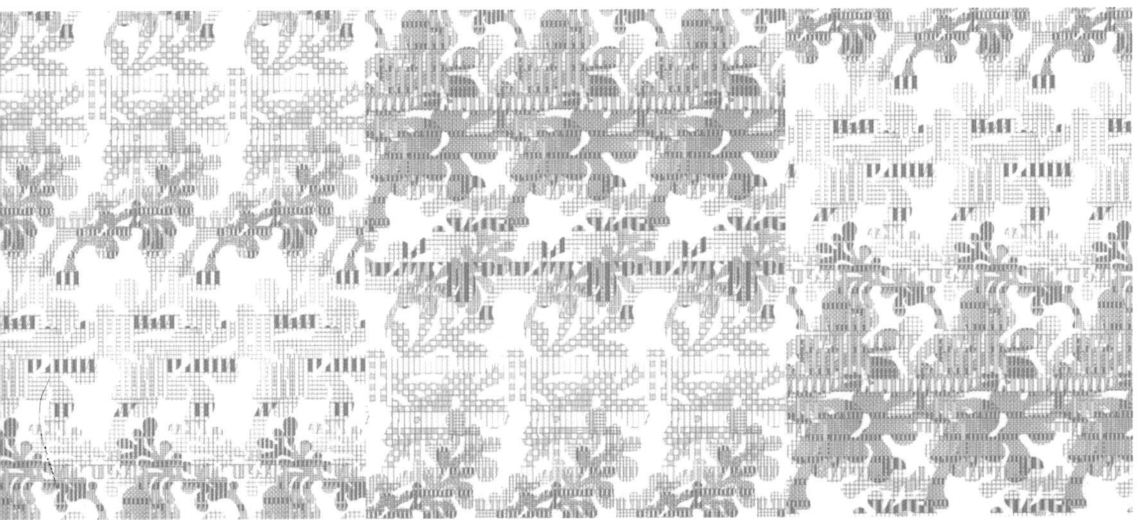

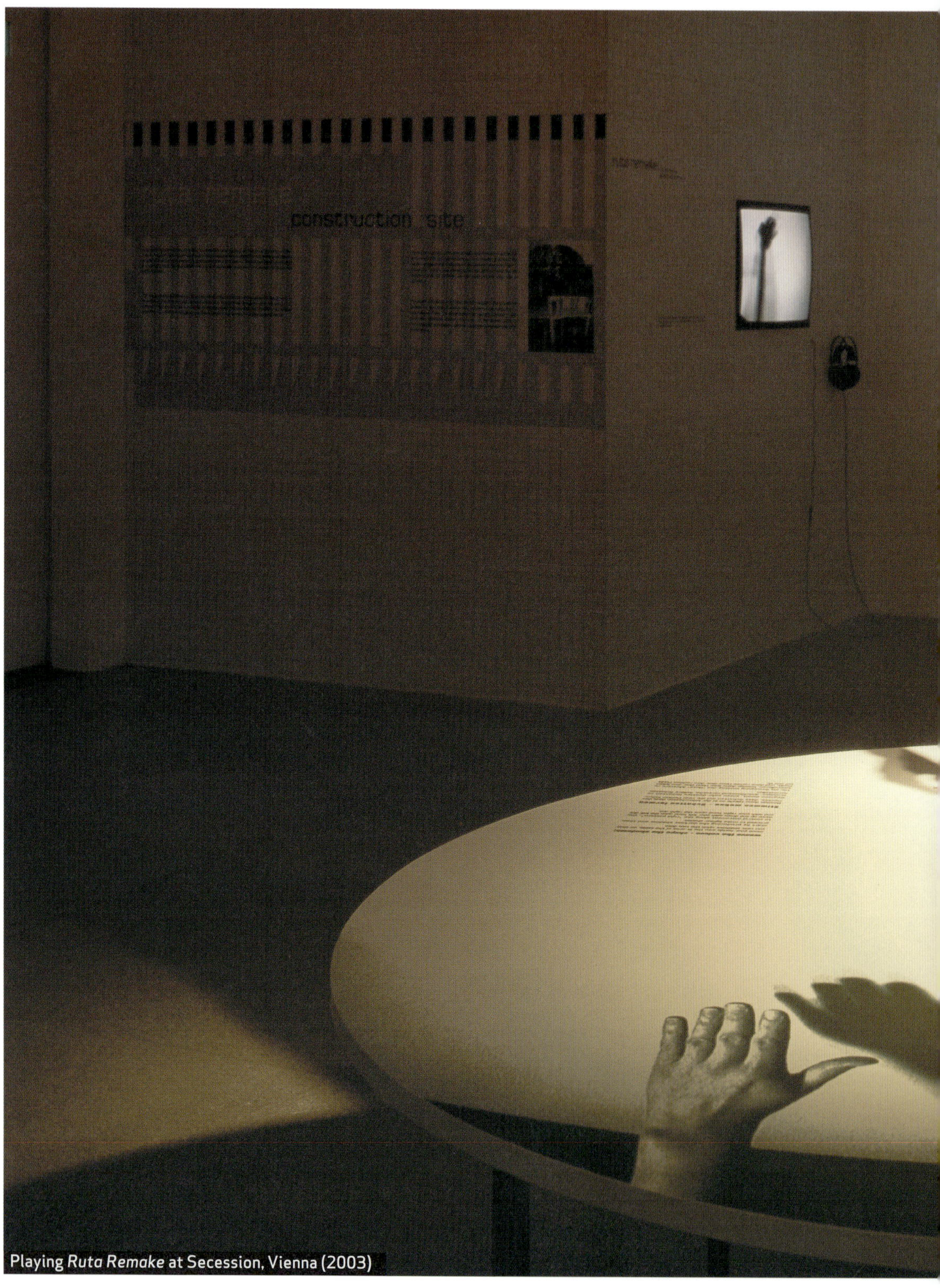

Playing *Ruta Remake* at Secession, Vienna (2003)

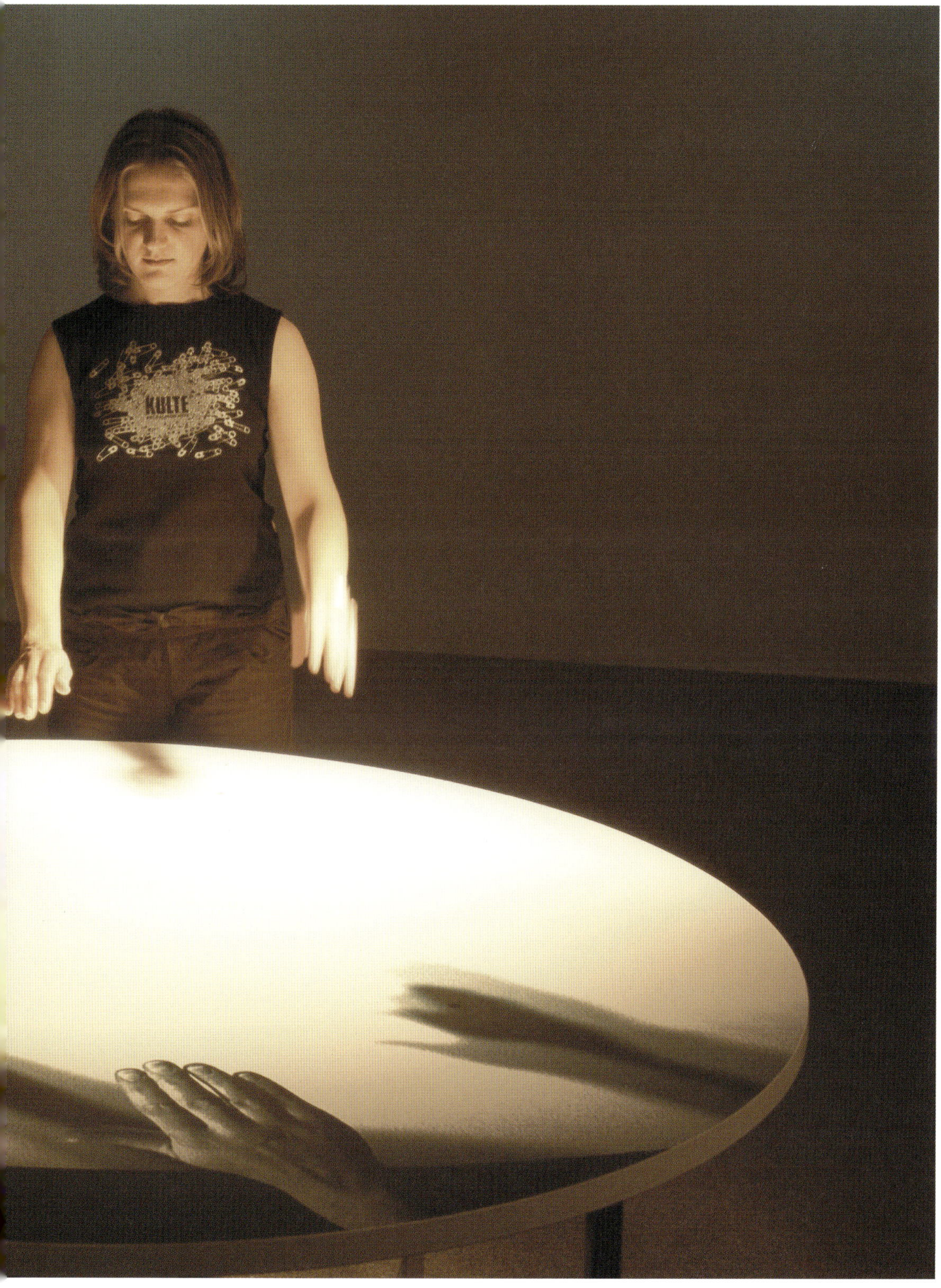

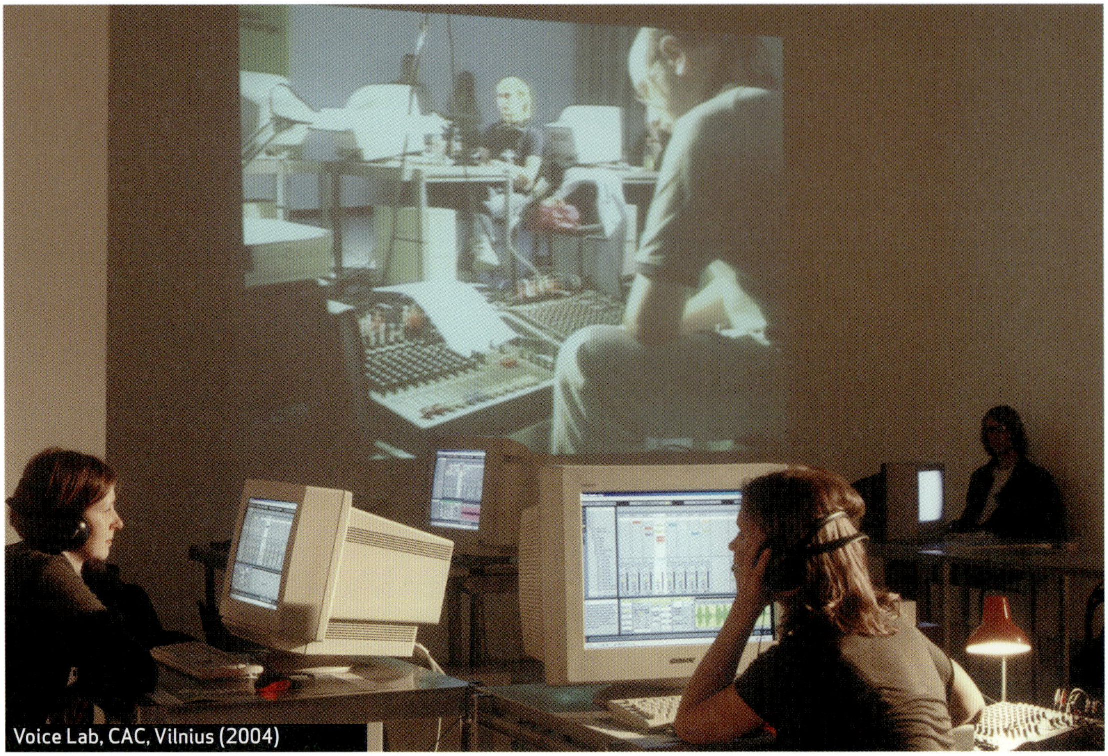

Voice Lab, CAC, Vilnius (2004)

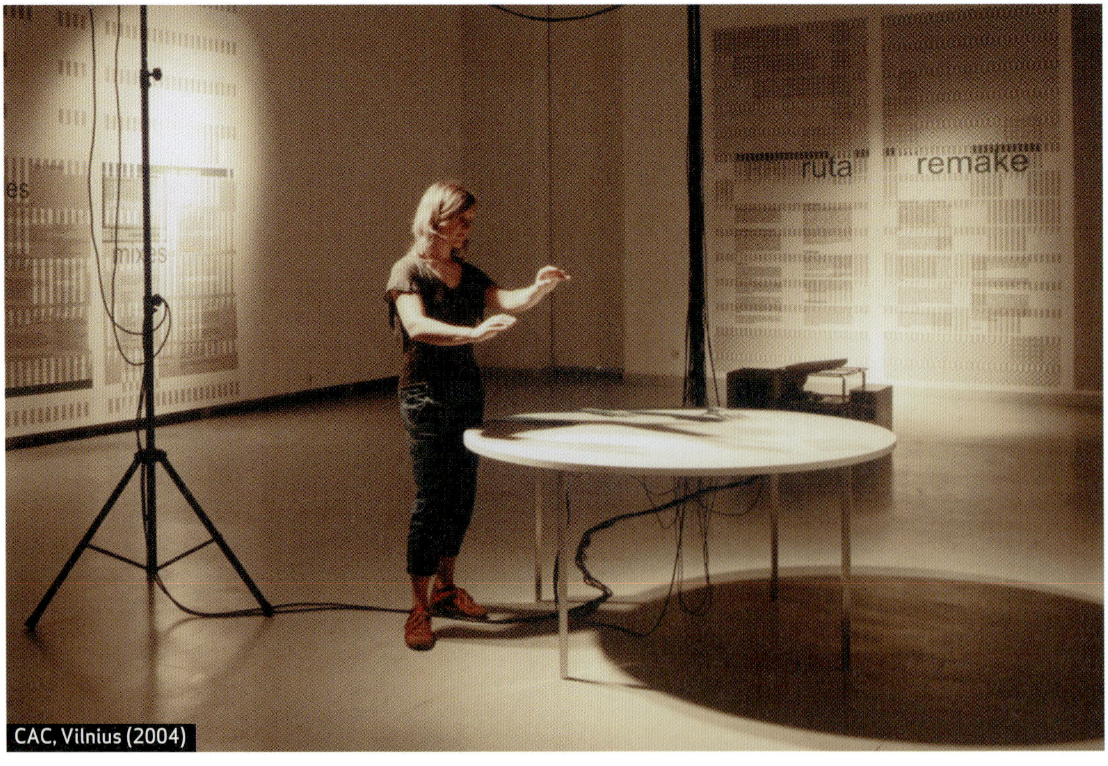

CAC, Vilnius (2004)

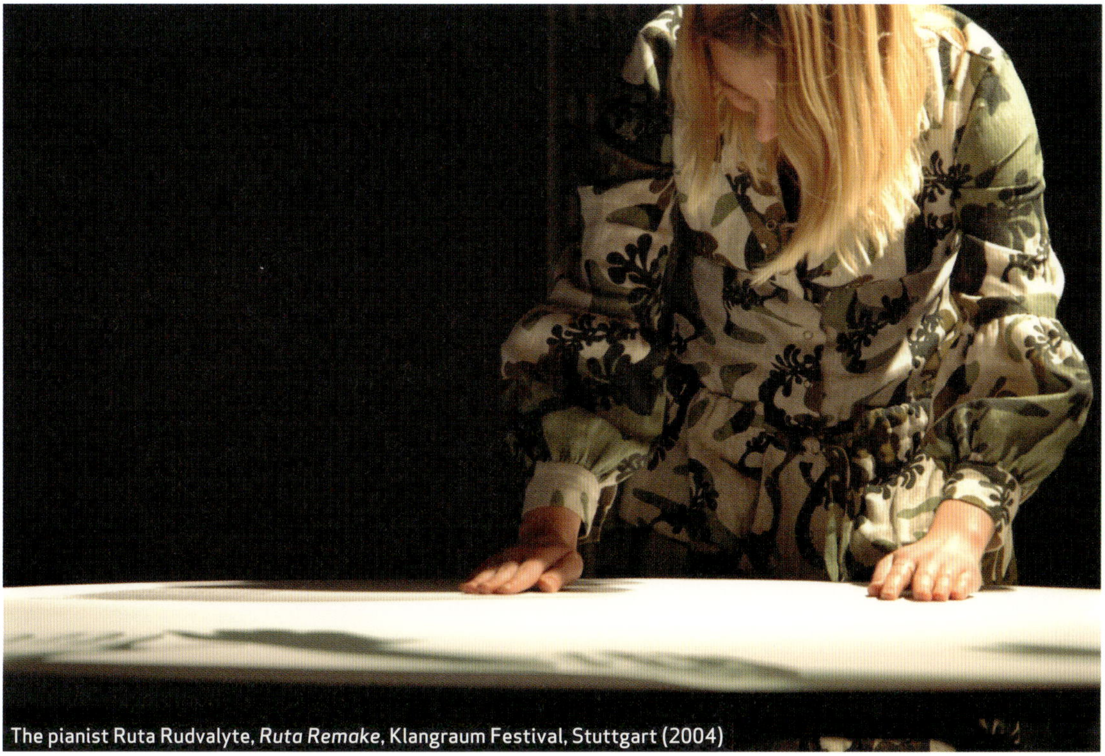

The pianist Ruta Rudvalyte, *Ruta Remake*, Klangraum Festival, Stuttgart (2004)

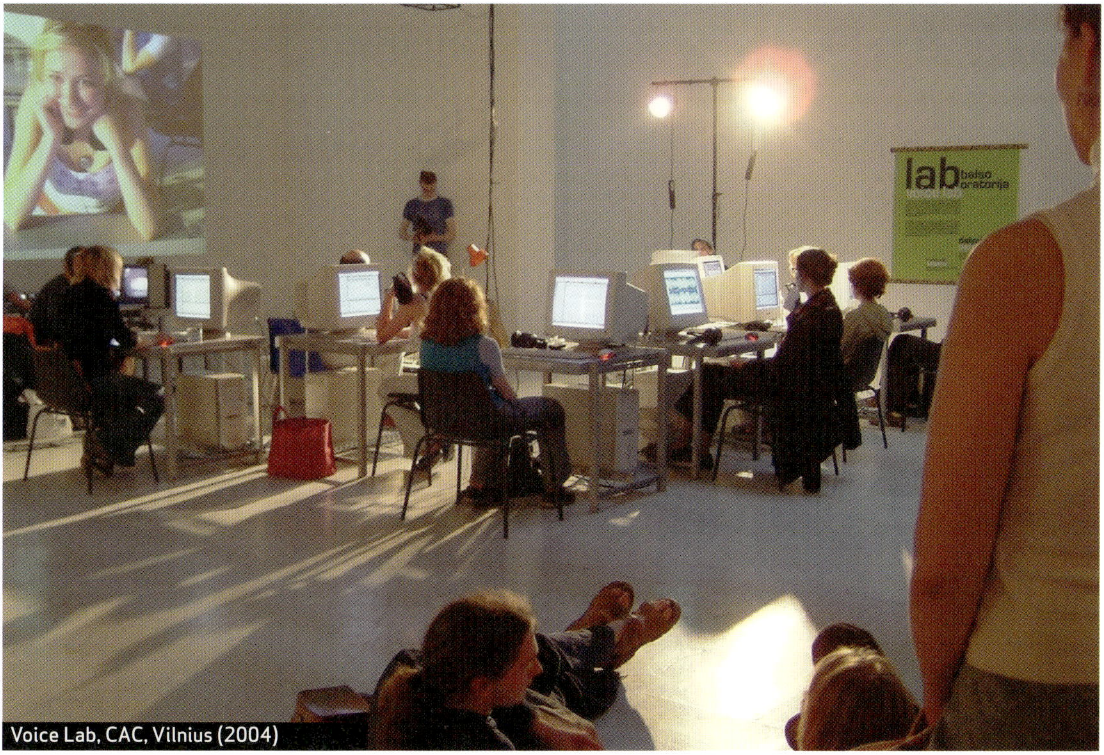

Voice Lab, CAC, Vilnius (2004)

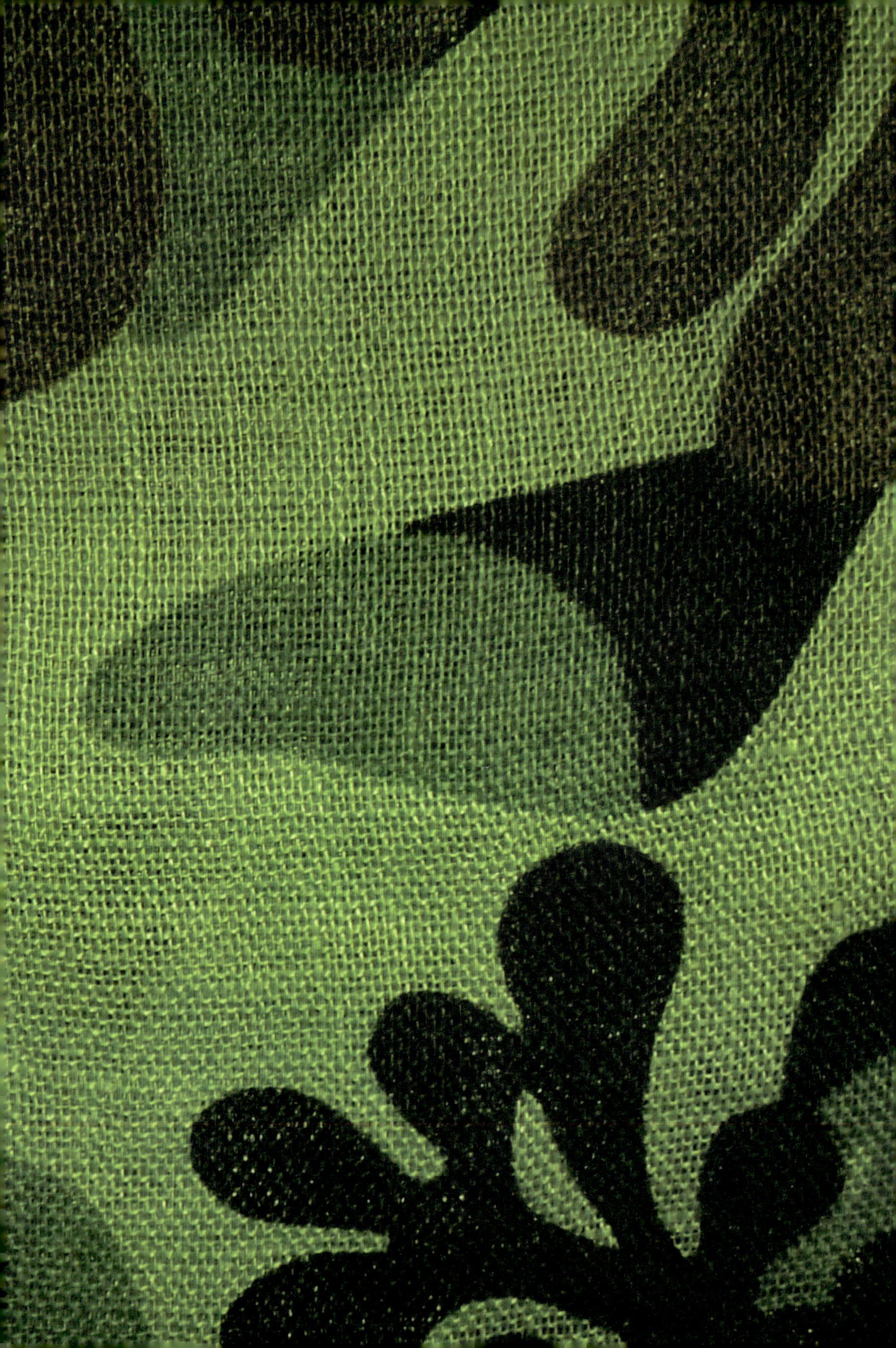

DRUZBA (2003 - ongoing)

The *Druzba* project is an attempt to create a reading of the cultural, political and geographical domains found in a fictional journey along the Druzhba, the world's longest pipeline, built in the 1960s and 70s under the Communist regime to transport oil some 4,000 kilometres from Russia to the Baltic states, the Ukraine, Hungary, Poland, Czechoslovakia and Germany. The Druzhba pipeline – *druzhba* means "friendship" in Russian – was built by the Soviets to control the Eastern bloc and much of Western Europe through its oil supply. It was constructed with the materials, machinery and equipment provided by "friendly" countries, which saw it as a source of wealth and security and a symbol of unification. It was associated with the abundance and power of the world's greatest country, which "would last forever" and also "lead the world into a new dawn."

The pipeline became a symbol of independence that protected the newly established Communist countries from the whimsical market economy of the West. The security of the energy supply was taken for granted and everybody joined the network, without realising it would become an instrument of colonisation and control. The golden handshake proffered by a comrade was soon devalued, however, since it led to forced unification and uniformity. Keeping to a set of common goals and rules, workers groups from the "brotherhood of Socialist allies" built the pipeline, thus creating what was probably the first transnational project of this size. The very fact that this set of countries managed to build it together was not considered to be enslaving.

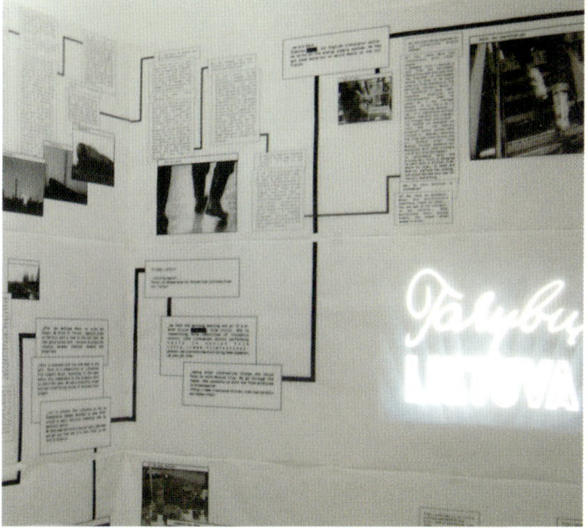

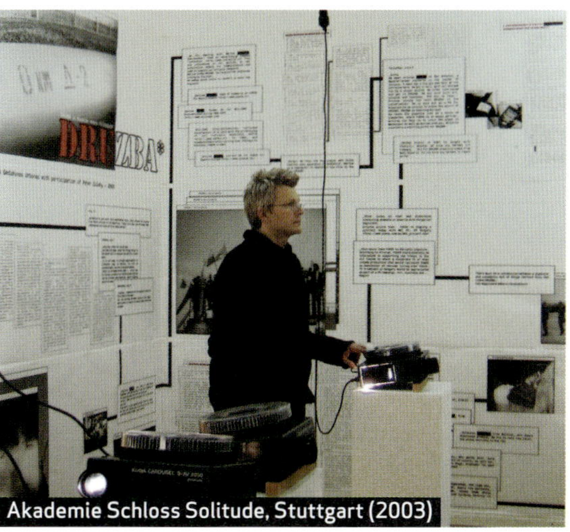

Akademie Schloss Solitude, Stuttgart (2003)

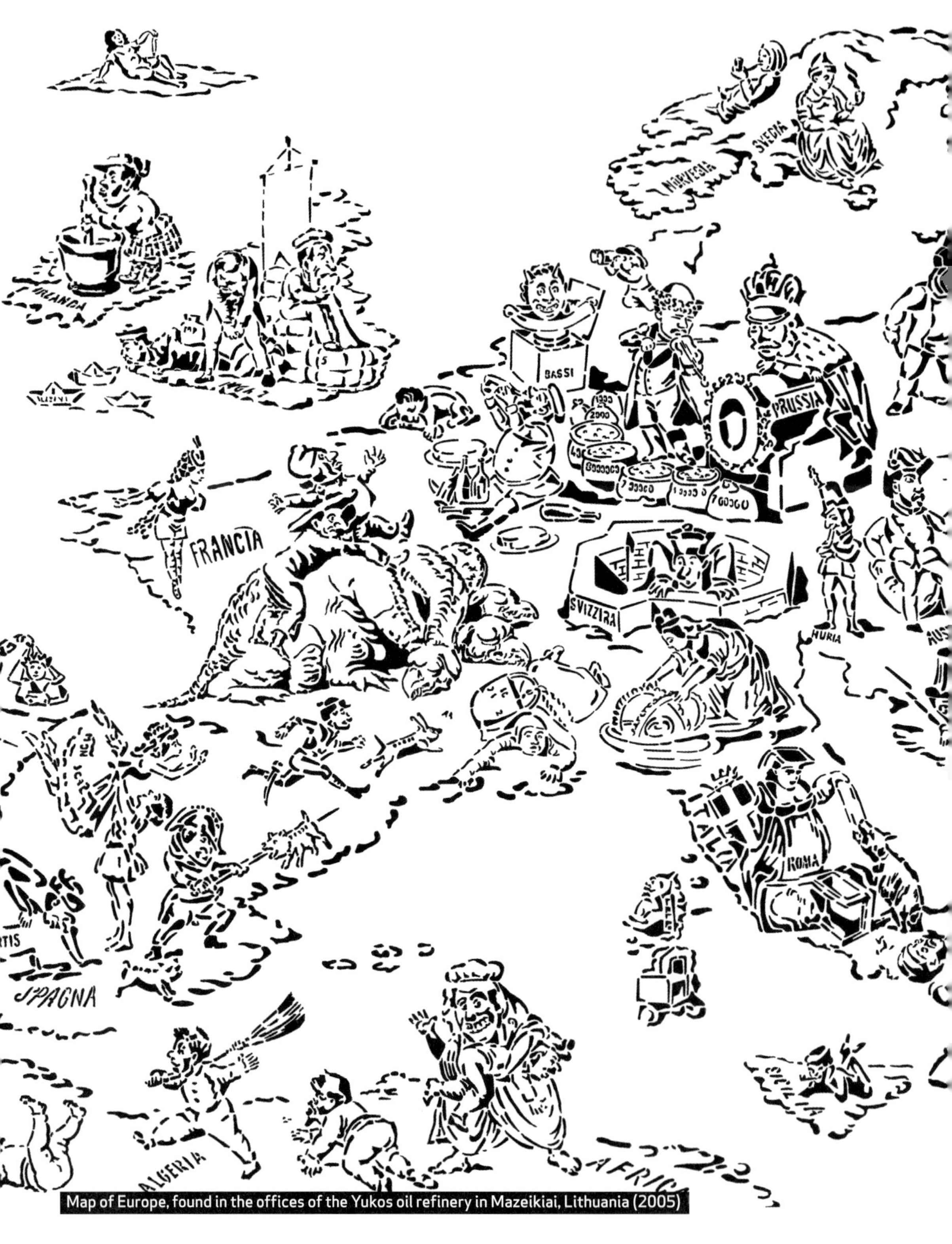

Map of Europe, found in the offices of the Yukos oil refinery in Mazeikiai, Lithuania (2005)

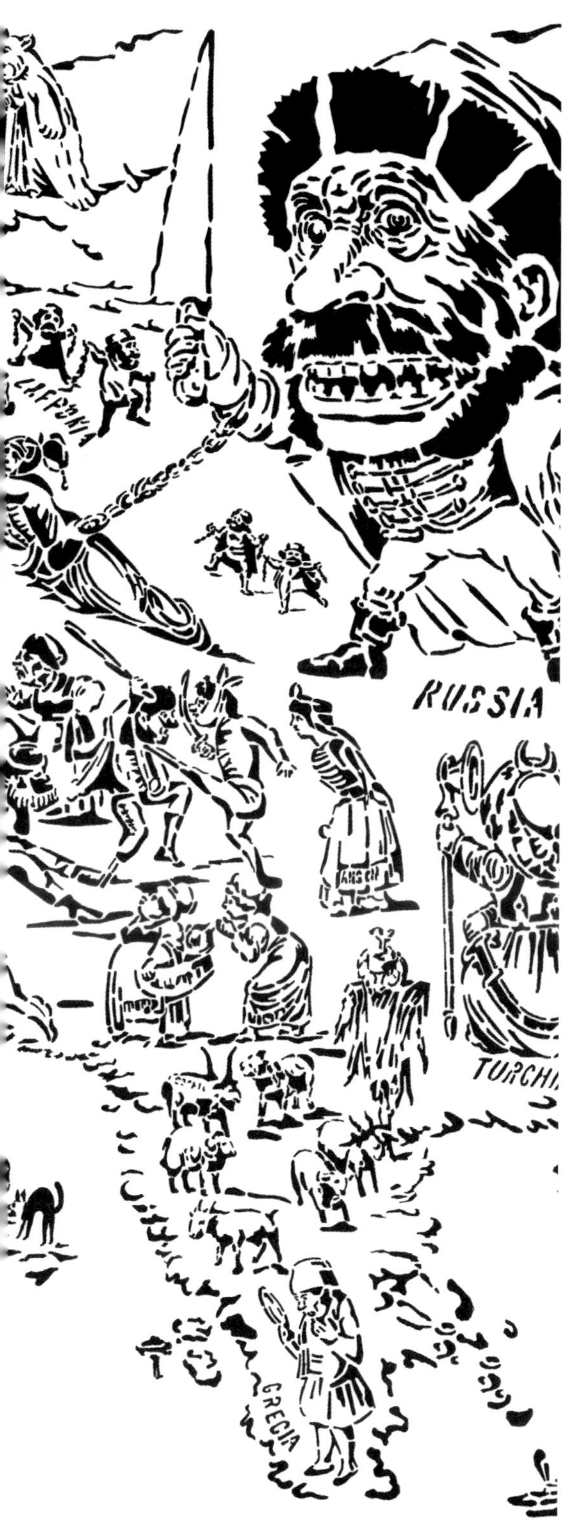

As the Soviet Union collapsed, the newly set up companies of the former Eastern bloc, now backed by American capital, began to use their old influence and to steal into the oil-rich fields of Siberia and the Urals. The privatisation of the pipeline infrastructure was seen to be a symbolic gesture indicative of the new West-oriented political direction. Power and colonisation had moved from one compass point to another: the shoe was on the other foot…

The *Druzba* project focuses on the search for, and the development and realisation of, a script for a media narrative which, within an exhibition context, charts the relation between economical and cultural development, inquiring into the techniques of the broadcast media (television and cinema) and the play of identity within the culture of contemporary migrant labour. *Druzba* sets out to construct a device for reading and navigating the network unfolding within a timeline of exhibition elements, creating subjectivities of negation that reflect upon capital, precariousness and colonisation, and suggesting a trinomial system that includes the documentary film archive, the community and the production of a performance. The *Druzba* project investigates the ambiguous area of exchange between economics and culture. It forms a circumscribed theory for charting the psychogeography of an imperial infrastructure, linking it to personal anxiety, the idea of friendship and the construction of power games.

People who abandon a network that has disintegrated move, migrate and transport labour power and the psychic baggage of common histories and experiences. This movement creates new "plantation worker" clusters and communities abroad, Druzhba branches that extend territorial demands by "colonising" and "challenging" local modes of cultural production and evoke possible

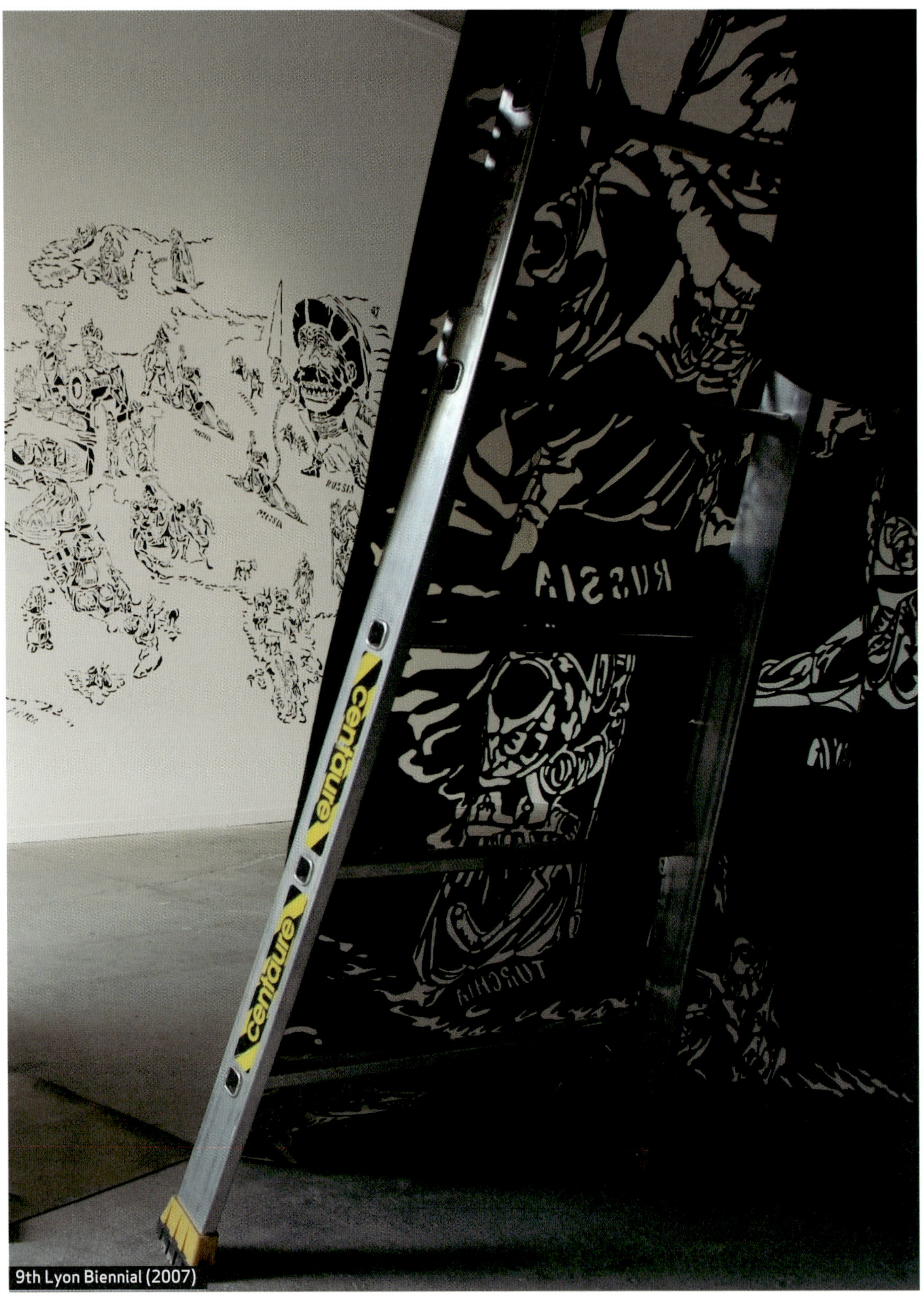

9th Lyon Biennial (2007)

territorial conflicts. The *Druzba* project studies the constructing of new perspectives within mobile communities and their diasporas, while also exploring the aspects of communication and transportation among migrant populations, their new cultural trajectories and the friction created by this new plantation economy.

Druzba at MACBA unfolds through a sequence of acts built around the minstrel show, a relatively limited form of entertainment used as a theatrical device for social comment or satire. Consisting of comic skits, variety acts, dance and music performed by white people in blackface, the minstrel show played an important role in shaping assumptions about blacks. However, unlike much vehemently anti-black propaganda of the time, the minstrel show made these assumptions palatable to a wide audience via a well-intentioned paternalism. An all-singing, all-dancing Al Jolson – and later Mickey Mouse – transformed blackface as a style of theatrical makeup (which turns white into black), thus enabling it to question widespread racist stereotypes, attitudes and perceptions. The caricatures that are the legacy of blackface persist to the present day and are a cause of ongoing controversy.

The *Druzba* project considers performance as a medium for understanding the mechanisms of different techniques of power. The project traces the methodology and aesthetic language developed by the avant-garde concept of the Kino-Eye by Dziga Vertov, whose revolutionary work from the 1920s evolved into a propaganda model of instant documentary reportage, thus providing a "psychedelic" experience that went against predominant socialist realism. Pipeline machinery forms the basis of the transformation of the mechanical model into an informational one, into a "system of signs". The geographical, historical, political and economic flows, through which the pipeline branches, intersect and bridge the spatial leap from self-contained work to open-ended scenario. Collaborating with the Lithuanian Central State Archives and the Russian State Documentary Film & Photo Archive at Krasnogorsk (RGAKFD), the project constructs its own archive by researching images from propaganda and educational newsreels and the private films of construction workers in order to contextualise the intersections where politics and the aesthetics of power meet.

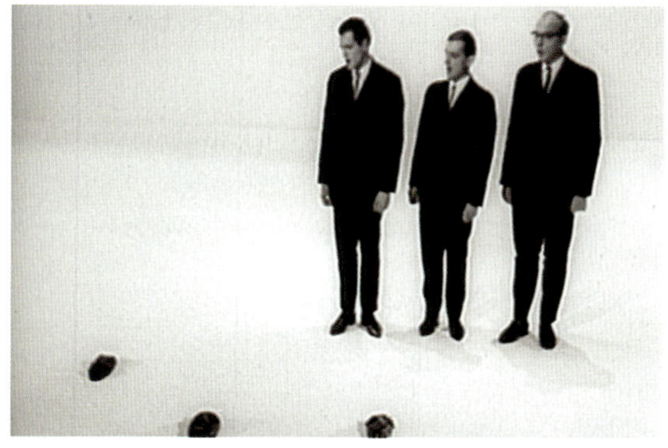

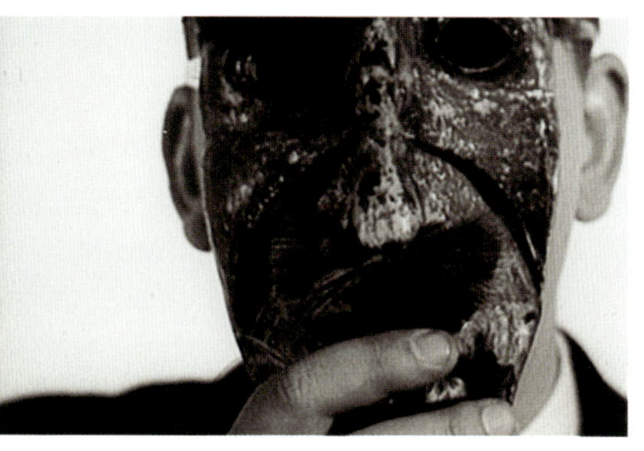

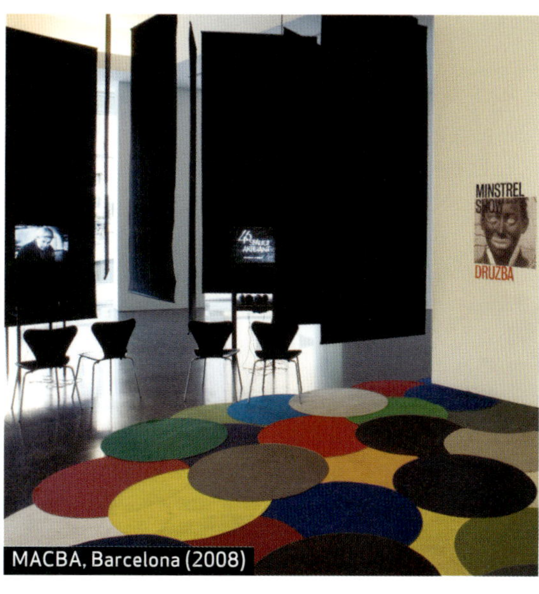

MACBA, Barcelona (2008)

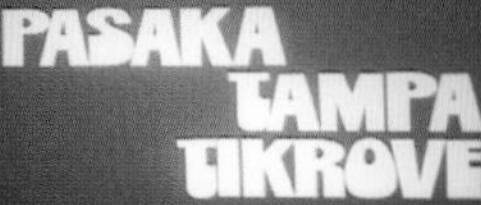

Children, I'm going to tell
you about black gold.

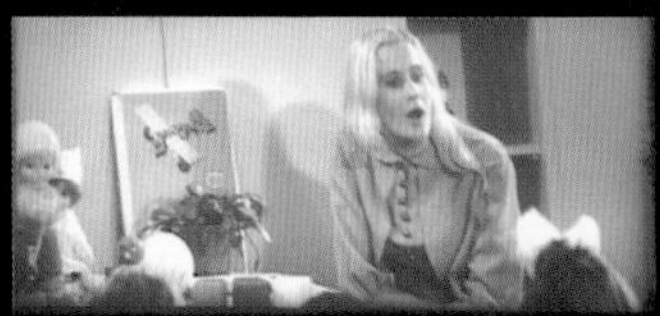

People call our oil black gold.

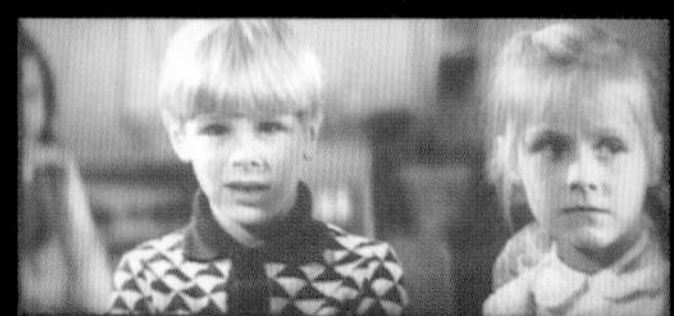

In the early days people used to
transport oil in leather sacks.

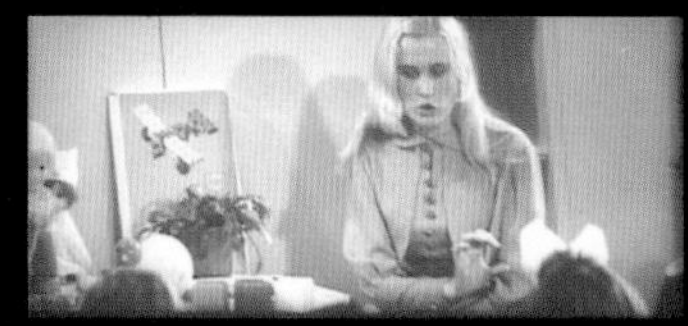

They'd pour it in, tie it up,
put it on the back of a horse
or a camel and off they'd go.

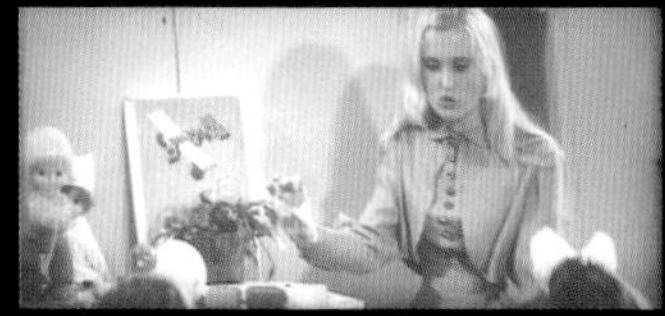

Then they started transporting
it by train, in cisterns.

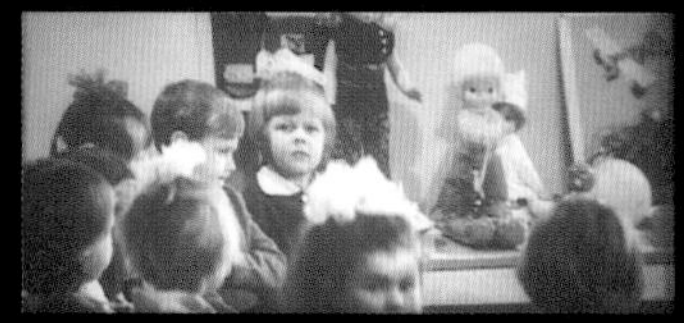

But not even this amount
was enough for people;
they needed a great deal of oil.

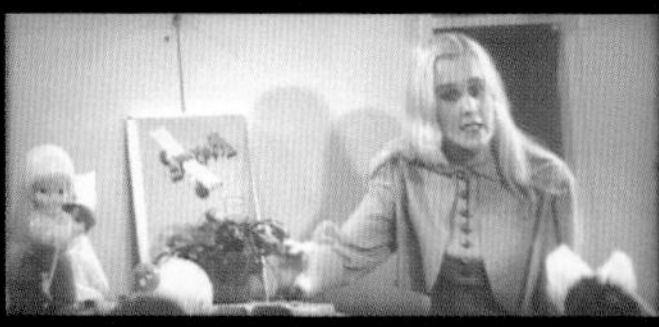

And so now they've built
long pipes deep down in
the ground

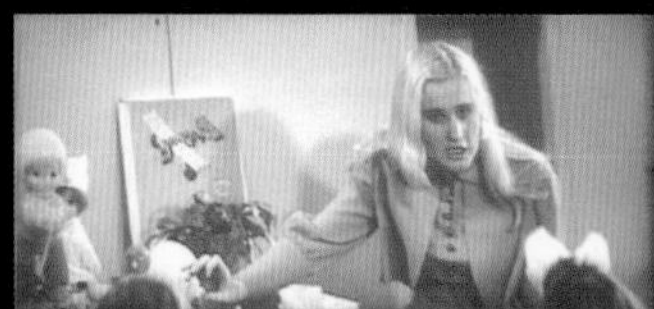

and these pipes
stretch really far...

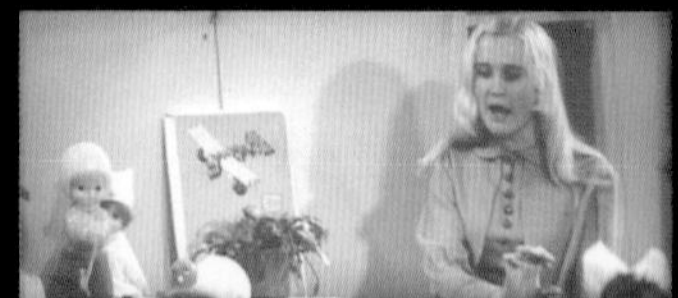

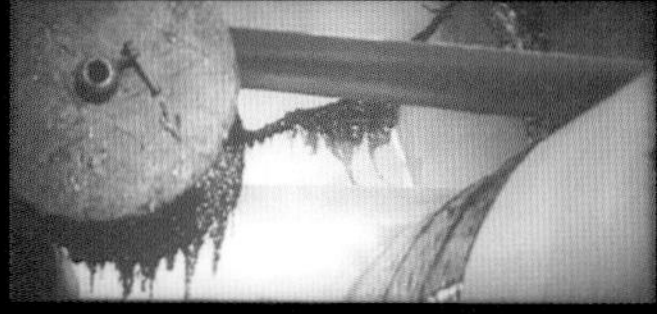

And through these pipes
the oil started flowing.

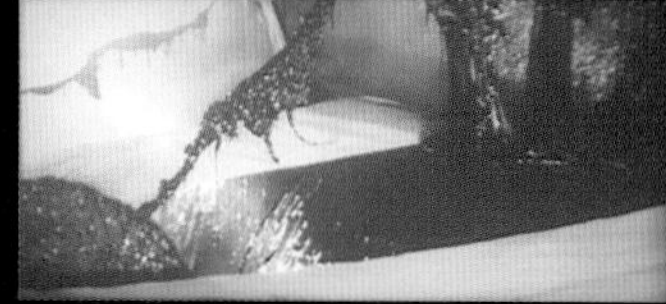

In Mazeikiai, fairy tale and reality
are so close to one another.

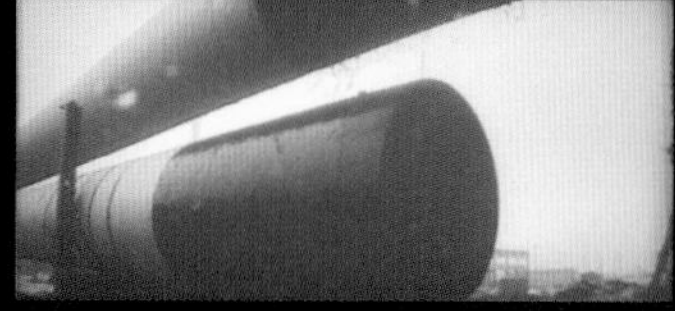

Pipelines may stretch for
hundreds of kilometres…

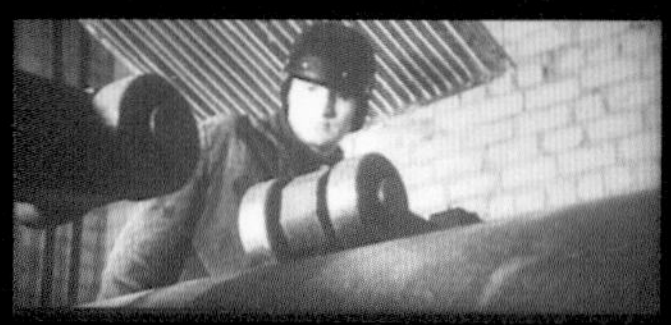

But before constructing them,
they have to be connected,
welded, smeared with black tar,
wrapped in insulation…

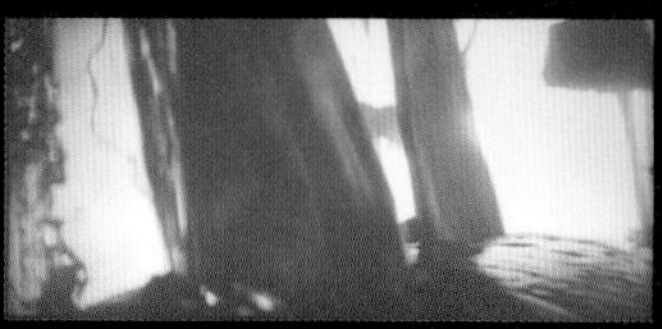

Heat will be controlled
from an automated panel.

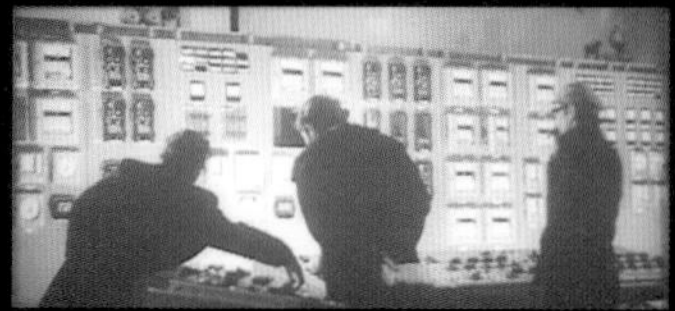

New streets are built.

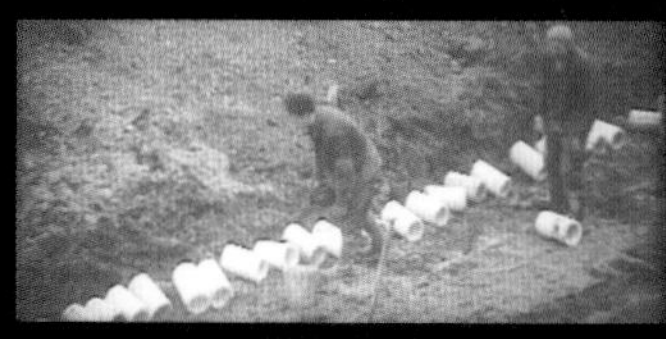

In the northern part of the town
there's an Oil Workers Avenue.

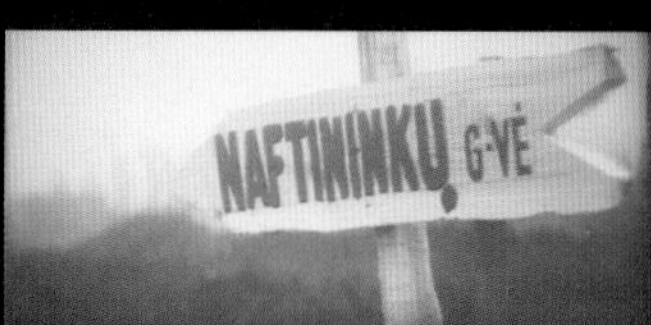

Just imagine, built from glass
and concrete,

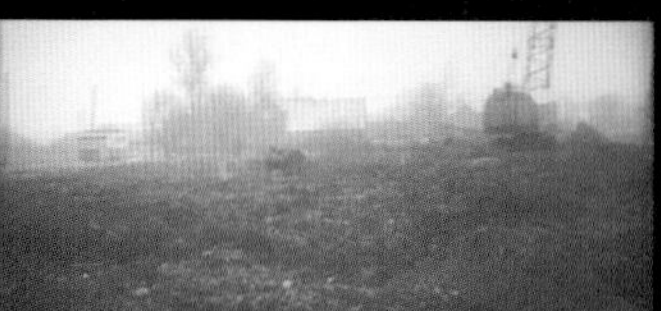

a supermarket, restaurant,
nightclub, neon lights.

Oil is used to produce
many things.

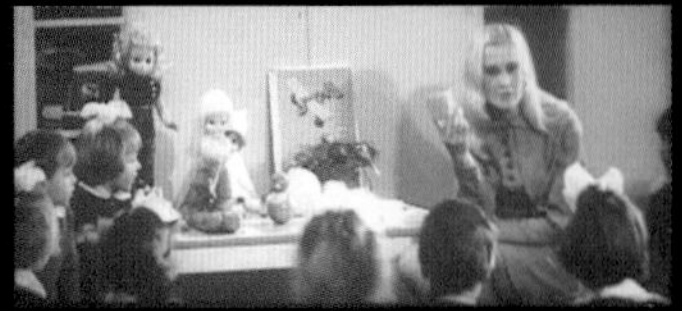

For example, the little toy cubes
we build towers with.

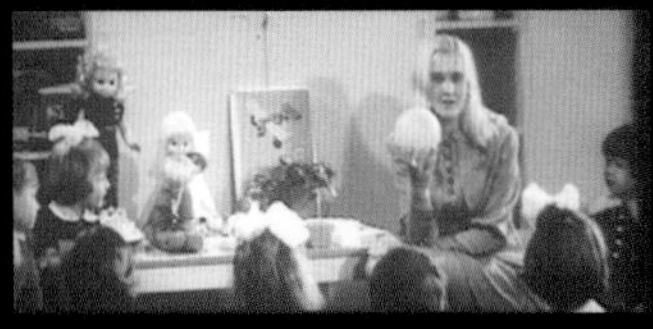

Then again, the little balls
we play outside with.

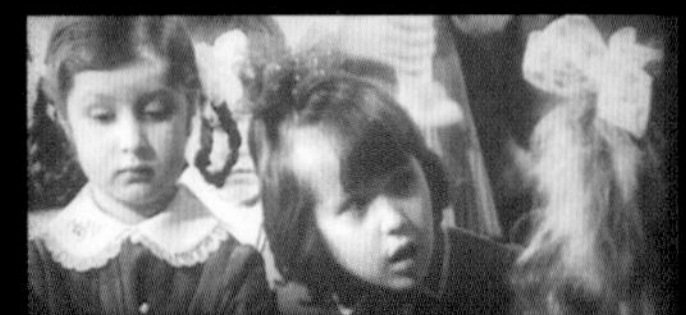

And this spaceship
is also made from oil.

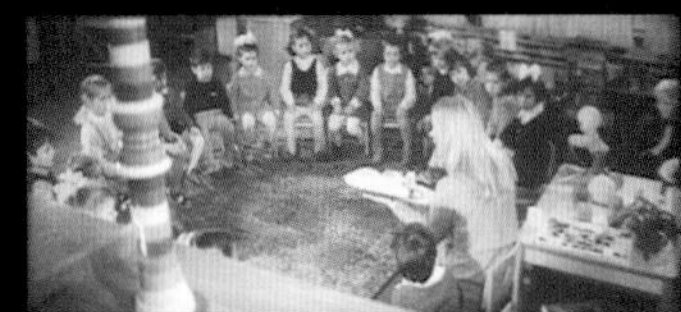

And sometimes when we
become ill, have a headache
or a sore throat after eating
too much ice cream,

we take medicine.

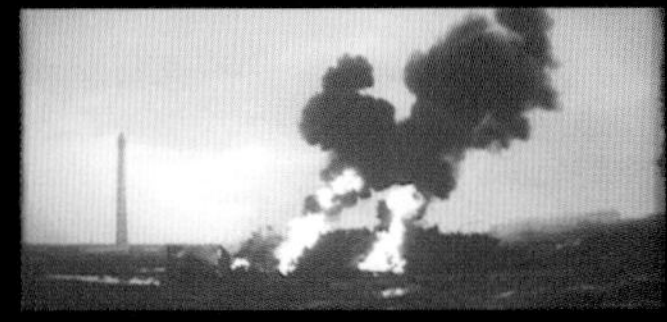

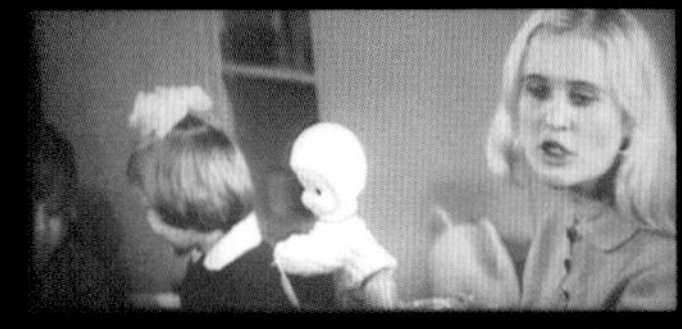

Medicine is made from oil, too.

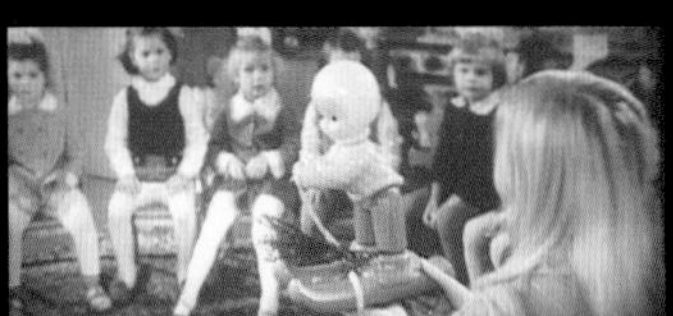

An oil refinery is being built in our
little town of Mazeikiai.

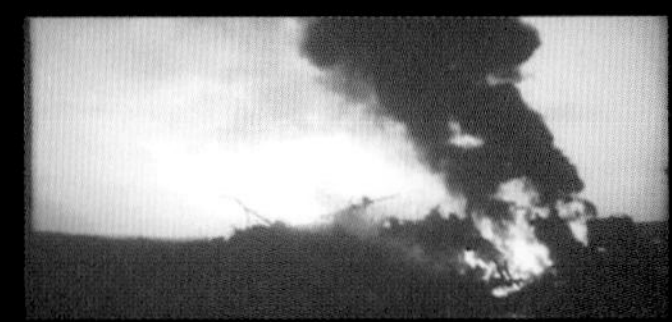

The parents have different
tales to tell.

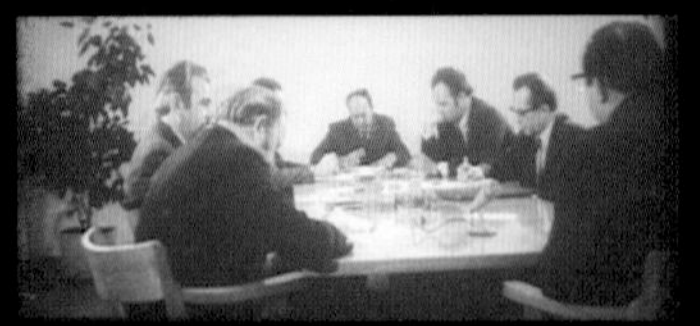

Fairy tale becomes reality (1975)

Ivan and his Druzhba, 2003

I started working in the oil industry on 25 July 1972, when I came to Lithuania to work on the Druzhba project. I hadn't worked in the oil industry before that. I started as the manager of the crude oil supply station in Poland. At each end of the oil pipeline there is an oil supply station. Between five and eight people are employed there and they supply oil and take meter readings. Each country – the Ukraine, Belarus, Lithuania, Latvia – has, since the introduction of private property, its own board of managers, but today the Transneft company in Moscow handles both the central dispatch and metering of oil.

I worked for Druzhba until 1999, when Williams went and fired me. I'm really angry the Americans came over to help us, although fortunately they left before they'd completely ruined everything.

Druzhba became a huge international project, with Hungary, Poland, the Czech Republic, East Germany and the Soviet Union making a deal to connect up their oil pipelines. The agreement was signed on 18 December 1959. The first chief oil executive of Druzhba was appointed in 1963, a man called Rais, an East-German. There have been only three chief oil executives during Druzhba's entire existence. And this man, who was 68 when he retired, died a year later. He'd become so deeply embedded in the system that he couldn't bear to be separated from it.

There is Druzhba 1 and Druzhba 2. There used to be one pipeline, but with the need to increase oil capacity, a second one was built. The direction is the same, however, they both keep to the same corridor. The centre of the whole Druzhba system used to be in Lvov. And then Druzhba began from Samara – the starting point of Druzhba 2.

All pipelines are interconnected. Siberia is the main provider of crude oil – from Nizhnevartovsk, Omsk, Tomsk, Surgut. Each of them is also connected to Almetyevsk and Perm. Everything is interconnected here. Now it comes from Nizhnevartovsk through the so-called upper pipeline to Nizhny Novgorod, through Moscow and over to Polotsk. The Surgut-Polotsk pipeline is called "nefteprovod", and the rest is Druzhba. Crude oil reaches Lithuania (the Mazeikiai Refinery) either through Surgut-Polotsk or through Druzhba. It also comes from Almetyevsk, from Tatarsk, from Bashkiria, but it contains a lot of sulphur. Crude oil from Surgut is better. When the Mazeikiai Refinery was commissioned, the Surgut pipeline didn't yet exist. It was launched in 1981, before Lenin's birthday. Back then we supplied the first crude oil to the refinery.

Everyone used to run around then, Moscow would lean on us. They'd say, everything must be done before Lenin's birthday, and it had to be. Now you can laugh, but it wasn't funny at the time. We had to work day and night back then. Those who've gone through the Druzhba school, they still work that way, they know their work and they do it honestly. There were huge quotas, excellent specialists; commissions used to inspect them and they'd want people to work hard.

In Latvia, for example, we constructed a pumping station. We built it in six months in the Soviet days and it's still working. When Brezhnev signed the Helsinki Agreements in 1975, he promised there'd be more oil for the West and it had to be done. It used to be tough working back then, my kids were little and I was away almost all the time. I used to work on site day and night. When summer came, we weren't allowed to take a vacation or go home, just like in the army – that's how strict the regime was. And salaries weren't very high, a mere 120-130 roubles a month. People used to work from enthusiasm rather than for money.

We used to work with the Polish company Energopol. They built part of the pipeline from Belarus to Lithuania and we worked with them all the way through. Energopol is a world-famous company, I've heard they're doing reconstruction work in Iraq. You can see it from their work, they do a quality job and they work fast.

But it used to be more interesting to work back then in the Soviet Union, when there was a unified system. There used to be different challenges. You had to dig out a pipe, cut it out, weld it, dig it back in, fill it with oil and test the leaks. Everything according to the book.

There was a jury which would stand and watch to make sure everything was done the right way. We used to visit Kuybyshev, Michurinsk or Novopolock. They'd visit us. There used to be such cooperation, just like that socialist race.

The hardest time was when the pipeline was separated. I remember we all gathered together with our specialists and were discussing how to deal with the issue. I got all the men together and asked everyone to think. There were many different opinions, but the priority was given to creating our own structure. We employed more people, bought equipment. We had the money and we dealt with the problems.

Everything depended on old links around Druzhba. There were old links with other people. They still operate, they can't be disconnected, just like you can't disconnect railway tracks. Of course, you may cut yourself off and drive around your own backyard, but if you want a connection with the rest of the world, you can't make it without links leading outside. It's exactly the same with the oil supply system.

I remember once receiving a call from Parliament inquiring as to whether we could pump oil from Chechnya to Lithuania. "Would it be feasible?" they asked. I said, "Feasible, yes. The pipelines are interconnected." "How?" they asked. I said, "Through Moscow." "Oh no," they said, "Let's do it without involving Moscow." I said, "It's impossible without Moscow." The system is designed so that the main dispatch centre in Moscow, NEFT, controls flows and distributes oil. Without an order from Moscow, neither Latvia (Ventspils) nor Lithuania (Mazeikiai) will load a single ton of oil into the tanker. In accordance with the procedures, first a telegram is sent with a written order where to load, who is to perform the loading and when, the price of the oil and who will pay for it – everything.

And this is economics. When politics gets in the way, there's chaos. You can see it in our country: when the politicians start giving orders, common sense goes out the window.

During all that privatisation, the minister used to refer us to Parliament. We'd listen. They'd say everything would be alright, they'd show us Western management methods and we'd see the way things ought to be done. I'd like to look that minister in the eye now and ask, "So, how are they managing things, after privatisation?" But that's the way it is…

I remember when the minister made us all appear on the stage and say if the staff and the manager supported the arrival of the Americans, of Williams International. I was quite diplomatic, I couldn't say I was against investment. I said, well it's good Williams or some other company comes, the important thing is that there's more crude oil, that people live a better life, that profit increases and all, no matter which company is involved. There should be a sense of moving forward, of progress. But there was no progress at all.

A different owner came, a different operator, who changed the contract immediately. It's against common sense to have such a contract, to have the loss of 240 million they did, and to compensate for the whole amount from the state budget. Where have you seen the

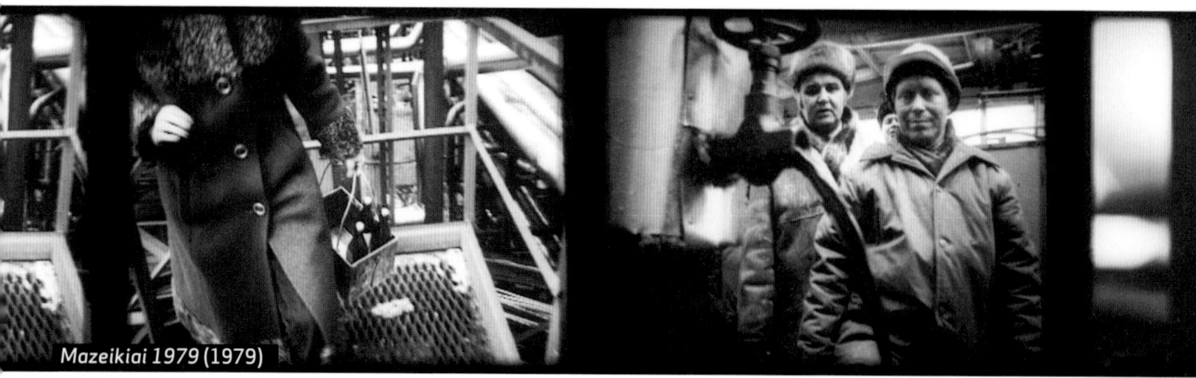

Mazeikiai 1979 (1979)

state compensate the loss to a businessman because he wasn't successful? It happens. I'm very upset.

Americans were there as advisers, the major ones. I understand: the advisers say how in their opinion it could be done better, we discuss it and do it that way. But if I see things going wrong, I say "no" to the adviser, and he calls the ministry, the minister blames me, and orders me to do it the way the adviser says. So what kind of adviser is that? But I put my signature anyway. He doesn't put his signature anywhere. If there's a problem – he's gone. How can you work that way?

There used to be a Kurdish fellow called Khalil. A phantom. Yesterday I found myself looking through some old papers and came across a picture of him posing with John Major, and I said damn it. After the deal Khalil disappeared. He was gone from that day forth, once Williams had signed the contract with the government. He is not there anymore. Perhaps he's currently "helping" someone else. There are many such types.

If I'm not mistaken, this Khalil fellow brought Williams to Lithuania. Or another shadowy businessman from America… What's his name?… Ka… Ka… Kazickas. Kazickas. As Paksas bluffed his way through back then, everybody around here ran. Kazickas and Adamkus from Montreal did a moonlight flit, while Landsbergis left his grand piano in Paris – he also ran here, and so on. Somehow it just so happened that everyone was abroad then. Paksas was a hassle…

I remember Brudno from Yukos coming to Lithuania. Brudno would visit and observe the situation here. Who can say where it all began? Maybe Yukos existed here from the first, its name was just different. It spent some time under the name of Williams, failed, took pots of money and walked away. And now Yukos comes and "sets to work." And now it makes a profit and everything. Out of a 240 million loss. It's absurd.

The only thing I'm upset about is that I've given twenty-seven years to the oil supply system, the pipeline, Druzhba. Now I'm more than fifty years old, and no one needs me anymore. No job, nothing. All the engineers and administrators were against Williams. We used to say we ought to do something about it, maybe someone would listen to us, but no one did. We used to say, maybe we should have got in touch with the Pope. Neither the Prime Minister, nor the President, nor the Minister, nor anyone else would listen to us.

There was some talk that the name of Druzhba shouldn't be dropped. Friendship with Germany and America was considered to be good, but Druzhba with Russia is not so good.

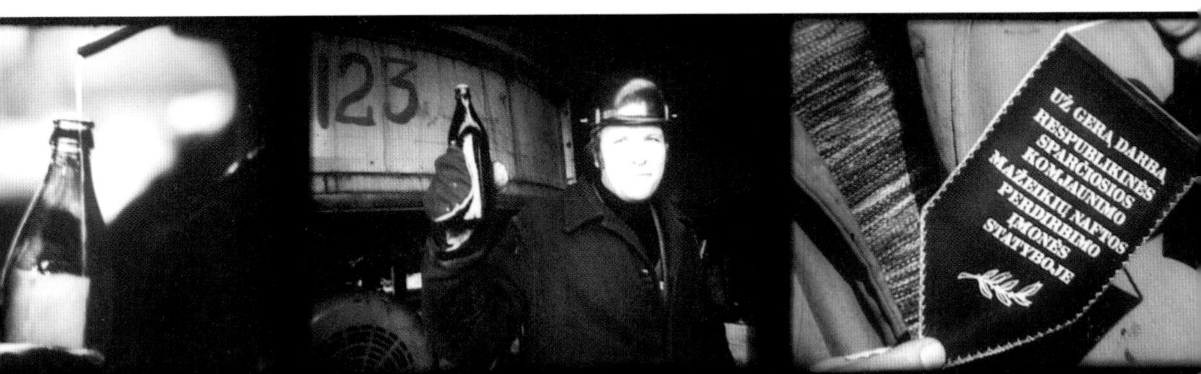

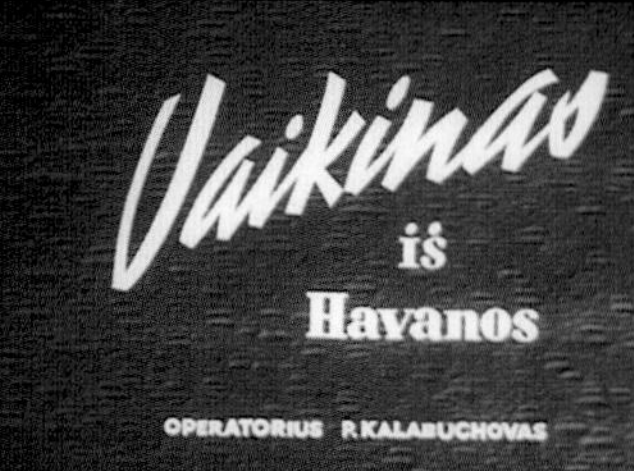

Terey Riso Pereira, a twenty-
year-old from Havana.

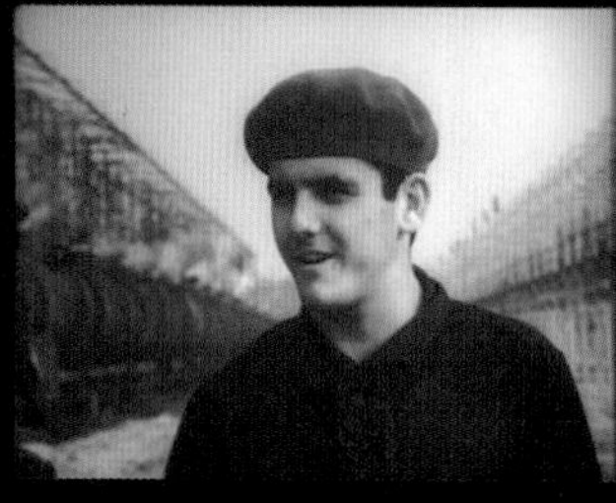

He came to Klaipida in the
Soviet Union to study.

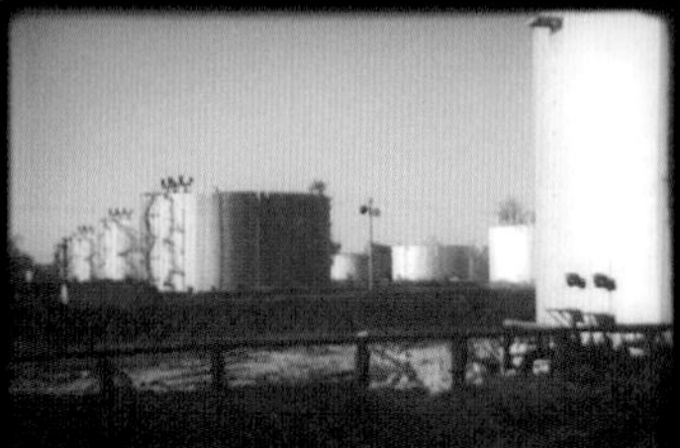

Young Cuba really
needs specialists.

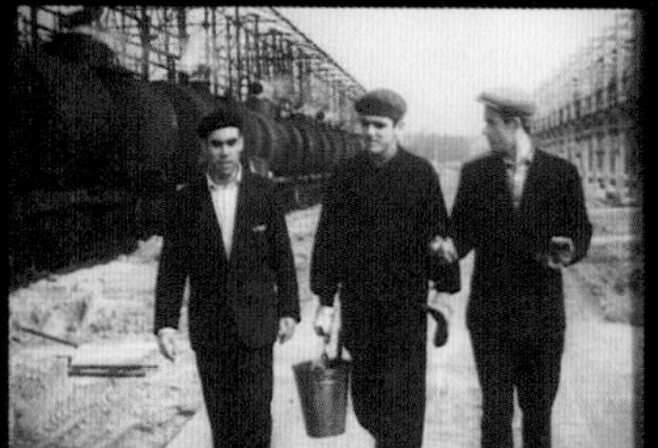

In Havana Riso will have to manage
an oil-storage facility similar
to the one in Klaipida.

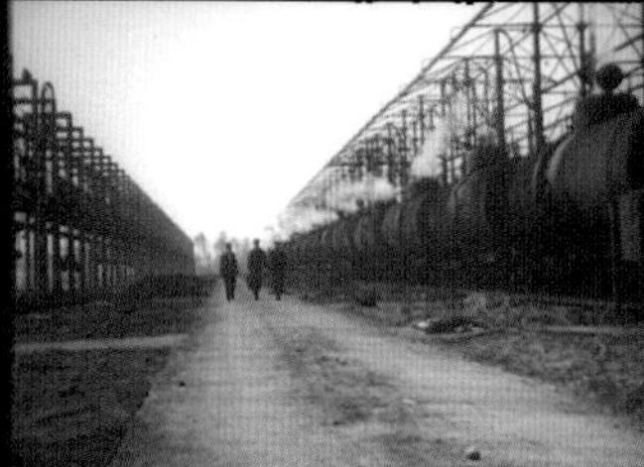

The port city gave him
a warm welcome.

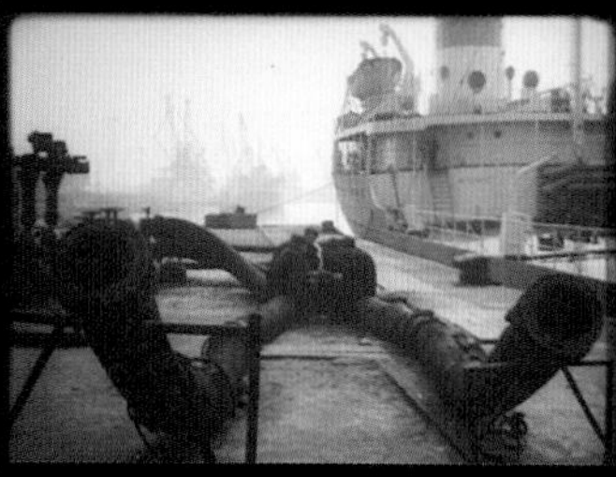

A short break at work and the
workers quickly surround Riso.

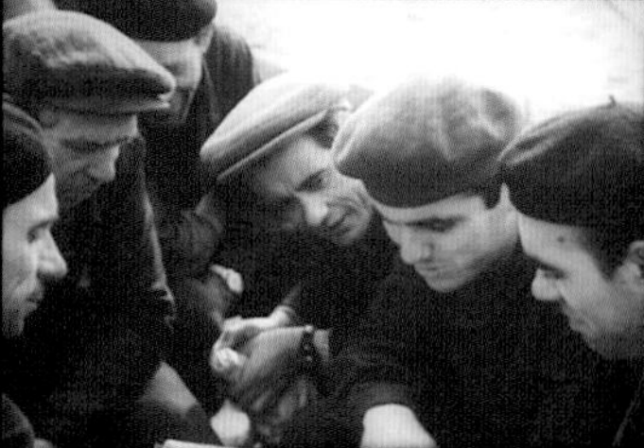

And even though the Soviet Union
is a great country, Riso feels homesick.
But in order to report to
Fidel when he gets back, he must
keep on studying.

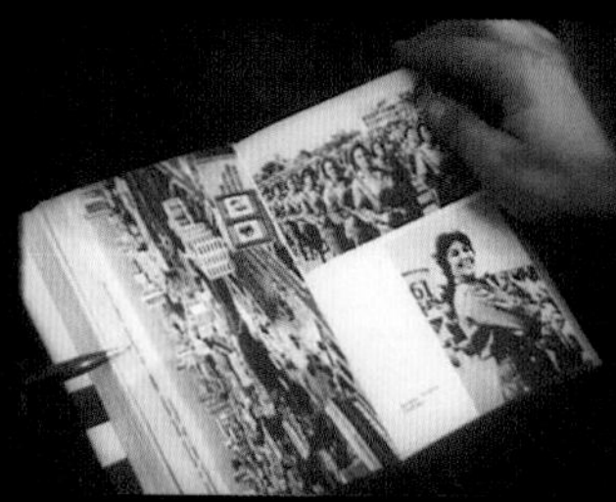

Soviet people give a huge amount
of support to him and thousands
of other Cubans.

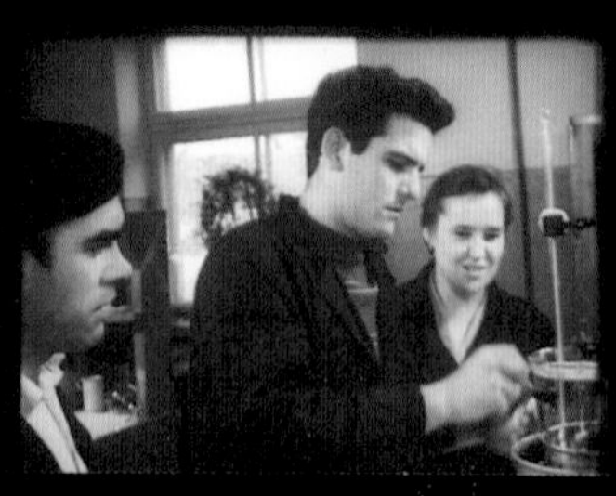

The Man From Havana (1963)

Fuel thieves have dug a hole to oil products supply pipe in the forest

JURGITA VITKAUSKIENE

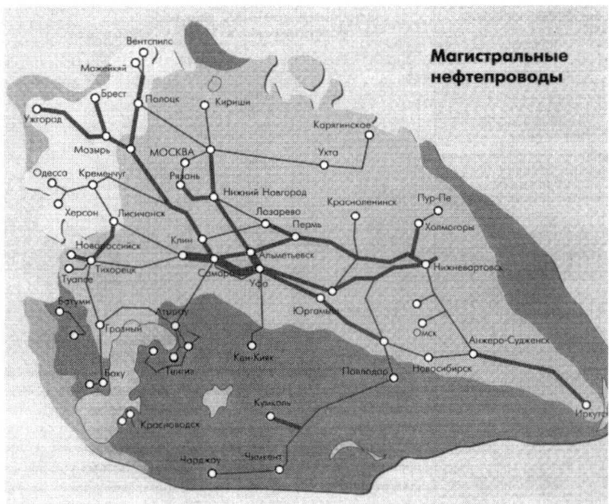

Yesterday, in a remote part of Birzai Forest close to the Druzhba fuel delivery pipeline, an illegally connected hose was found. Placed some 25 centimetres under the ground, the professionally connected (and expensive) pressurised hose snaked through the trees. It must have been a painstaking piece of work, as the hose even passed beneath stumps and roots. At the end of the almost 160 metre-long hose, a manometer and tap were found. The hose was pressurised and there was evidence of the escape of diesel. The end of the hose was found 200 metres from the road, and it is possible it might have been extended under the ground further on, to make it accessible from the road. The diesel was probably loaded into canisters and carried manually from the forest. Repairing the pipeline will cost the oil company nearly 2,000 litas. This is the fifth time this oil delivery line, located in a remote village surrounded by forest, has been illegally tapped since 1999. The police have been unable to find the guilty party. ■

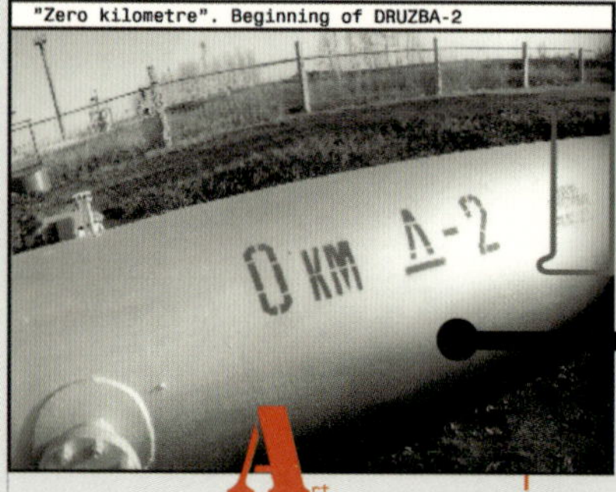

DRUZBA

Our hands are burning to start immediate report, which should mark (finally!) beginning of a...pipeline.

DRUZBA in Russian means FRIENDSHIP

Art **S**cience **B**usiness

July, 21
_we decide to just start this spontaneous diary, that reflects our journey from Peters arrival to his departure. Travel in a timeline of 9 days that interweaves the tracks of film, magic and oil

Tuesday, July 1
_sunny day. Peter arrives at 5pm.
_we take him home, leave the things and go to the water mill to discuss the plan for a next week.
_it is not easy to arrange appointments in Lithuania long in advance. As life is unpredictable, we have to be spontaneous.
_Peter is stressed after IKEA... + still has to finish a preface for the Solitude edition and we already see Damocles' sword hanging above his head

Wednesday, July 2
_raining...temperature is unusually cool for this time of the year.
All the morning we make calls to the magic world and oil empire to build some links and bridges

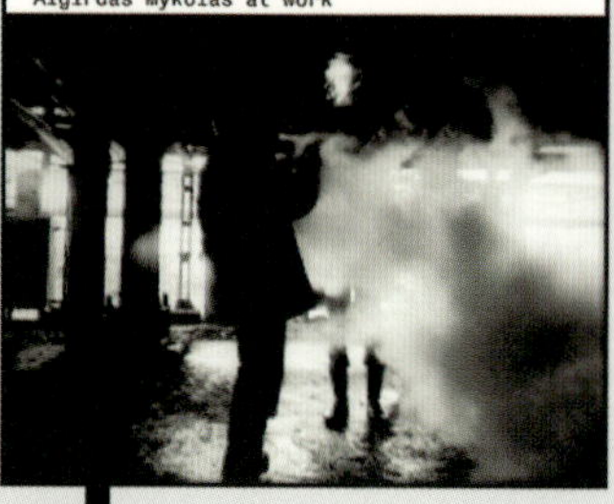

_Algirdas ███████, the head of Spiritual Academy and Kazlauskas from the Academy of Parapsychology are hard to convince.
<Http://www.parapsichologija.lt/v_kazlauskas.htm>
They work to get people back from out there. We are not dying yet and they are just busy with the almost dead. Next week?

_we are meeting with Marius ███████, businessman, head of advertising company "Lukrecija" <http://www.lukrecija.lt>
They are interested in our ability to set alternative models for communication and used to support our artistic research.
Marius likes DRUZBA, he recalls few relatives living by the pipe.
He makes phone calls to connect us with the big guys:

_Sarunas ████████, head of commerce at YUKOS for Baltic states <http://www.yukos.lt>

_Darius ██████, former PR for WILLIAMS International during 1999-2001

_WILLIAMS International(US) confirmed satisfaction of ex-pats with the privatizing of oil refinery MAZEIKIU NAFTA <http://www.nafta.lt> in 1999, and disappointment after turning over the keys to Russians, YUKOS in 2002

_Arturas ███████, current PR for YUKOS for Eastern Europe <http://www.jonkus.lt>

_Bingo! We have the key player who holds control over apparatus of mediation. Marius is a character in search of his role in the play DRUZBA

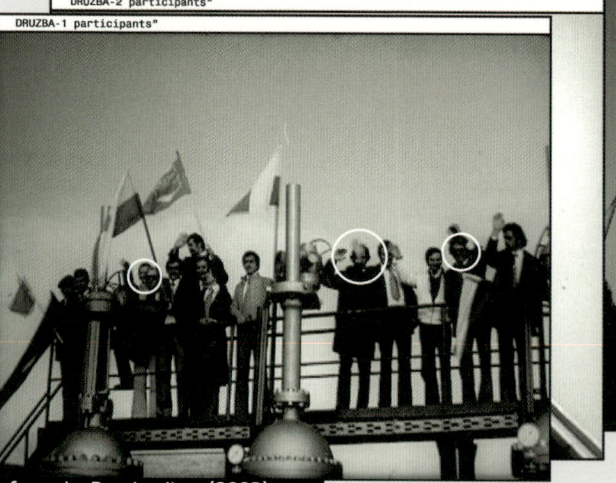

Excerpts from the *Druzba diary* (2003)

Thursday, July 3
_sunny
we meet Arturas ▮▮▮▮ at San Antonio, a Mediterranean pizzeria in the center of Vilnius. A week ago a big guy was shot at the entrance here. He got a call, went out and was hit by a sniper bullet. We order shrimp soup and get to DRUZBA. We take tuna salad and wine and mix it with science, business, Solitude, us as artists, Peter as a writer. The mix is fine, but DRUZBA... Arturas avoids DRUZBA in the talk. He is o.k. but as a PR for Russians he is careful with attempts to evoke spirits of DRUZBA. DRUZBA is haunting Europe?
He reads the pipeline just as a bunch of companies, where YUKOS is an equal partner. Arturas can help us to visit the plant in Mazeikiai as well as Birzai station, which he considers a starting point for DRUZBA

_DRUZBA branch in DDR? he laughs with rhetoric: whether we know any German oil company... Oil for DRUZBA pipeline comes from West Siberia. Do you know any German to reach so far...

_Peter hooks on that and elaborates connecting shamans in Siberia with Hungarian magicians. Arturas points that YUKOS is signing a contract today with MOL Rt. of Hungary <http://www.yukos.com/ep/MOL_project.asp>

_this would lead YUKOS to Adriatic pipeline. According to Arturas, YUKOS could possibly be interested in supporting the travel to the oil fields to shoot a corporate TV or even cinema production that would represent YUKOS as benefactor of natives living over there. TV broadcast in Hungary would be appreciated as part of a PR campaign. Art, business and... Magic?

_after business we change the track to a spiritual world: we meet with Henrikas ▮▮▮▮▮▮, TV journalist at TV3 channel. Henrikas is a producer of entertaining program that searches for people with unusual and magic powers. He introduces us with names and abilities of his favorites. We look through videos. Few to mention:

_woman eating sand (a bucket a week, almost nothing else)

_witch of witches, Vilija ▮▮▮▮▮▮, from the Witch School

_Vytautas ▮▮▮▮▮ from Moletai, who hears mushrooms growing. We try to call him later, but phone switches to the fax

_Dalia from Kaunas, who works with "aura soma" method, theory of colors, we call her, but she is gone to Riga, promises "an open house" for us in a week

_so called Doctor Jegerskas, the rude one, he is really violent, beats his patients, shakes their heads, kicks them while smoking, shouting and cursing heavily in Russian

_Henrikas is skeptical, even for the best things he shows, but then he says: "there is a serious one, that I believe to, whom I never filmed, his name is Vasilijus".
We feel, he is serious. And we sniff oil

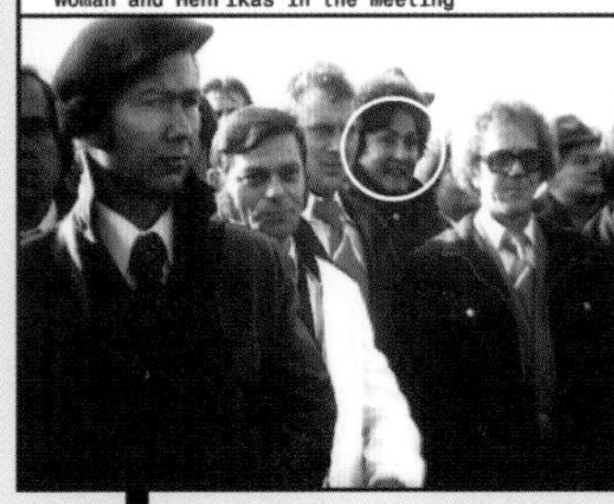
Woman and Henrikas in the meeting

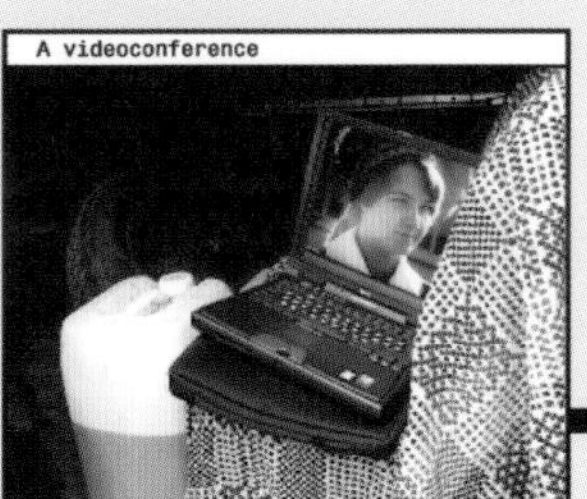
A videoconference

_after two meetings Peter is tired and hungry. We drive to "Torres", Spanish place on the hill with a view to the old town. We take spicy turkey with red wine to grasp the relation between Siberian shamans and Hungarians

_Peter is obsessed with view down in the park. We hear voices and sounds of national folk singers

_just to pretend that Lithuania is not so homogeneous Nomeda decides to show Peter around a small Karaites community near by medieval castle.
We take some Karaites kibynlar with lamb away and get our feet wet in a lake. Peter is one foot in Siberia

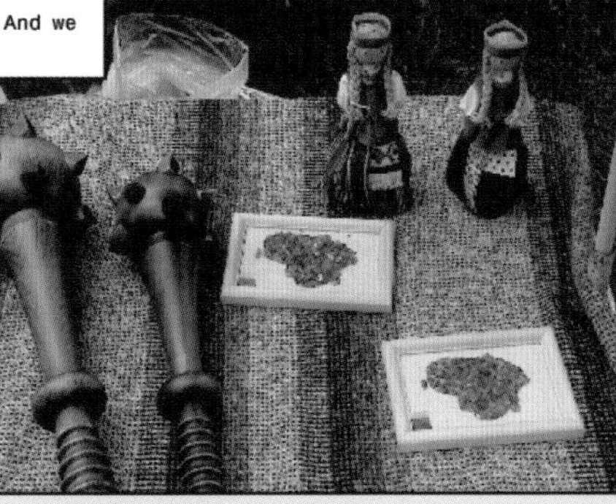
Tools maps and fetishes

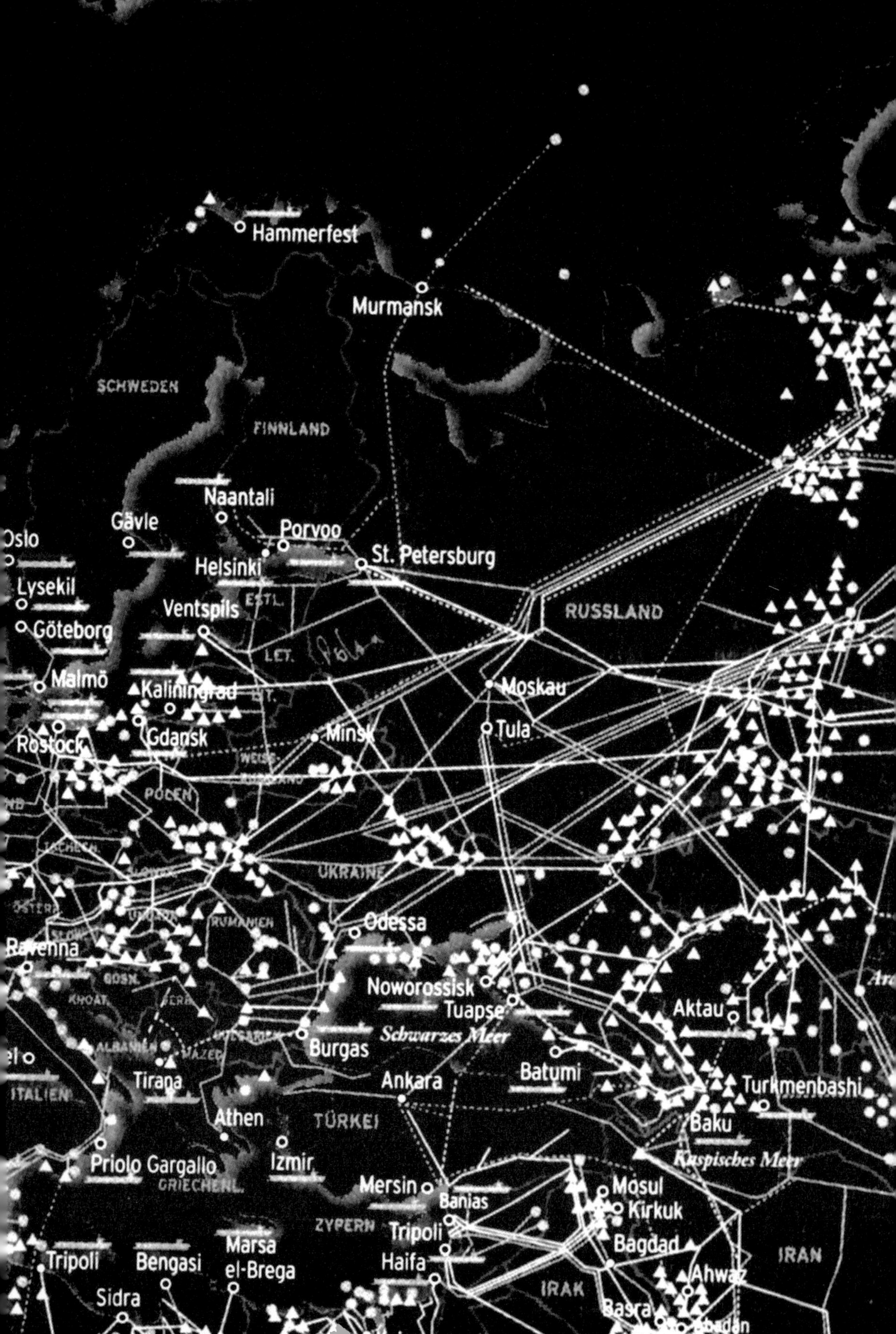

Hammerfest
Murmansk
SCHWEDEN
FINNLAND
Naantali
Gävle
Porvoo
Oslo
Helsinki
St. Petersburg
Lysekil
ESTL.
Ventspils
RUSSLAND
Göteborg
LET.
Malmö
Moskau
Kaliningrad
LIT.
Rostock
Gdansk
Minsk
Tula
WEISS
POLEN
RUSSLAND
TSCHECH.
UKRAINE
ÖSTERR.
UNGARN
RUMÄNIEN
Odessa
SLOW.
Ravenna
BOSN.
KROAT.
Noworossisk
SERB.
Tuapse
Aktau
ALBANIEN
MAZED.
Schwarzes Meer
Burgas
Batumi
Tirana
Ankara
Turkmenbashi
ITALIEN
Athen
TÜRKEI
Baku
Kaspisches Meer
Priolo Gargallo
Izmir
GRIECHENL.
Mersin
Mosul
Banias
Kirkuk
ZYPERN
Tripoli
Bagdad
IRAN
Tripoli
Bengasi
Marsa
Haifa
Ahwaz
el-Brega
IRAK
Sidra
Basra

www.vilma.cc/DRUZBA

PRO-TEST LAB (2005 - ongoing)

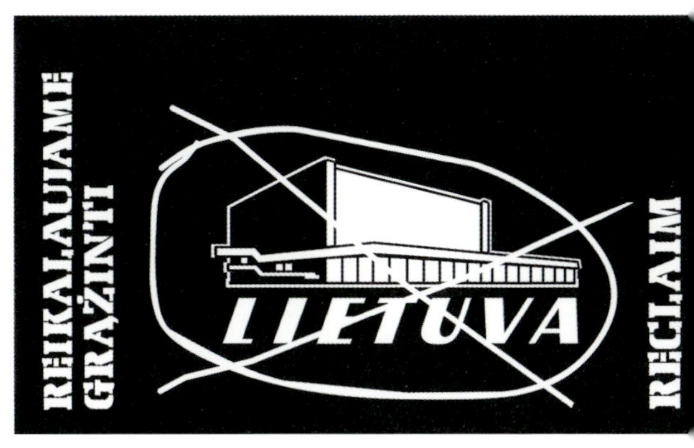

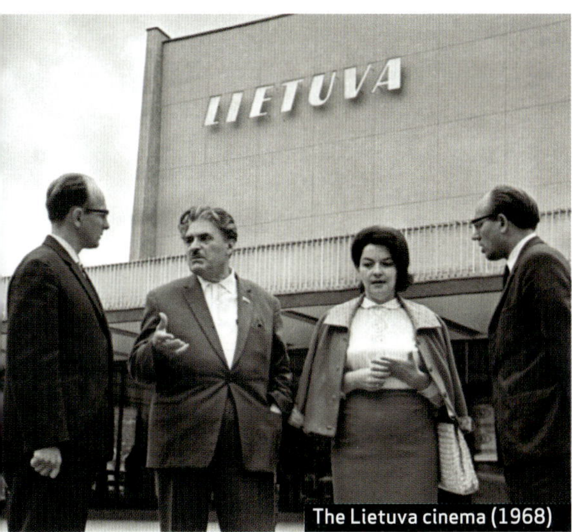
The Lietuva cinema (1968)

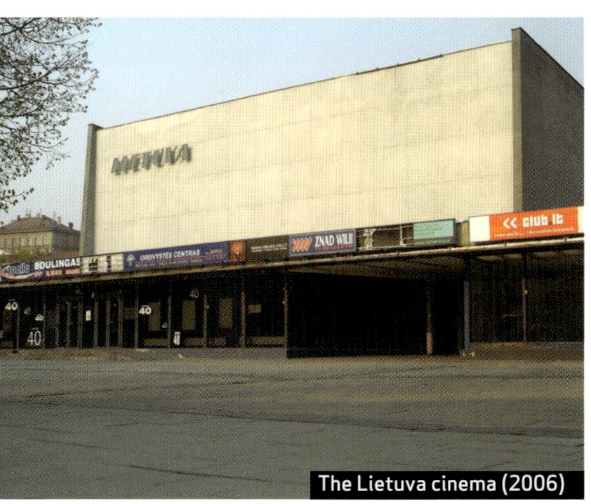
The Lietuva cinema (2006)

 Since independence in 1990, Lithuania has been caught up in a mad period of privatisation, property development and demolition. Like a Wild West land-grab or a gold rush, speculators and real-estate tycoons have joined forces with corrupt municipal bureaucrats to redevelop the country at an insane pace. Profit has been their only motive. Their method is simple: tell the population that a market economy is good for everything. Convince them that capital is king. Remind the public that making Lithuania look like any big capitalist city is the best way to erase the Soviet past – and to make the country attractive to even more investment and development.

Cultural and political change shattered Lithuania as all of post-Soviet space was hit unexpectedly by the ultra-rapid implementation of a shock doctrine.[1] The transformation from Soviet planned economy to capitalism mixed neo-liberalist privatisation and the effects of globalisation with the potency of a Molotov cocktail. Today, all would agree that "independence did not bring freedom".[2] Freedom and modernisation in post-Soviet space is uniquely understood as the free market and privatisation. The concept of a free market serves, here, as an imperative which guarantees that one's Western tutors will not be disappointed.[3] Put simply: the totality of one regime has been exchanged for another. This totality became a natural law implemented by a new ideological institution: the notorious Free Market Institute[4] – which exerts undue influence over government. Under this rubric, public space, landmark buildings,

69

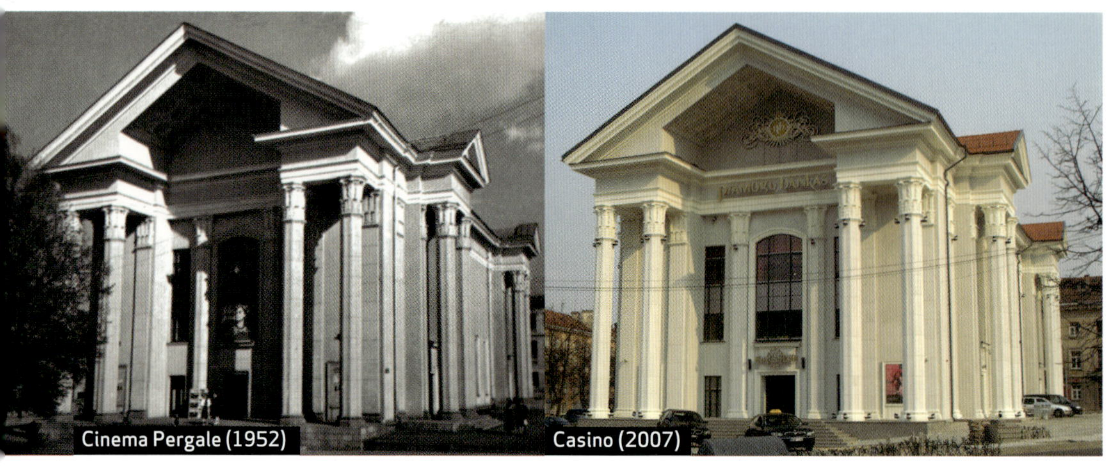

Cinema Pergale (1952)

Casino (2007)

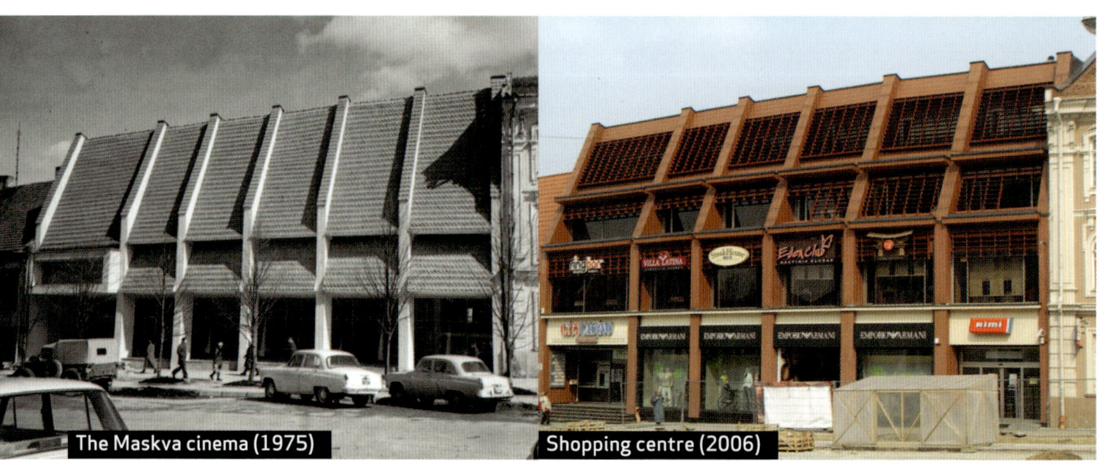

The Maskva cinema (1975)

Shopping centre (2006)

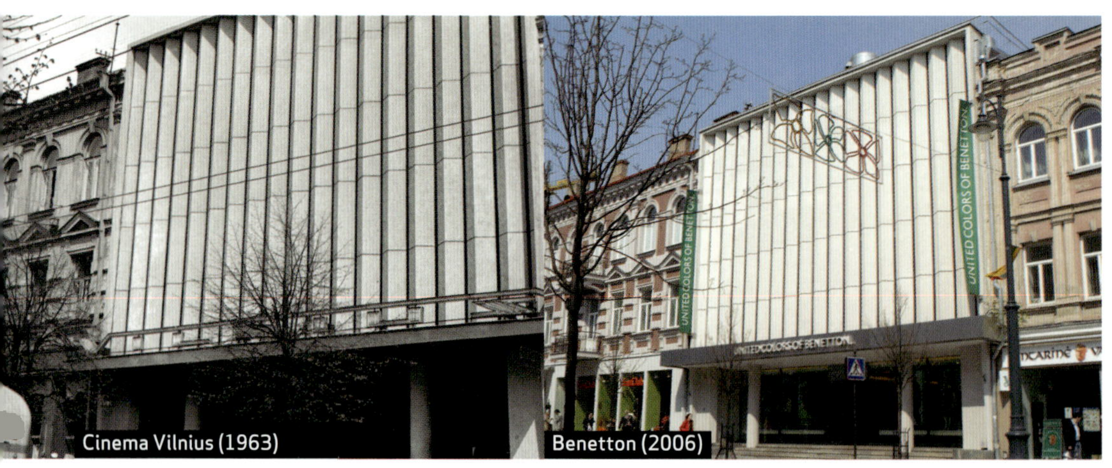

Cinema Vilnius (1963)

Benetton (2006)

cultural life, and public opinion have been the main victims. Who needs a municipal park in the light of wild capitalism? Under the former Soviet regime the idea of public space was introduced via notions of architecture and city planning that captured the contemporaneity of the moment during the period of "Socialism with a human face".[5] Cultural entities, facilities for recreation and sports, and premises for gathering and socialising used to be planned in the centre of the city. Despite their modernist aesthetical value and utility, examples of Soviet architecture are now considered to be derelict monuments of the past, memorials to Soviet ideology.

There were those who hated Soviet architecture, hated modernism, longed for the multiplex experience, those who claimed that public squares were a deformation affecting the old parts of the city. The ideal of the Soviet modernist infrastructure and its concept of common space was suddenly reconstituted in an idealisation of privatised, closed off space. Without being romantic about the past or defending modernism, a thorough assessment is needed of the ideological premises that replaced it – namely, the destructive rhetoric of today.

During the Soviet period cinema was crucial to the cultural life of the country, with huge movie theatres being built in the centre of many Lithuanian cities.[6] These cinemas played an important role as places for public gatherings. After independence, as Soviet structures crumbled in a wholesale fashion, cinema buildings became a focus of attention for the real-estate market. In a short period of time private enterprise managed to take over and destroy almost all the cinemas in Vilnius, turning them into apartments, supermarkets, casinos and shopping centres.

More than twenty cinemas disappeared, including such urban landmarks as the Ausra (Dawn), Zvaigzde (Star), Spalis (October), Pionierius (Pioneer), Pergale (Victory), Tevyne (Motherland), Kronika (Newsreel), Aidas (Echo), Planeta (Planet), Neris, Vingis, Lazdynai, Vilnius and Maskva (Moscow). As a poor replacement, and echoing the tragedy of cities the world over, two huge multiplex cinemas were constructed: the Coca Cola Plaza in the suburbs and the Akropolis Cinemas beyond the city limits. The latter, which is part of Lithuania's largest shopping mall, is representative of the *mallification* of the country.

With the multiplexes came multiplex Hollywood movies: thus, the demolition of cinematic space encoded the demolition of independent film programming.

It is symbolic that the last cinema to be privatised and destroyed during the past decade is named after the country: Lietuva.

"Let's meet at the Lietuva"

On the lost battlefields of privatisation Lietuva has become a significant rallying point. The Lietuva was built in 1965 as a piece of Soviet modernist architecture, becoming the biggest cinema in Lithuania with more than 1,000 seats and a 200-square-metre screen (offering an ideal image size). It was home to the Vilnius Film Festival and as such has played an important role in the imaginative life of a whole generation of local people. Its name, Lietuva, is also an important signifier of national identity, as it never bore any Soviet overtones (i.e. it wasn't called the cinema of the Soviet Republic of Lithuania). To say to somebody "Let's meet at the Lietuva" really meant something during the Soviet occupation. In front of the cinema a vast public square offered an ideal space for gathering, debating, chatting and hanging out.

In 2002, the Vilnius municipal authorities quietly sold the cinema to private property-developers with a caveat that it had to operate as a cinema for a three-year period.[7] That term ended on 1 July 2005. Is it not strange that during all these years no voices of protest were raised in Lithuania? Why were people silent, indifferent, during this time of change? Why has there been no protest at all since the years of "singing revolution"?[8]

It might be thought that the cultural, urban, activist practices that call for protest, for the reclaiming of public space, come from the Western cultural tradition of democracy. A repressive Soviet past simply erased such activities from people's memories. Nowadays, the discourse of protest is not possible. Protesting means looking over one's shoulder, longing for a past; it connotes Stalinism and the massive repression deriving from the Gulag. Hence the notion of protest, and Leftist practice as such, has a negative meaning for many people in the post-Soviet world.[9]

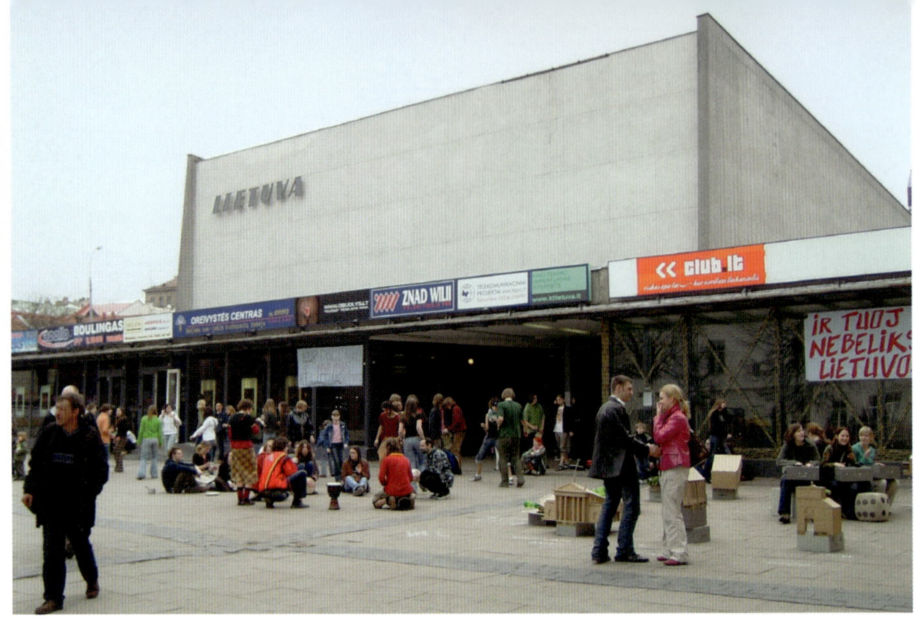

Lietuva. Sold out

When I was a child I enjoyed going to this cinema. It seemed so big to me, so modern, so desirable. There was that cafe, where I'd always get my favourite milkshake. The huge facade could tell a tale about endless Soviet optimism, one big utopia.

The word *Lietuva* on the facade seemed outrageous in Soviet times. As a sign at the border crossing, as a border post, it marked the forbidden world, where Fellini, Antonioni, Visconti, Godard, Kieslowski, Tarkovski and even Buñuel dwelt.

Only through cinema could you see another culture, the Western one. The cinema was like a bridge, like a mediator between this and another reality.

There was also a planetarium near the cinema, where teachers would take us to gaze at the celestial sphere. We would sit in the darkness and watch the planets go round. Just like in the cinema. It seemed as if I could touch the Moon, feel its skin with my hand. The planetarium and the cinema together. They were like a local dream factory. Cosmos and cinema. Two big Soviet passions. A bridge between two systems where Communism and capitalism meet.

People would always gather in the square in front of the cinema. They would queue from dawn to dusk to get tickets. Tickets for what?

Films were important to people since they created the illusion that things were better elsewhere. Or that everything was going to be alright. Or...

The square near the cinema used to be a popular place for dates... Like bridges favoured by suicides, wailing walls and poets' graves, this place had a good aura.

Everything was happening so fast, all that stuff... I don't know when it

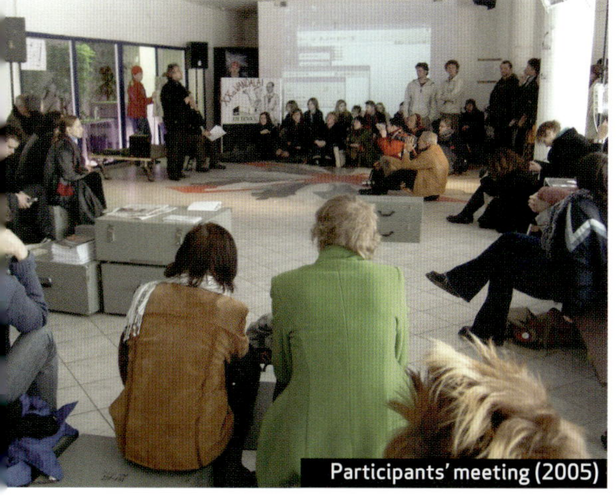

Participants' meeting (2005)

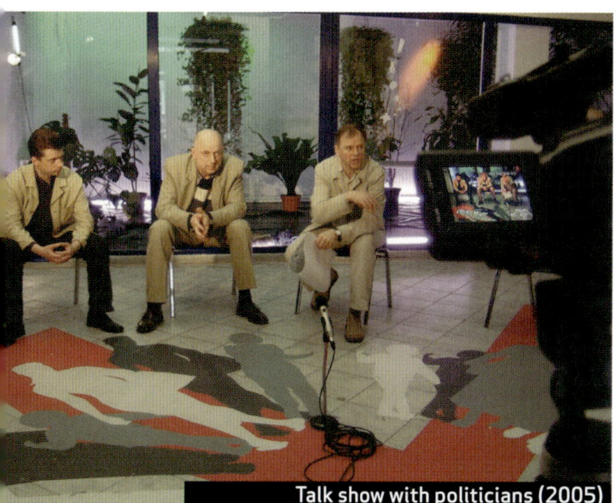

Talk show with politicians (2005)

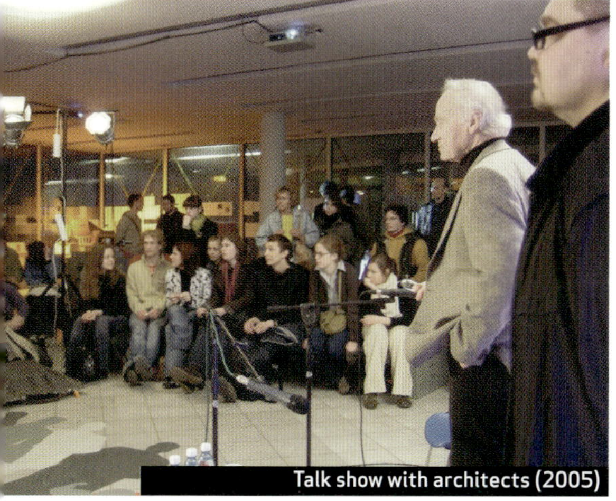

Talk show with architects (2005)

The state and market forces also stand in the way of protest. But democracy is conflict and antagonism, not consensus. Are we maybe dealing here with an imitation of democracy that rejects antagonism? Neoliberal conformity means, of course, avoiding antagonism while at the same time making use of it. In such a context it is very difficult to speak of protest.

If protest is impossible, if resistance is unimaginable, what kind of artistic strategy might be used in order to generate some kind of protest? And if there is no protest, can we maybe bring it about, make it happen? How do we open up the contradictions hidden on site?[10]

Towards the collective action

In March 2005 the former Lietuva ticket office in Vilnius was squatted and converted into a *Pro-test Lab* inviting people to propose different protest scenarios; to both inspire action and make it happen. Beginning as a case study of the destruction of the Lietuva movie theatre – the largest Soviet modernist pavilion-type building in Lithuania – it has developed into a space and an archive of various forms of protest (and legal proceedings) against the corporate privatisation of public space.

Artistic praxis ought to reflect change, let's say. Although the question is, once more, how does it contribute to change, in fact? Is it possible to construct a work that wouldn't just analyse or reflect change but actually generate it? How does one organise the capacity to provoke it?[11]

The *Pro-test Lab* addressed collective production and participation and was aimed at creating a community to activate people's cultural and political imagination. The citizens of Vilnius who've joined the *Pro-test Lab* come from different, sometimes antagonistic, communities and social groups, young and old, students and pensioners, intellectuals and workers – but all trying to imagine what a positive kind of protest might be. With a bit of dash, turning *pro* and *test* into action, they have constructed a new identity for the place, as well as creating a site for testing the potential of protest.

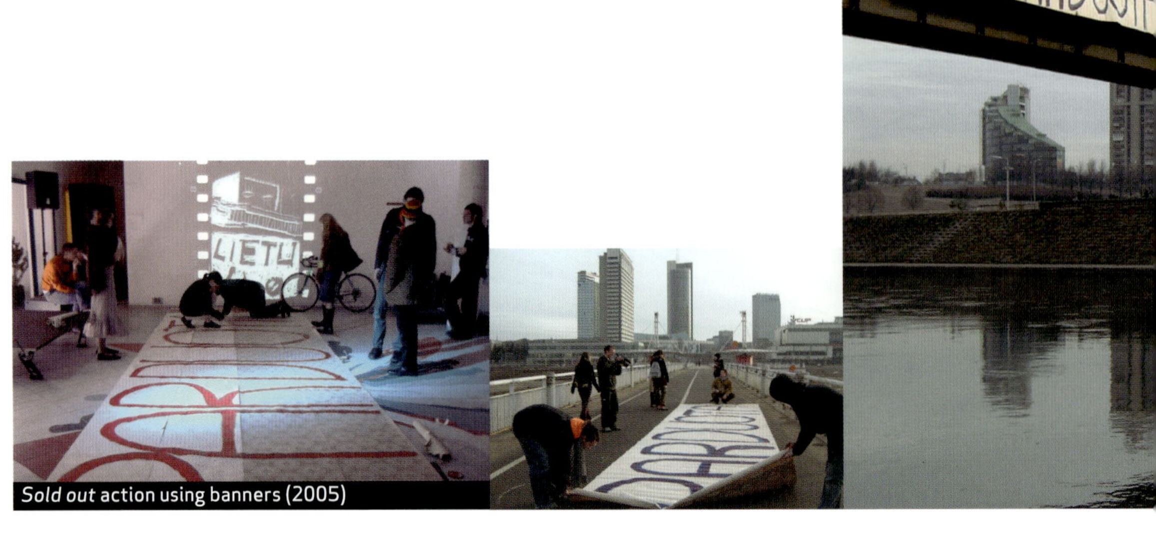

Sold out action using banners (2005)

was sold. I even failed to notice when the cinemas disappeared. They were privatised in a moment. In my childhood Vilnius had a lot of them, maybe twenty. Vilnius was the city of cinemas. Dziga Vertov, Ladislaw Starewicz, Werner Herzog. Sartre, Greimas. Structure and cinema city. Had Mekas not gone to the West, he'd now be talking about Vilnius, not New York.

It was a hard time for cinema then. After the Fall of the Berlin Wall, the cinemas began falling, too. All that time people were silent. Nobody noticed. Everybody minded their own business. That's normal. Competition. We reject the past. We take steps towards the free market. Struggle for survival. Attempts of adaptation. Ultimately, mutual distrust.

No kind of protest is possible. There aren't protests in Lithuania like they have in France. Is it a grim aftermath of occupation?

The great euphoria after reclaiming independence. Today we are free and nobody forces us to march in demonstrations. Not like in the recent past. We are free in our choices. Finally, we have a possibility to choose.

Finally we don't have to protest. Finally, we no longer have to march in demonstrations. People don't like Soviet architecture today. It brings back depressing and even painful memories about the empire. This architecture: concrete, massive walls, grey monsters. Extremely thick walls. Now it is a ghost that should be banished from the city. Just like what happened to the monuments of Soviet ideology.

I like skyscrapers and all that is new. I've heard that the cinema is going to be demolished and that some people set up a community to save it. I felt sceptical like most of my acquaintances.

"Join in, participate, offer your own protest scenario."

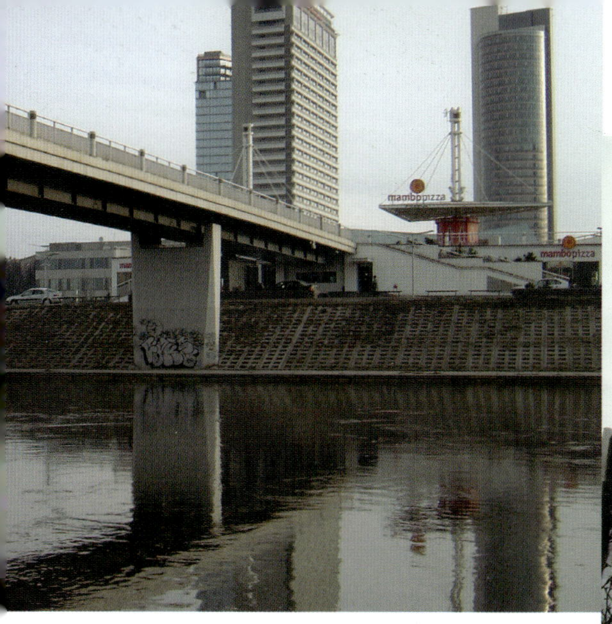

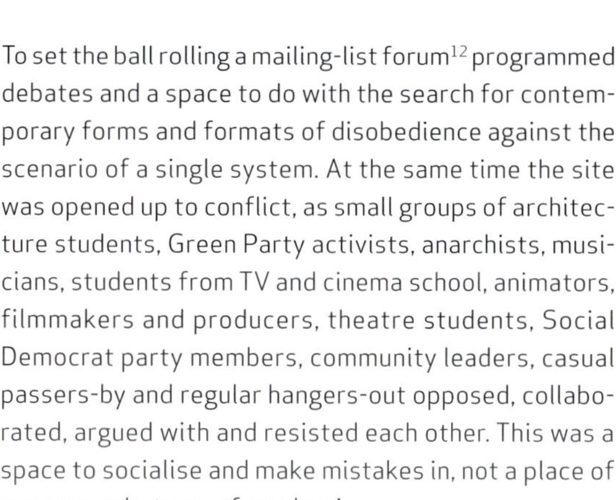

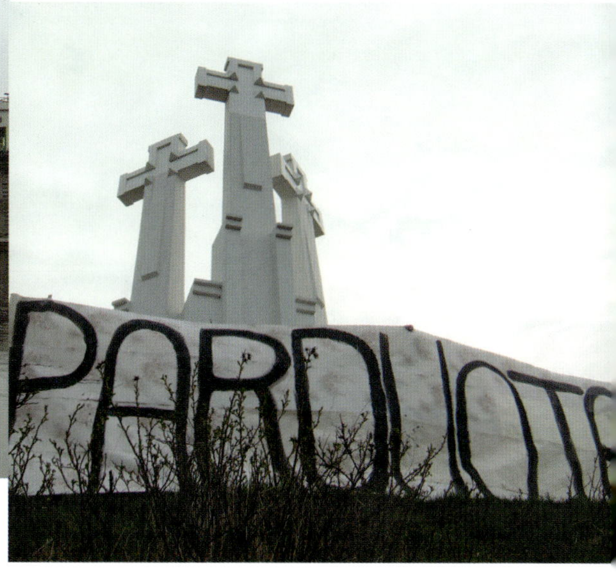

To set the ball rolling a mailing-list forum[12] programmed debates and a space to do with the search for contemporary forms and formats of disobedience against the scenario of a single system. At the same time the site was opened up to conflict, as small groups of architecture students, Green Party activists, anarchists, musicians, students from TV and cinema school, animators, filmmakers and producers, theatre students, Social Democrat party members, community leaders, casual passers-by and regular hangers-out opposed, collaborated, argued with and resisted each other. This was a space to socialise and make mistakes in, not a place of consensus but one of production.

The *Pro-test Lab* archive

The *Pro-test Lab* archive organises a collection of images and props, and the relationships they produce with the act of protest. The archive maps attempts to stage an autonomous platform for action through an art project that can penetrate reality through political acts. This develops both inside and outside the art system by simultaneously considering the tension that such a relationship produces.

The *Pro-test Lab* has performed the function of a recording device, and gradually built up an identity and a scenario for both space and archive. Referring to the early model of the Lumière Brothers' camera, which had a twofold function (to shoot film and to project it), this recording device has generated actions and registered different forms of protest. It captures the protest, which accumulates, matures, and yet remains unidentified, unvoiced, ever in search of a format and a way of becoming vocal. It has developed into a rallying point that extends artistic claims into political resistance.

The archive is constructed through the events of artistic production staged as a campaign of reclaiming public space as their method of protest. It acts to initiate the debate elicited by the conflict between privatisation and publicness, art and ethics, activism and production. Starting as an art project that investigates the energies of the productive side of protest, the *Pro-test Lab* is archiving all the possibilities of impossible protest that rally people against the privatisation of public space.[13]

From art project to juridico-political process

It was apparent from the outset that the public effectiveness of the *Pro-test Lab* would be tested against its profile in the mainstream media. Popular media in Lithuania – and around the world – is retreating from hard news coverage and in-depth issue-based reportage. And a strategy for finessing the media to put a positive – and constant – spin on an essentially insur-

With such words the group of young utopians invited everyone to protest. Students, the Greens, artists, fun-seekers.

Lanky youngsters, enjoying their temporary freedom. Some weirdos, doing nothing, waiting for their hour of success. Exhibitionists who experience sexual satisfaction fighting for the truth.

I didn't feel like the right person for all this action.

Of course, most people saw them as some kind of freaks. But they were attractive.

Every day on my way to work I would observe the young guys gathering near the cinema. They played Monopoly in the street. They put the city on sale. Everyone in this game was able to buy the cathedral or city hall of Vilnius. It's good to be rich.

I joined in. Everyone was overwhelmed by a sort of collective enthusiasm. I felt solidarity with them. Together we arranged events. A lot of events.

Somebody brought some old wallpaper. We made enormous posters and wrote *Parduota* (Sold out) in huge letters.

On Sunday morning at 7 am I went with people I didn't know yet and hung huge *Sold out* posters on the bridges of Vilnius. I walked the streets of this city and my voice cried "Sold out!"

I was surprised that so many people came to stand up for Lietuva. They chatted, danced, drank and smoked, cooked, just spent time together. Then I realised that they just wanted to identify their place. That place was as important to them as their own place. As the place created by themselves. The place of spending time together.

Was I an observer or a participant? Did I participate in this action as a collaborator?

It was really interesting to understand what other people thought. What are their intentions? Why do I hear their voice only now? Why were they silent before, when it was possible to change something?

Today is not 1968, and the Lietuva is in Lithuania. Here, protest is understood as a demon, only not black but red. And instead of horns it has a hammer and sickle.

I'm a sceptic. A realist. A grown-up. I will not protest against Bush. I want safety for my small country.

Anyway, you can't change anything. Barking dogs will not disturb the clouds. We arranged such an event near the cinema. The Lietuva will be pulled down, nobody doubts it anymore. Now this building is really grey and dead, like an alien body from another planet.

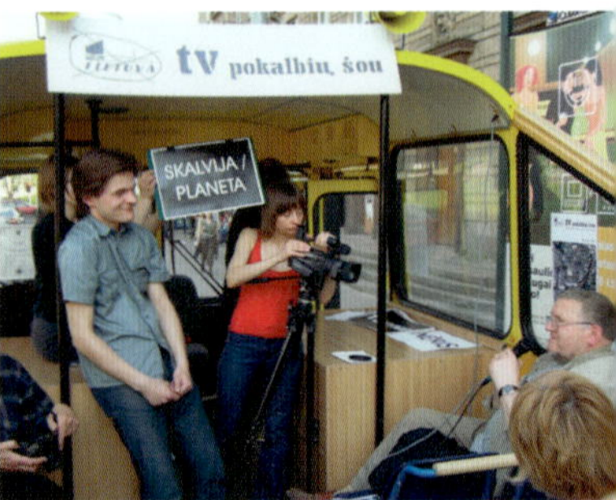

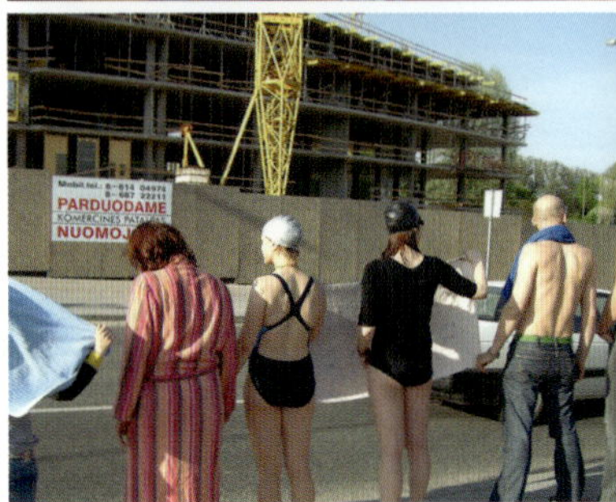

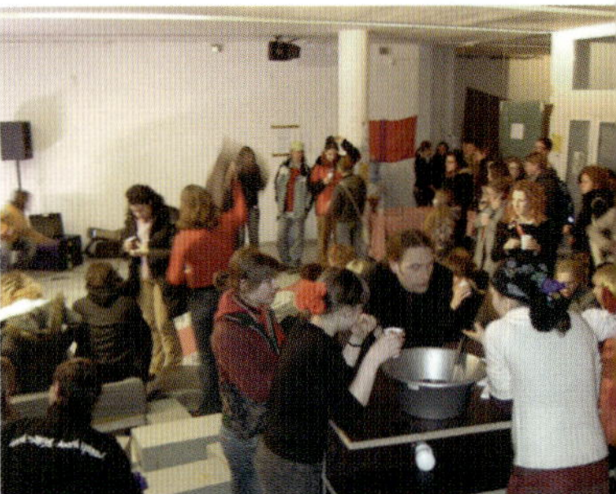

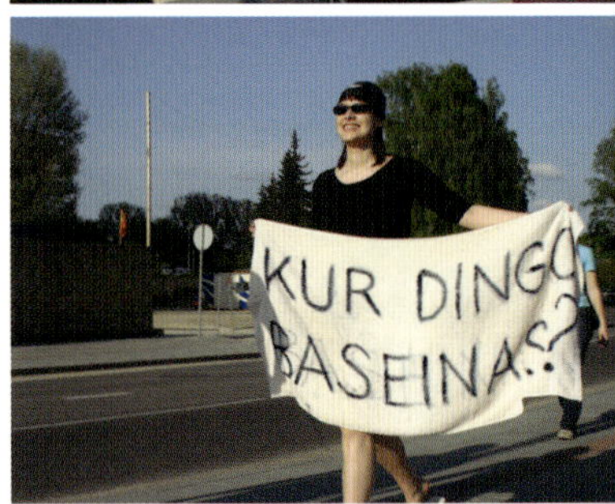

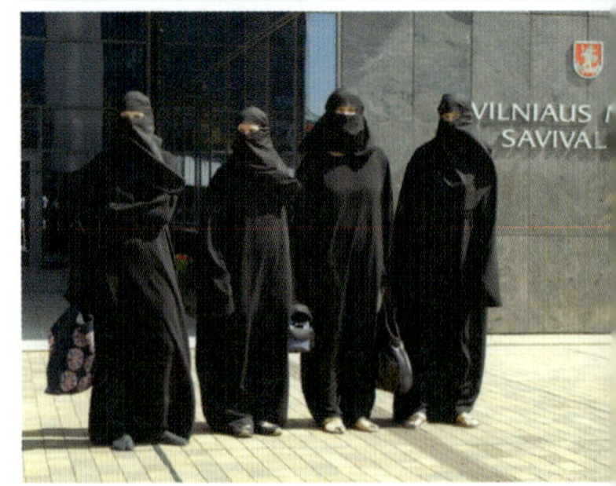

rectionist project was needed. The *Pro-test Lab* had to make sure that the media was regularly supplied with attractive and newsworthy material, so a series of performances and events that manipulated populist forms were developed to keep the project in a constant state of animation and "going public". (The inverse is also true; property developers and neo-liberal politicians can bury information by *not* scripting a press release and *not* posting information on websites.)

The Internet has become a bona fide news source and stories that begin life in cyberspace are re-reported in the dailies and on television, so significant efforts were also channelled into building a constant electronic information profile for the *Pro-test Lab*. And the profile of the Internet chat resource, and linking to other sites and discussion spaces, was constantly being built: as was the issue of public space via constantly commenting in the webblog resources of other web portals. In this way a shadow identity for the *Pro-test Lab* could be constructed within public discussion taking place in other quarters. At a certain point an online interview was republished on several websites and in a number of newspapers, which started the broader public dissemination of information.

The invitation to participate in the international exhibition *Populism* – taking place in Vilnius, Amsterdam, Frankfurt and Oslo – also delivered a strategic platform to the project. Firstly, the *Pro-test Lab* would be reported on in the framework of the exhibition (the Lithuanian media always concentrate on local participating artists) and would be delivered to a larger international audience. The *Pro-test Lab* archive has also been presented in major exhibitions in Austria, Italy, the Republic of Korea, and Russia. Appeals could also be made to international solidarity as the issue of redevelopment is a contested topic throughout Europe. Moreover, as in many small countries, Lithuanian corporate executives, politicians and bureaucrats set disproportionate store by international opinion – lest it threaten future inbound foreign investment. And high levels of investment are drawn from Norway, the Netherlands, and Germany where *Populism* was being presented.[14]

As the electronic and media profile of the *Pro-test Lab* began to rise, new names and new activists began to appear within the web-community specifically associated with the project. This was manifested in June 2006 when a call for a public citizens' meeting of cultural producers was held at the Contemporary Art Centre (CAC), Vilnius, and sixty producers attended with the aim of generating an alternative vision for the site of Lietuva cinema, which culminated in a weekend-long workshop.[15] At the same time, opinions began to appear accusing the *Pro-test Lab* of instrumentalising, or becoming, "the authority of protest" and "privatising" the discourse of protest and harnessing the potentials of networking to a selfish end.

A month later the owners of the Lietuva site, Plot 17, Pylimo Street, made their mandatory public presentation of the plans for the site. Outside the Municipal Offices appeared several figures dressed in full black *burqa*-like costumes, staged by a new group of protesters associated with the *Pro-test Lab*. In Lithuania (which is mono-cultural) the sight of a *burqa* potentially triggers associations with Islamic terrorists, or freedom fighters, among them a group known as *shakhidi* or "black widows" that were first active in Afghanistan and more recently in Chechnya.[16] The following month the citizens' movement *For Lithuania without quotation marks* addressed an open letter to the members of UNESCO World Heritage Committee expressing concerns that the building was being developed in contravention of the Vilnius World Heritage Protection Order (the Lietuva is located within the boundary of the World Heritage Zone).[17] In stark contrast, the Lithuanian Green Party, supposedly representative of shared concerns, rejected a protest action coinciding with a public protest action that they were making (and had got proper permission for), arguing that it placed them in a negative light.

The next step, and as a reflection of the growing public support for the actions being taken, a public petition *For the Lietuva cinema and the cultural policy relating to it* was launched, the intention being to present the petition to the Government and to initiate two laws: one to pursue a definition of "public space" and the other to define "public interest".[18] In one month the petition was signed by 8,000 citizens and was presented to the government of the Republic of Lithuania for mandatory future deliberation.

It turned from the centre of attraction into a grey spot. Now nouveaux riche types will have apartments here. Maybe scenes from old movies will haunt them, maybe they will hear voices.

I work a lot. Sometimes during weekends, too. It's important for me to rest. To recover. I like to relax well. I'm still looking for new experiences. New emotions.

I liked protesting on behalf of the Lietuva. It was like a vacation at the same time. To compensate what I do every day.

I met people with other ways of thinking here. What is the product they produce? Is action essential?

It's good to feel united. To have an idea worthy of your effort, worth fighting for. To feel important and to do something meaningful. Unfortunately, it's no longer possible.

Protest is based on a logic different from my job. It gave me the possibility to be in someone else's shoes. I felt as if I did something forbidden. Something illegal, beyond what's normal. The strange excitement that you feel when crossing the line of what's allowed. It's been a long time since I last experienced it. Maybe way back when I skipped classes because of the cinema.

Am I a rebel? No, it's just a kind of masquerade. I'm a weekend rebel. On Fridays, after work is a good time. I buy a strange sort of pastime.

Protest highlights my style very well.

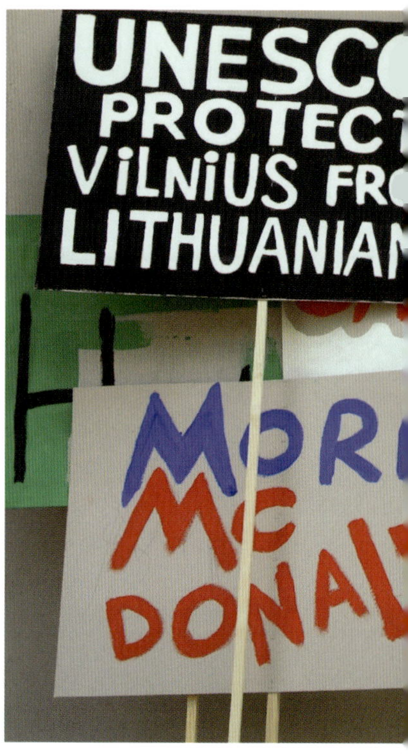

Lietuva. Sold out, 2006
Script for the film, based on the narratives posted on the mailing list generating *Pro-test Lab* space and its activities.

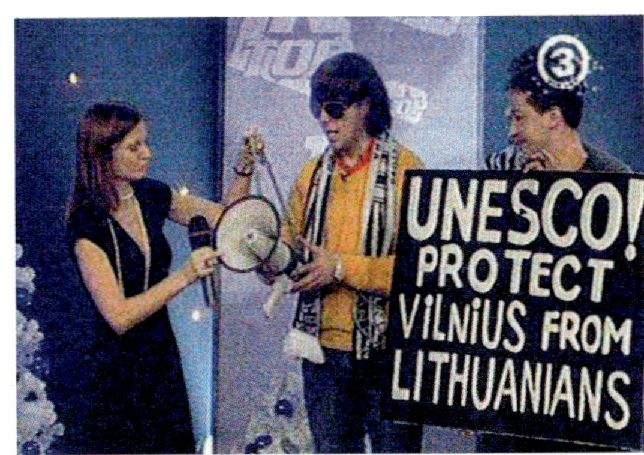

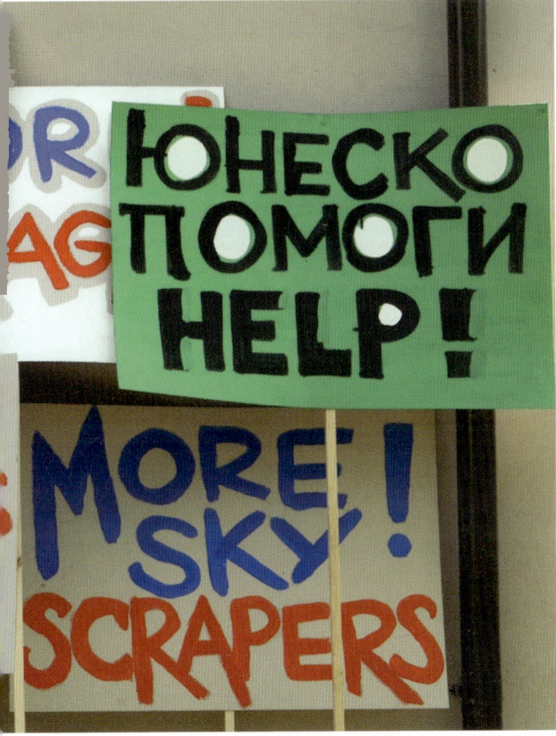

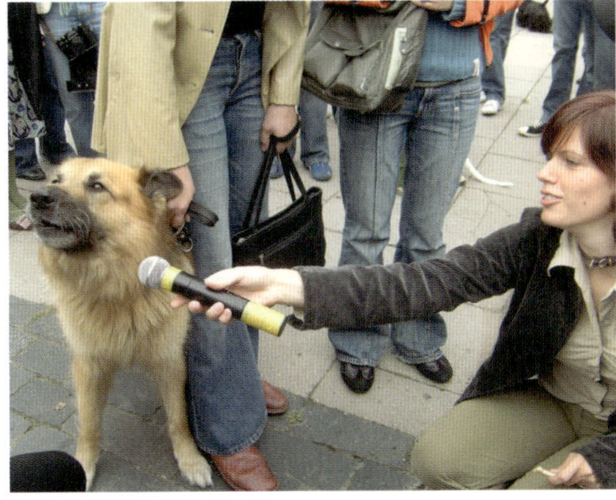

At this point, entering the national legislative arena, the actions of the *Pro-test Lab* began to test the limits of an art project and also defied the temporal limitations of what is commonly understood as the work of art: a clearly defined and delineated *gestalt* object and action (concerned with aesthetic institutions). It also began to question the matter of public interest and who, if anyone, is responsible for it in Lithuania as 8,000 signatories represent a voting block or constituency large enough to influence a public election – yet no politician associated themselves with the movement. It also started a debate about what constitutes public interest, who has a right to represent public interests, and their proper value in relation to private concerns.[19] (Profit and not the people remains the mantra.) So why not an artist as a public representative?

For Lithuania without quotation marks

The *For Lithuania without quotation marks* movement began a campaign of writing open letters to the shareholders and trustees of the holding company controlling the Lietuva cinema site (to deflect attention from the ultimate owners of the concern). Private space in this case is equal to privacy, as corporate directors don't want to besmirch their public political image and damage possible future influence over matters involving the public domain. And their profit motives want to maintain the status of Lithuanian public space as "for sale" to the highest bidder.[20]

From October 2006 to January 2007 the Petition Committee of the Government of the Republic of Lithuania addressed the petition of 11 July submitted by the movement *For Lithuania without quotation marks*. The Committee instructed the Ministry of Culture to form an advisory sub-committee on the matter of the nature of public space and cultural artefacts, that included members of *For Lithuania without quotation marks*.[21]

In full exercise of their citizens' rights, the *For Lithuania without quotation marks* movement made a submission to the Vilnius District Administrative Court pursuing an "abrogation of responsibility by the Vilnius District Planning Commission for rewarding redevelopment rights and building consent for the Lietuva cinema site".

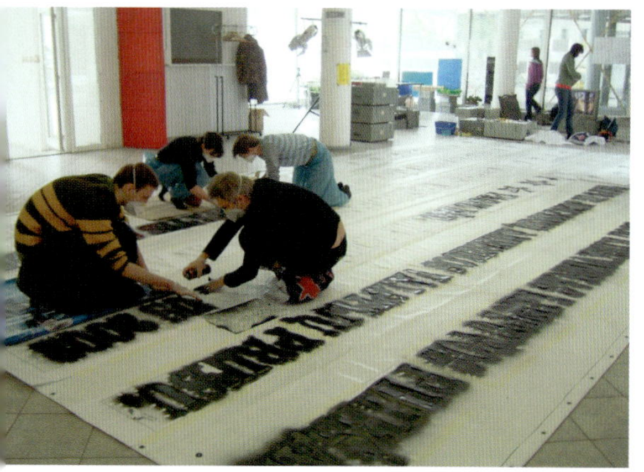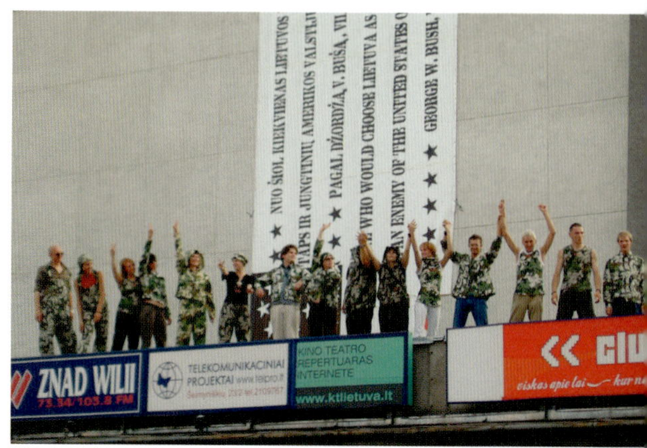

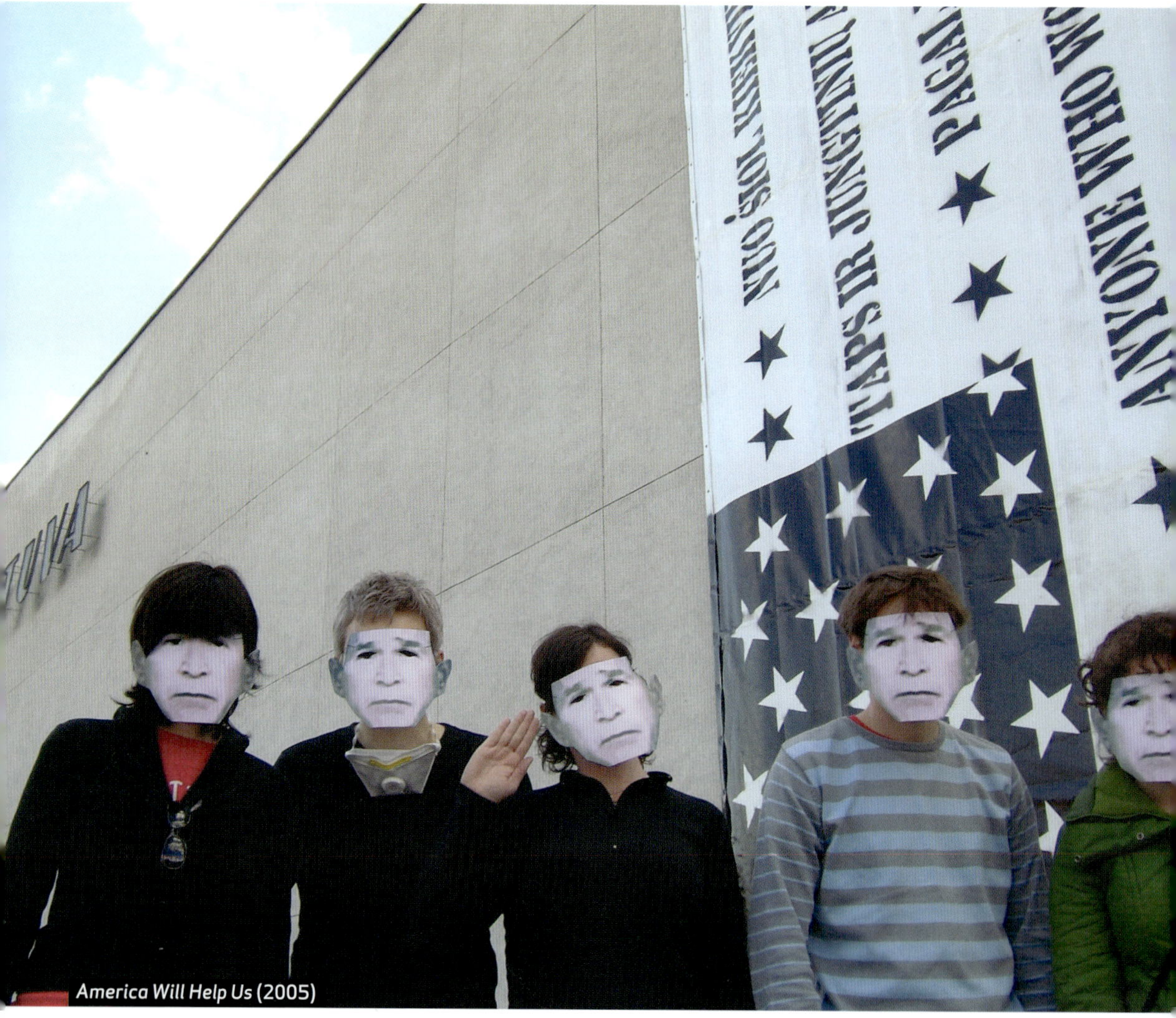

America Will Help Us (2005)

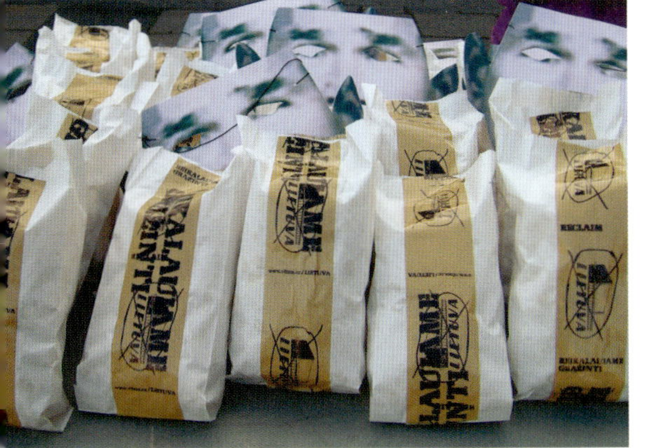

Parliament House and the monument to the fallen heroes of independence, this is becoming an urgent question for Lithuanians and their political representatives. Particularly as Vilnius is going to be caught in the glare of being European Capital of Culture in 2009: a politically motivated project that is supposed to celebrate the national spirit of creativity and to be a public celebration – which needs public spaces – of Lithuanian national culture. And not its wrecking by the forces of privatisation and consumption.

And on 8 May 2007 the four principal members of the movement were subpoenaed to appear before the Court to address their submission to delay the development of the site. And in support of the claim the *Pro-test Lab* made an action at the site, measuring the effects of the granted permissions in terms of scale, to prove to the public just how intrusive the proposed new building would be: obscuring the view of neighbouring properties and subsuming both the square and footpaths used by thousands of pedestrians every day. Their daily commuting routes, and space, were clearly set to disappear into the belly of the developer's beast.

In counter-claim the developers counter-sued the four principals of the movement in the District Civil Court[22] for loss of trade valued at hundreds of thousands of Euros as development has been halted while the courts make their findings. And that is where the process stands, straddling the legal divide: in a public face-off between a commercial Goliath and an activist citizens' David.

The Lithuanian political and legal system is being forced to confront the monster and decide between the spatial will of the agora or the atrium: which simulation of public space is enclosed within a commercial complex. Is public space a space of ambulation and aggregation free of commercial imperative, or is the space to wander through necessarily linked in the future to the necessities of consumption? As private glass-and-steel monuments to consumption start to hem in the Lithuanian

NOTES

1. Naomi Klein: *The Shock Doctrine: The Rise of Disaster Capitalism*. New York: Metropolitan Books/Henry Holt, 2007.

2. Gayatri Chakravorty Spivak: *Subaltern Studies: Deconstructing Historiography*. Oxford: Oxford University Press, 1988.

3. Slavoj Zizek: "What Is To be Done (with Lenin)?", *These Times* (21 January 2004).

4. The statutes of the Lithuanian Free Market Institute clearly encourage that freedom is the right of access to a free market, the rights of the individual to own private property, the rights of the market to set value.

5. "A process of mild democratisation and political liberalisation that would still enable the Communist Party to maintain real power" (Wikipedia).

6. By the time that Lenin dispatched *agit-trains* (with Dziga Vertov films on board) to propagandise about the revolution, cinema was already considered to be the most important of all the arts in the Soviet Union. As part of Communist policy, but also due to Stalin's personal fascination for cinema, a great many film theatres were built around the country. It would be too reductive to say that cinemas were merely places of ideology. Those built in Lithuania played a crucial role as places for public gatherings and for the production of cultural awareness.

7. The Lietuva was privatised by the company VP Market, a national supermarket chain. VP Market has made inroads into other fields, such as real estate, the supply of energy, etc. As well as its overall domination of the Baltic market, it also extends as far as Bulgaria and Rumania.

8. "The Singing Revolution is the commonly used name for events between 1987 and 1990 that led to the regaining of independence of Estonia, Latvia, and Lithuania" (Wikipedia).

9. Here we should mention that all Leftist discourse in Lithuania smacks of Stalinism and of state-controlled demonstrations. It just so happens that during the last fifteen years no serious attempt has been made to reintroduce Leftist discourse into politics. After the collapse of the Soviet Union, all the one-time Communists became hardcore capitalists. They were capitalists in the Soviet period, too, having all the privileges that European Union bureaucrats have in Brussels today. After the re-establishing of independence, the ex-Communists merely changed the name of their party, since the CP was made illegal, just like the National-Socialist Party was in Germany after the Second World War. The Communists became Social Democrats. And those who did not change their name – the real Communists, so to speak – are now in prison.

10. The site is always structured symbolically, architecturally and ideologically, and the job in hand is to reveal hidden contradictions.

11. We started discussing the idea of creating an experimental model for resistance in the autumn and winter of 2004 with the curators of the *Populism* exhibition.

12. vilma@vilma.cc, which had almost two hundred participants.

13. More than seventy events have been organized at, or in relation to, the *Pro-test Lab* from April 2005 till now.

14. As part of the *Pro-test Lab* programme, on the 23 August 2005 there was a TV bridge between Vilnius and Oslo organised by the Office for Contemporary Art (OCA) in collaboration with Atelier Nord. It brought together artists, architects, activists and politicians from both countries for comparative study of gentrification processes in Norway and Lithuania and how they lead to the privatisation of public space.

15. The workshop titled *Bezpridel* was organised as a three-day session discussing the proposal for the Gwangju Biennial brought by curator Cristina Ricupero. Reflecting upon the notion "the abundance of Asia," it was interesting to think about the constraints framing Europe and Asia. This kind of thinking about two positions is essential for the local Vilnius and Lithuanian context as it is striving to resolve historical bonds with Asia and articulate its relations with Western Europe. It is thought that Europe constitutes itself as a constant building of borders, whereas Asia is borderless,

and it could be framed as *Bezpridel*, a Russian word that is hard to translate, meaning "go as you please".

16. Several figures dressed as "black widows" of Islam (although they were not only women), with their faces covered, all except the eyes, walked through the main streets of the capital, visiting a large supermarket and spending some time at the fountain next to the Parliament. An hour after they paid a visit to the Parliament fountain the participants were apprehended by the security services.

17. An appeal to UNESCO *Concerning the Destruction of Cultural Heritage and Cultural Open Spaces within a Cultural Heritage Object: the Historic Centre of Vilnius* was presented during the UNESCO World Heritage Committee 30th session in Vilnius on 8-16 July 2006.

18. A Lithuanian version of the petition http://www.culture.lt/peticija/ was signed by more then 8,000 citizens. There is an ongoing version to express international support for this petition at: http://www.culture.lt/petition/

19. Such a discussion was organised in October 2007 by the Parliamentary Committee for Law and Order in collaboration with the Free Market Institute to analyse the decree that defines the "defence of public interest" and came to the conclusion that "as regards the often occurring complex economic, social processes in society, it is difficult to identify public interest and to distinguish it from private interest or the interest of marginal groups of people."

20. In October 2005 VP Market sold their shares of the Lietuva cinema to a real-estate developer, Rojaus Apartamentai (Paradise Apartments), and today the owners of Lietuva are: Cinema Scotland shareholders Peter Baker (Chairman); M2Invest shareholders, Arthur Simonsen (Vice-chairman) Dalius Kaveckas, Amit Majithia and Per Moller (shareholders).

21. The committee decided to partially meet the demands of the petition and to approach the Government to create working groups at the Ministry of Environment, including a working group to initiate a law that would define a public space within the framework of "territorial planning and consent", and to organise, at the Ministry of Culture, a survey of cultural spaces in the urban environment.

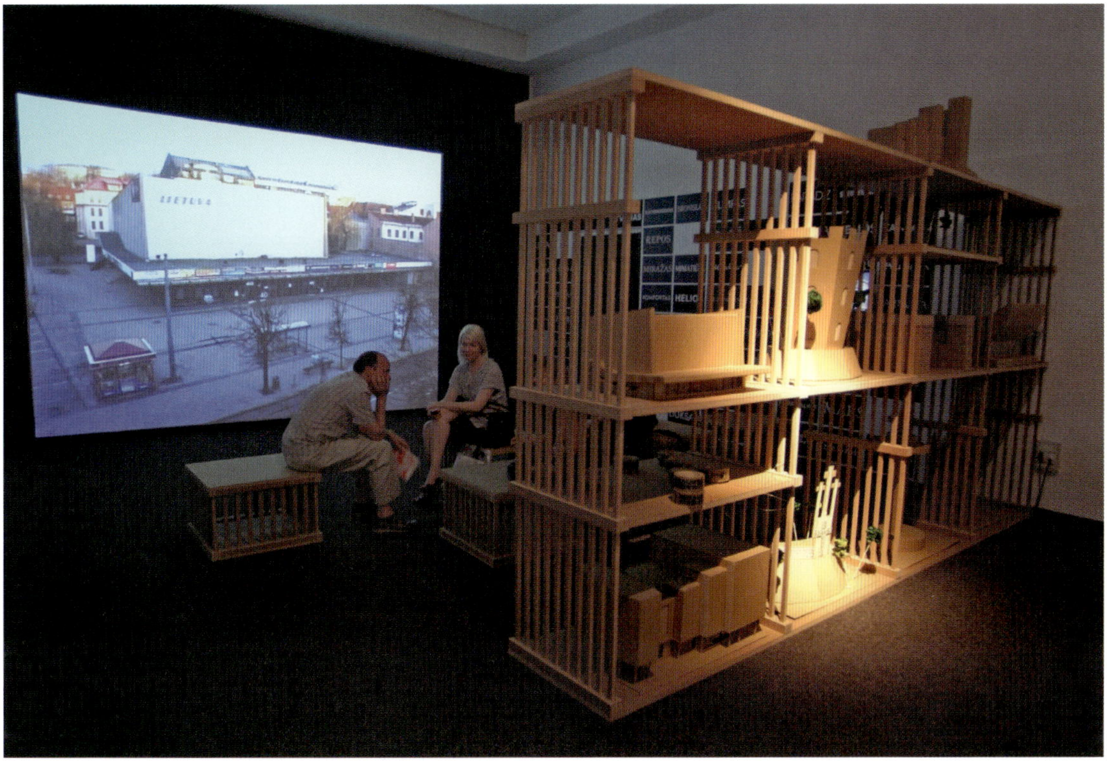

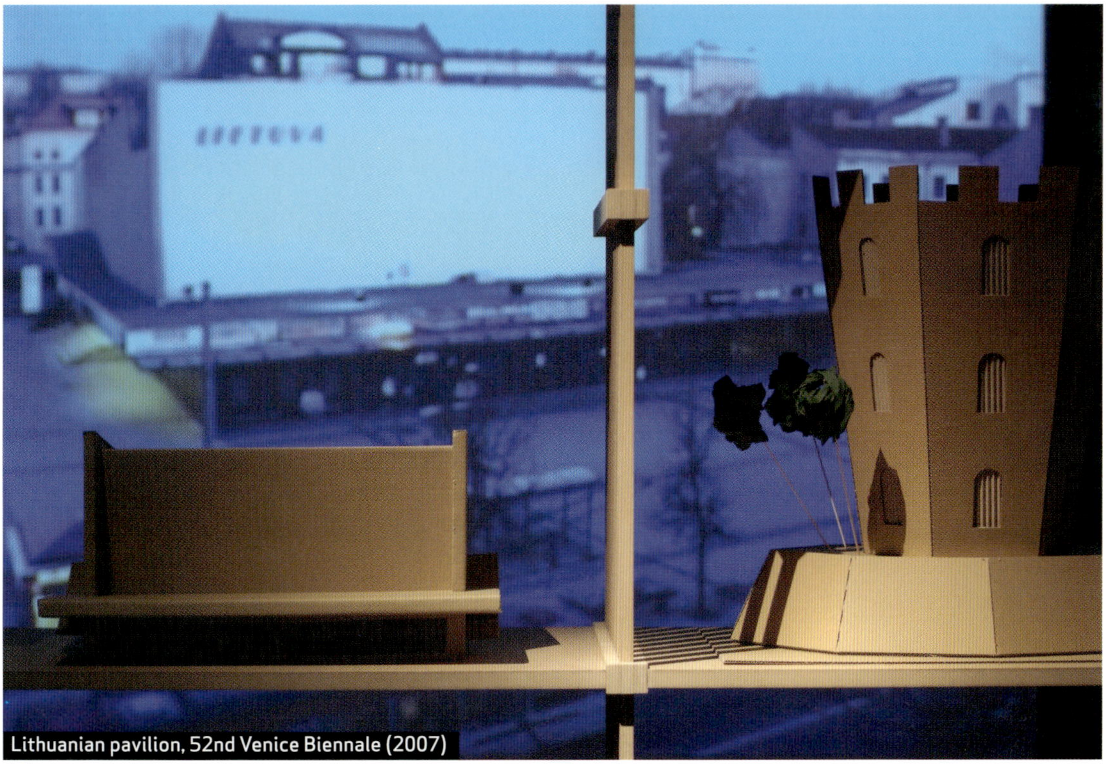

Lithuanian pavilion, 52nd Venice Biennale (2007)

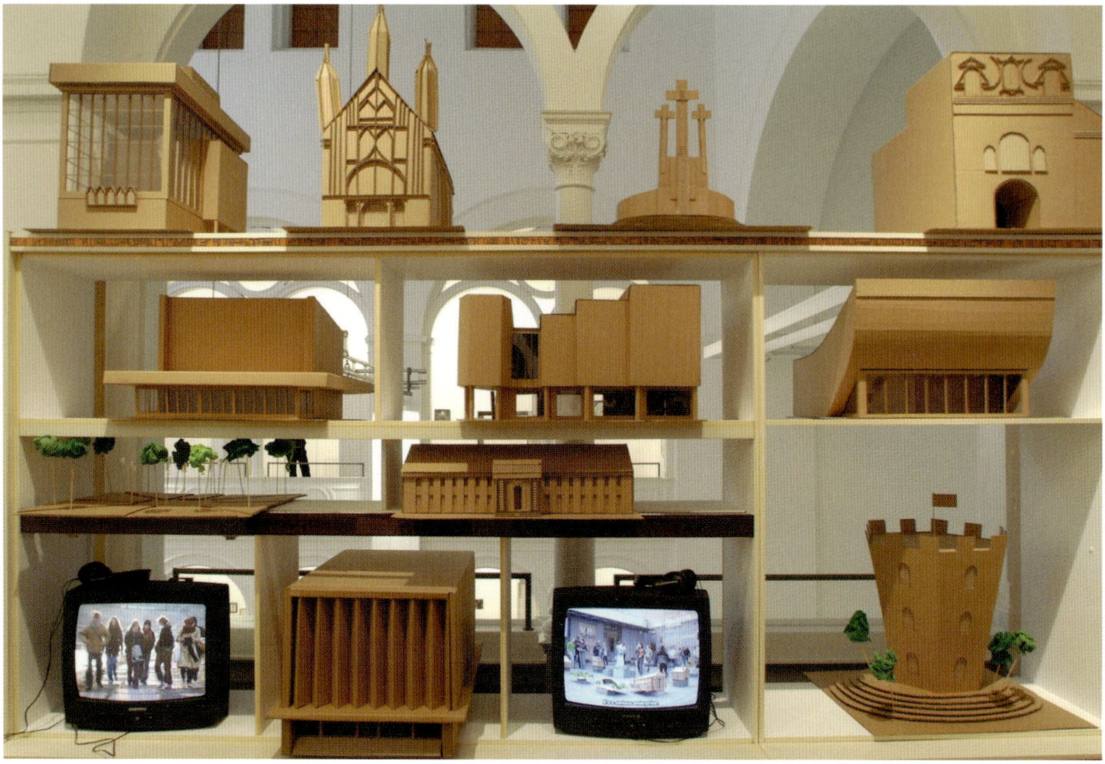

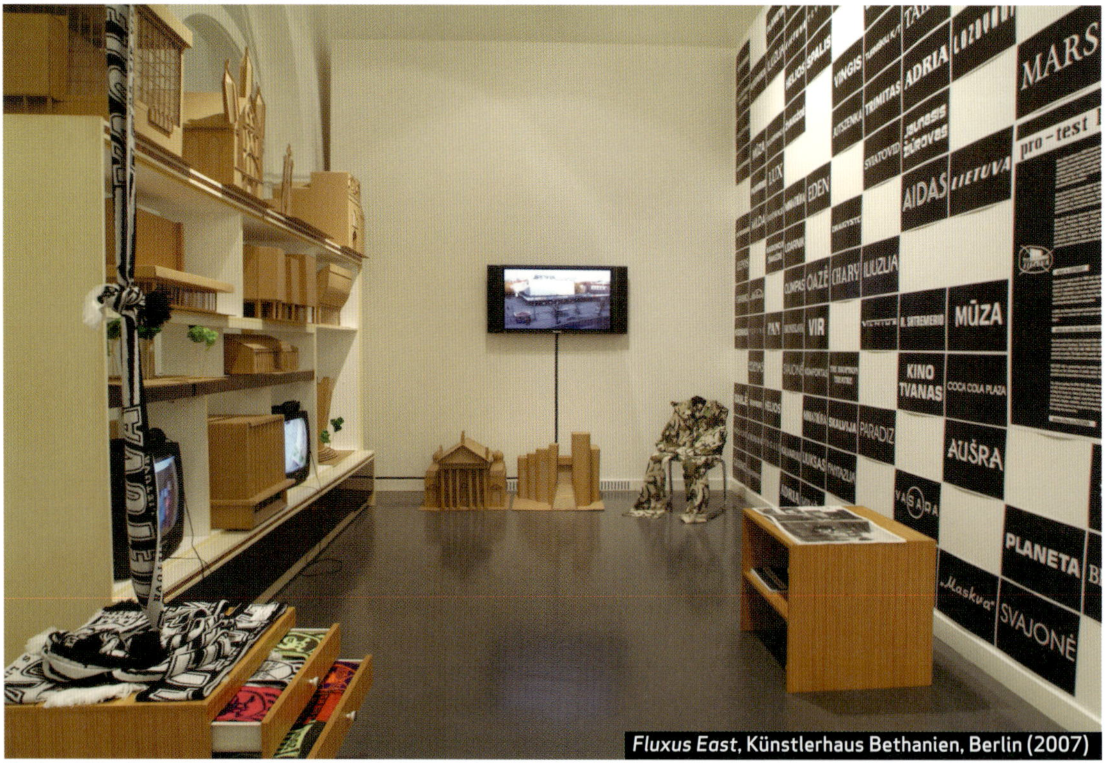

Fluxus East, Künstlerhaus Bethanien, Berlin (2007)

VILLA LITUANIA (2007)

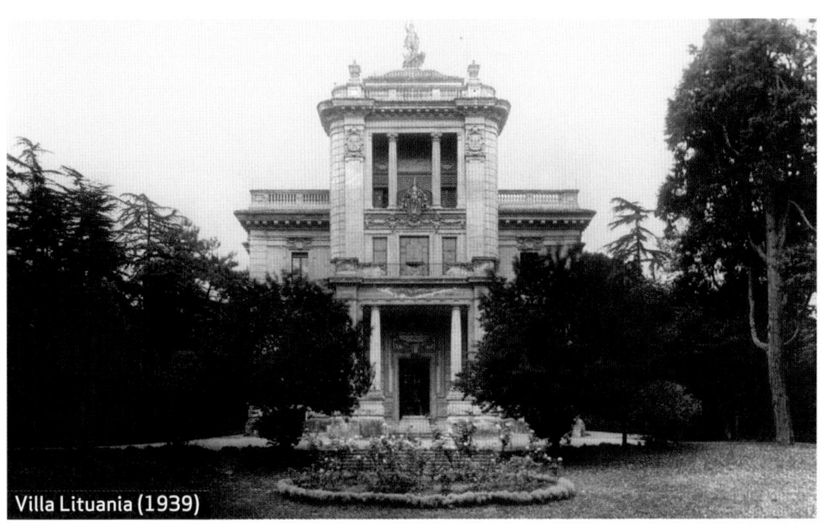

Villa Lituania was conceived as a context-specific project addressing the invitation to represent the country at the Venice Biennale. The project explores a prescient and problematic chapter in the complicated 20th-and 21st-century history of Europe. Villa Lituania was the Embassy in Italy of the first independent Republic of Lithuania (1918-1940). The Embassy operated from 1933-1940, but became a possession of the Soviet Union after the occupation of Lithuania. Fascist Italian government representatives handed over the keys to the property to Soviet officials in line with the alliance of powers signalled by the Molotov-Ribbentrop Pact (1939),[1] despite the safeguarding attempt on the part of the Ambassador.[2]

Villa Lituania provided a subject that could generate a sense of "productive nationalism" that could in turn reflect upon the political status of the national representative role of the Venice Biennale. Villa Lituania is a long-established symbol of national emancipation and is considered by many inside the country to be "Lithuania's last occupied territory", as it remains the property of Russia. Over recent years, however, the status of the building and stories about government efforts towards its return, or restitution, have been elided in national mainstream media coverage (to percolate in electronic media space alone). Salvaging an unofficial history for the type of project expected to traffic popular national symbolisms and icons represents an iconoclastic act, one that would undoubtedly refocus public attention on the fate of the Villa.

Moreover, in recent years, as competing Western art histories of the 20th century have been written, many Westerners have become increasingly fascinated by the legacies of Communism in general and Soviet Communism in particular. This audience tends to focus its attention on the Russian avant-garde practices that formed around Rodchenko and Malevich at the very beginning of the 20th century. It is an opinion that tends to be exclusively focused on Russia and blurs the distinct character of each of the Soviet states: moreover, it arrests the time of interest in these localities, so that history seems to stand still from 1918-1991. And this romantic inclination or nostalgia towards cultural artefacts of Soviet-era architecture, furniture, fashion and the applied arts is completely devoid of any awareness that Soviet culture was a colonial culture – a culture of occupation. The story of Villa Lituania reminds us that this occupation continues today (and that Russian art is by no means innocent).

The project, which also refers to histories of pavilion architecture, reflects upon the fact that Lithuania – like many nation-states that only began participating in international affairs after the First World War, such as the Republic of Ireland, Turkey and the PRC – does not have a permanent pavilion located in the Giardini in Venice. Pavilion architecture only had a short independent history in the first Lithuanian Republic – before it became involved as a state representing the Soviet techno-modernisation project that developed a mono-form: a palace of achievements. Soviet pavil-

Villa Lituania – for a day

He was a famous architect – Piacentini. You've probably heard about Piacentini, as he built a number of houses here in Rome. At that time he was probably one of the most famous architects in Italy. He also, as I mentioned, built a few villas in the Via Nomentana district, where various embassies appeared later. He also developed his own style, as you can see in the Via Nomentana building, and he specialised in designing palatial houses and representative buildings.

The house was really impressive both inside and out, but it was not entirely rational. The first floor was devoted to official functions and the lobby alone was quite impressive because of the four marble pillars, and a marble staircase with six stairs, I think...

They were white. And were very impressive, made from marble. The material was superb quality, shiny. The lobby was absolutely stunning, the first room was an antechamber, but large. Then there was my father's office. One salon, not too large, then the grand salon, which stretched through the whole house. There was a hall. That's one, two, three, then there was a dining room, four, and then another room for various functions, that's five, but these were large rooms. Five or six huge rooms. On the second floor there were private rooms. And there were also one, two, three, four, five, maybe six rooms. So all in all there were about 12-13 rooms. The first floor, for official functions; the second, for private rooms. And between the bedrooms on both sides there was a large hall, another so-called salon.

We lived there from 29 July 1939 until the beginning of August 1940. So, a year and one and a half months.

When we arrived in Rome in 1939, I was still a child. The arrival in Rome seemed like a fairy tale. Of course we hadn't seen such buildings in Kaunas, so huge. And the reception at the railway station: an impressively uniformed representative of the Protocol Office of the Fascist Government came to meet my father, dressed in a white *fascisti* uniform, because it was already high summer, a Fascist eagle sitting on his hat, and so forth. We were absolutely astonished at what we saw.

From what my mother's diaries say, the officer escorted my father to the car, but got distracted and went out the wrong exit. We were supposed to go out through an exit with the red carpet, as honoured guests. Therefore we went back into the station, my mother writes, and made a grand arrival at the proper exit. Outside the station a huge car was waiting for us, a brand new American Buick, a gleaming limousine. We went in the incredibly beautiful car to the Villa: palm trees, huge grounds, and a lit-up house, because the secretary had turned on the lights before the ambassador's arrival. It seemed so stunning, all that beauty. And we had the whole year ahead of us. It was a very, very happy year for us.

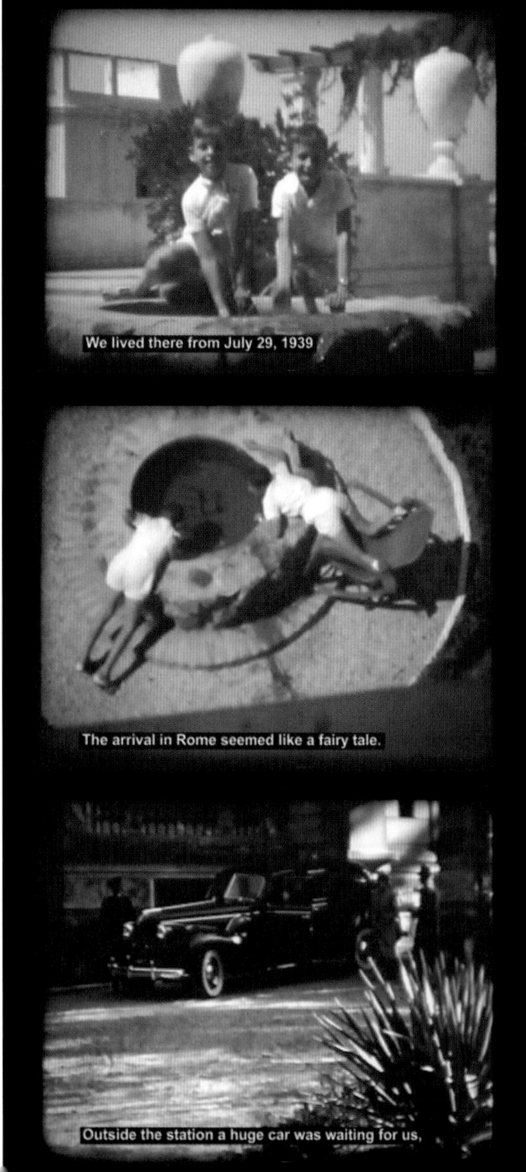

ion culture was launched with Konstantin Melnikov's pavilion at the 1925 Paris Exposition of Industrial and Decorative Arts and played an important role within the propagandistic "All-Soviet" exhibitions and festivals held in Moscow. For this reason, and despite the formal beauty of a number of buildings made for leisure and sport in parks and resorts, pavilions have become a discredited form and have fallen into disrepair in Lithuania. The *Villa Lituania* project reasserts the utopian desires associated with pavilion architecture and harnesses it within an analysis of the traumas that such desires provoke.

Occupied and privatised

Today, Villa Lituania functions as the Russian Consulate in Rome (a lesser annex to the Russian Embassy). Successive Lithuanian governments have lobbied internationally – with varying degrees of insistence – for its restitution. Since Lithuania's accession to the European Union in 2004, Parliamentarians have been able to press the case in this new chamber of influence – although they appear to be acting independently of parliamentary processes at home. Berlusconi's exit from power in Italy and the ascendancy of the Prodi government seemed to provide a different ear. Consonant with its post-imperial will-to-power, Russia's Putin government has, however, refused to give ground on the issue and Lithuania's politicians are meek in their diplomacy and public relations in that quarter.

Even though the project engaged with populist strategies – via nationalist sentiment – from the outset it met with confrontation and hostility from local politicians and government institutions, which were manipulated by the mainstream media. It was clear from the very first requests for assistance and support with research and fact-finding that the Ministry of Foreign Affairs and the Embassy of Lithuania to Italy considered the Villa Lituania project to be "invading their territory" and "possibly harmful to the delicate negotiations with Italy" associated with compensation for the occupation of the property. While effusively reminding people that as representatives of "a democratic state they would not restrain artistic expression," they still insisted on the fragility of the case, because

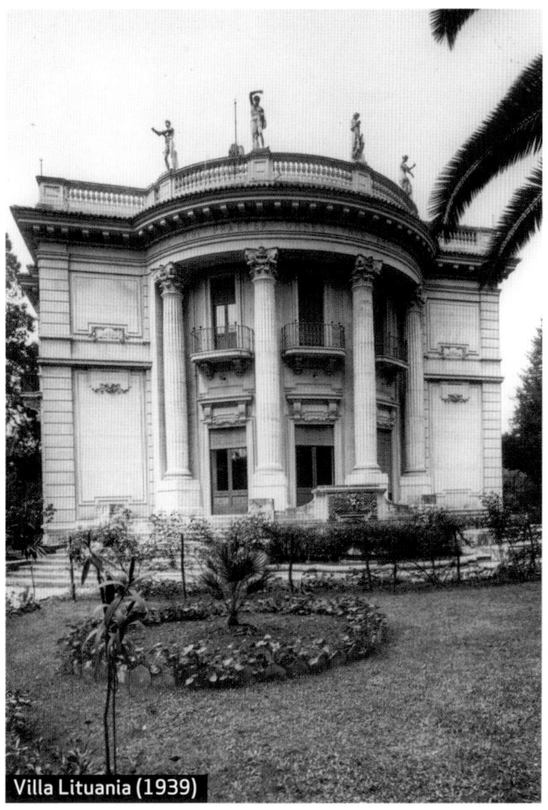

the "Russians and Italians are over-sensitive about the mention of the name Villa Lituania." In a sense, the project provoked a performative process of new identification that made the "powerful oppressor", the victims of its oppression and its collaborators uncomfortable and vulnerable, morally as well as politically.

As an art project, however, *Villa Lituania* was making no material claim on the house. Instead, it was reclaiming the public discursive space associated with the Villa and generating new discussions about its predicament and traumatic history – and the implications they have for Lithuania's current socio-political situation. Public discourse is currently divorced from contemporary Lithuanian politics, as is the sense of responsibility of the politicians to a public constituency, and a sense of commonwealth in general. In that respect *Villa Lituania* is a plug-in of the *Pro-test Lab* project, as it is also dealing with the idea of reclaiming space. It is, in a certain sense, a continuation of the process engendered by the Lietuva cinema. The artists are interested in the connections between these projects, which deal with strategies for

I read in the diaries that later each room housed the families of Soviet embassy staff and that there were at least three or four beds and a kitchen per room.

The grand hall was like a haven for refugees, more or less like a camp. And so in the grand salon, which was huge, they installed a cinema with a platform, a stage, and of course there were banners, portraits of Stalin, slogans, as my mother writes, about Stalin and the Sun, etc.

The Soviets were there from August 1940 to June 1941, when the war broke out on the Russian front. The Germans and Italians went to war and, because Italy was in alliance with Germany, when they declared war on the Soviets, the Soviets had to leave Rome immediately.

Diplomats of a country at war, as is the tradition, depart promptly. Then Villa Lituania was taken over by the Swedes representing the USSR in Italy. As a neutral, non-militarist country, the Swedes were entrusted with Soviet interests. They immediately sealed the gates, as the property of Sweden. Not a seal, actually, but a note saying that this was Swedish property. It had the seal of the Swedish Embassy. Then my brother, and some others, broke into the Villa and tore off the note.

They broke in on 6 July 1941, as I re-read in my mother's diaries recently. The war broke out, I think, between 15-20 June 1941, a few weeks later we tried to get Villa Lituania back. Immediately, Swedish embassy officials turned up, enquiring who dared to remove the Swedish seal. A former Lithuanian military officer, Lt. Gabriunas, who was a part of the campaign, joined my brother. He said, "Swedes had no right to leave that note, it is not their property, nor is it Soviet property, it is our property and we can do whatever we want."

The Swedes protested saying, "Let's go to the Italian Ministry of Foreign Affairs, and complain about this action." According to my mother, an hour later Italian officials came, and politely said, "We understand the problem and we will try to solve it. Please abandon the villa, we will take possession and officially return it to you later. The Italian government will cede it to

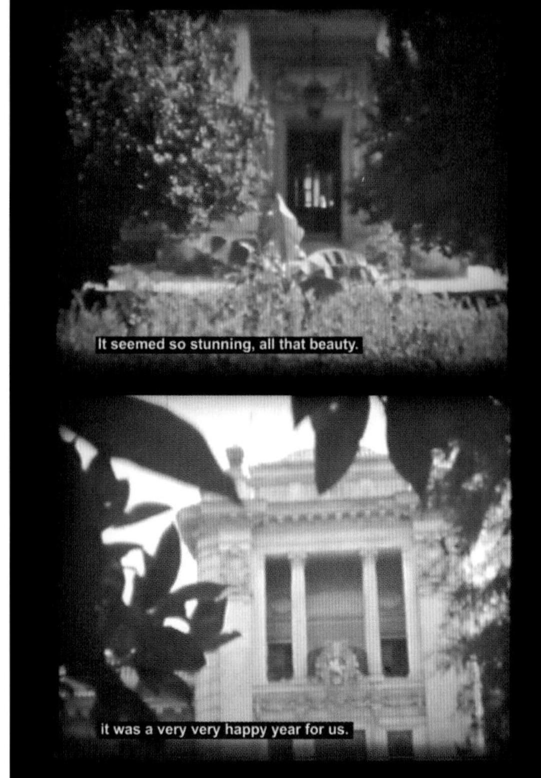

the Lithuanian community." Clearly, it was an empty promise. Nothing materialised and of course the Italians didn't return it. But, as my mother writes, they were very polite. The Fascists simply requested that we leave Villa Lituania immediately, but promised to give it back to us!

When did you and your brother re-occupy the Villa?
I wasn't involved, because I was a child, and too young. My brother strictly refused to take me there.

You were ten years old then.
My brother was in his teens. He was about seventeen. Naturally, he didn't want to take a boy of eleven. So my mother and I went to visit them later after they took their positions – for one day. Other community members came, as soon as they heard, and they flew the Lithuanian national flag on the building. The news spread in no time and everyone gathered, joyful that we'd got it back, got back Villa Lituania – for a day.

Kazys Lozoraitis' story (*Ambassador in Exile*, 2007)

embodying protest by taking into account identity, architecture and politics, but most of all with negotiations between spaces, private and public. The project has a particular interest in reversing already existing perspectives: in the case of *Villa Lituania* it is not asking for the house but invading the territory – not the building itself, but the territory of political negotiation and *absent* diplomatic negotiations. Negotiation is a political tool that forms an active arena for a project, gradually building up into a meta-territory that connects the two places, Villa Lituania and the Lietuva.

According to Edward Said, "ignorance is not an adequate political strategy for a people, and therefore each in his own way must understand and know the forbidden Other." By entering the forbidden (and occupied) territory of trauma and calling on the Russians (or Italians) for collaboration and play does not mean giving up on the defence of justice or solidarity with the oppressed, neither does it forget identity. Instead, the project addresses the issue of how to become a citizen in a situation suspended between reason, understanding and intellectual analysis on the one hand, and the organisation and encouragement of collective passions, such as those that seem to impel the "fundamentalists" – be they nationalist or neo-liberal – on the other.[3]

What is important to stress when speaking about these two projects – *Villa Lituania* and *Pro-test Lab* – is that they both confront the debates about expropriation and seek to re-appropriate lost territory. The *Villa Lituania* project makes claims not only about the lost building but metonymically refers to the damage that was inflicted by Soviet occupation, which has never been discussed in public in terms of compensation or symbolic recognition. We should bear in mind that nothing historical is frozen in time, and nothing is immune to change, and despite the tyranny of the majority, artists and intellectuals have the right to provide a refuge for dissent, for other kinds of views. The *Pro-test Lab* project makes claims not only about the building, which became the object of post-Soviet capitalist privatisation, but refers to the absence of a civil society that would have enough courage and initiative to defend the public interest. Both projects function as an interpellation creating new collective subjectivities, and in that respect they attempt to stage a performative work.[4]

Left-wing performance

A personal remembrance of quixotic leisure activities pursued during the Soviet era – and a flight of the imagination – generated the central conceptual gambit of the project. Working with racing-pigeon fanciers in Italy and Lithuania, the project evolved towards the presentation of an international pigeon race from Venice to Rome. This provided the project's brute symbolism: to send *colombi della pace*, "doves of peace",[5] to the territory of Villa Lituania. Two pigeon races were planned. The first during the Biennale *vernissage* (on Saturday, 9 June 2007) was conceived as an all-international championship race with birds from Italy, Lithuania, Poland and Russia. The second race was intended for the autumn as a special one-loft race from Venice to Rome, but did not take place.

The idea of the pigeon race is grounded in the abolition of the genre restrictions that often form a certain basis for fascination in particular media practices. The project attempts to get free of these restrictions and to "flit the nest" by considering the birds as a technology/media, or software, that performs and maps a directional will and territorial desire. The birds could also be considered as space invaders. The Tim Burton film *Mars Attacks* (1997) presents the audience with a number of stereotypes that construct and reinforce the imperial imagination. There is a scene in which some hippies release a white dove (clutching a fig leaf in its beak) as a symbol of peace to greet the Martians, and the Martians open fire and kill the symbolic emissary as they think it is a weapon (an air force of one!)

As technology, the race needs to be installed and launched – observing its operational protocols – with the risk of *crashes*. There is a fascinating networking from the domain of sport to art that intersects with the fields of politics and aesthetics. Like a biennale, the race has its commissioner and representatives from different countries; it starts in Venice and ends in Rome. There are similar factors involved in both the race and the art event, like movement, the weather, vitamins, training, ability, talent, distance, elevation, predators, winners, prizes, illegal betting and even an auction that summarises the whole event.

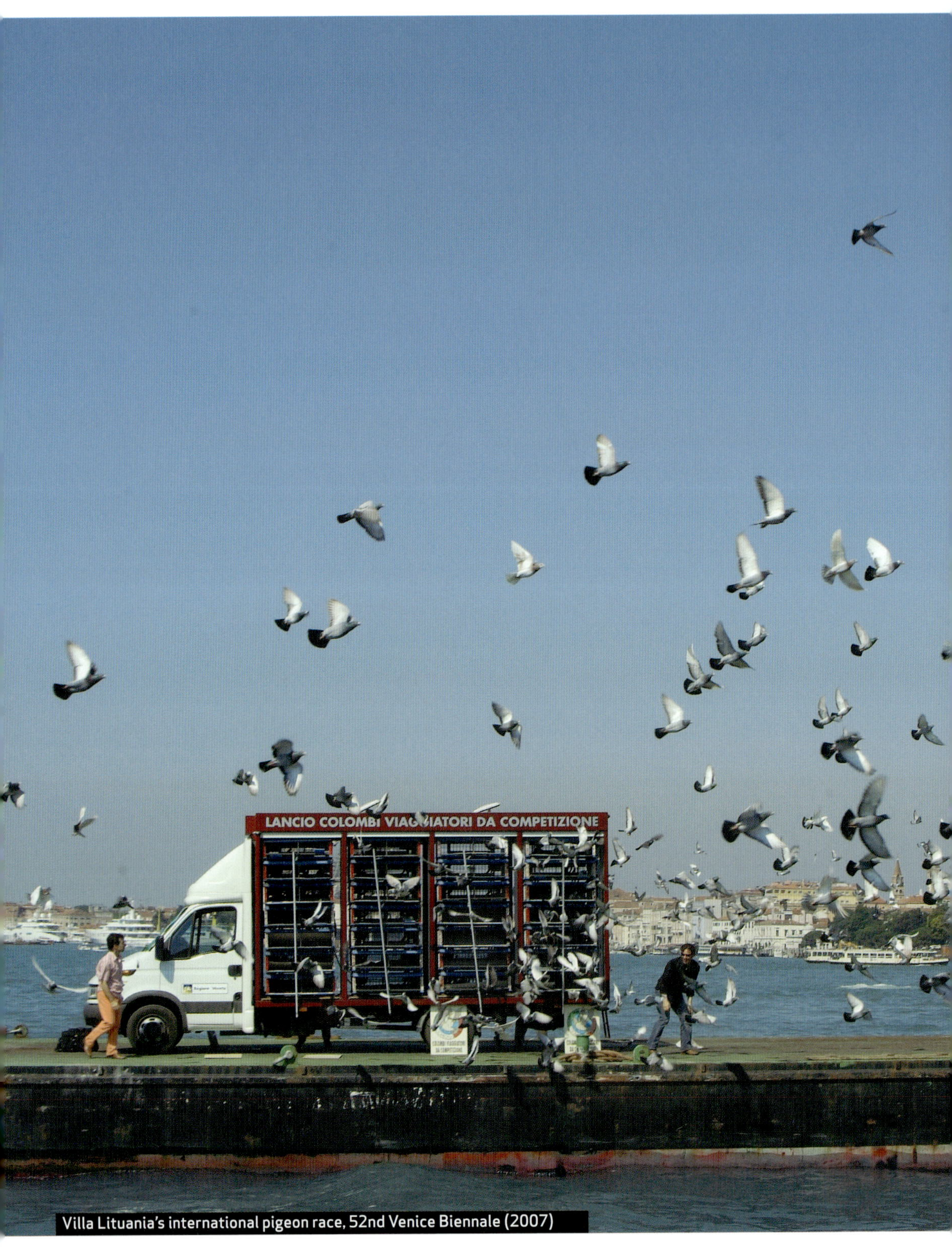

Villa Lituania's international pigeon race, 52nd Venice Biennale (2007)

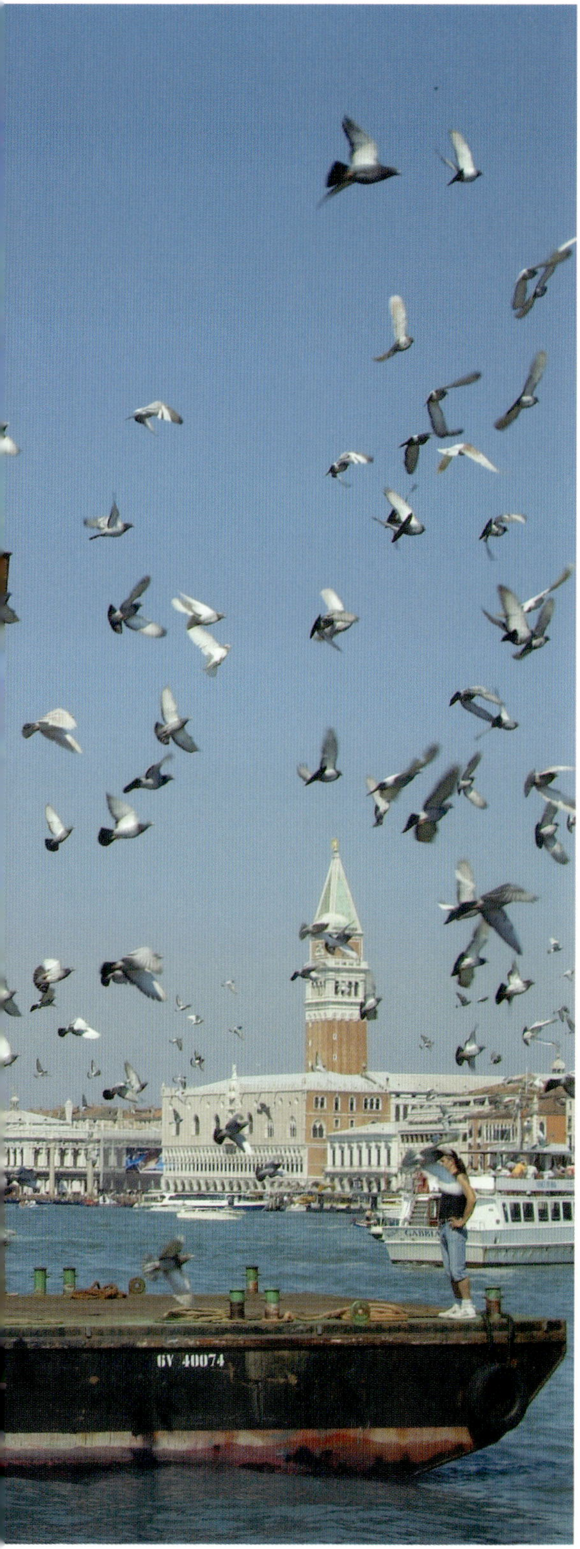

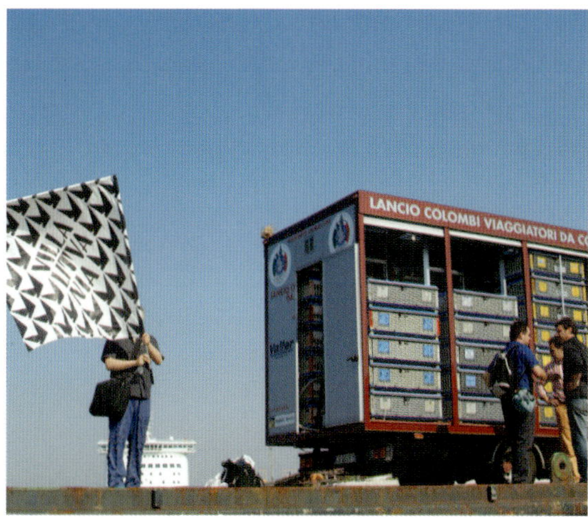

To achieve the ideal race from the pavilion in Venice to Villa Lituania in Rome, a pigeon loft (for pigeons from Italy, Lithuania, Russia and Poland) would need to be constructed on the grounds of the Villa. Pigeons triangulate the loft they make their first flight from as home and always return to that location when released: hence the term *homing pigeon*. Herein lay the tactical conceit of the project, as it would need to occupy territory or invade the space of the Russian Consulate situated in Villa Lituania. Once requests to build in the grounds at Villa Lituania were ignored by the Russian authorities, the artistic team turned their attention to alternative sites within the Eternal City.

Pathways: redrawing the borders

This process rerouted the project from the purely symbolic domain into the realm of *realpolitik*. To begin with, efforts were concentrated on the construction of a loft in public sites close to Villa Lituania, mainly Villa Torlonia (best-known as the old palace Mussolini made his home in) and Villa Paganini. This was a painstaking and protocol-heavy procedure requiring permission for occupation of the land (and building consent) from thirteen different departments of Rome City Council. After enquiries and requests made about sites close to Villa Lituania proved unworkable, efforts were shifted to a location in the EUR-park near the Mussolini-era Palazzo della Civiltà. The site was suggested by architect Massimiliano Fuksas (a Lithuanian exile) who is

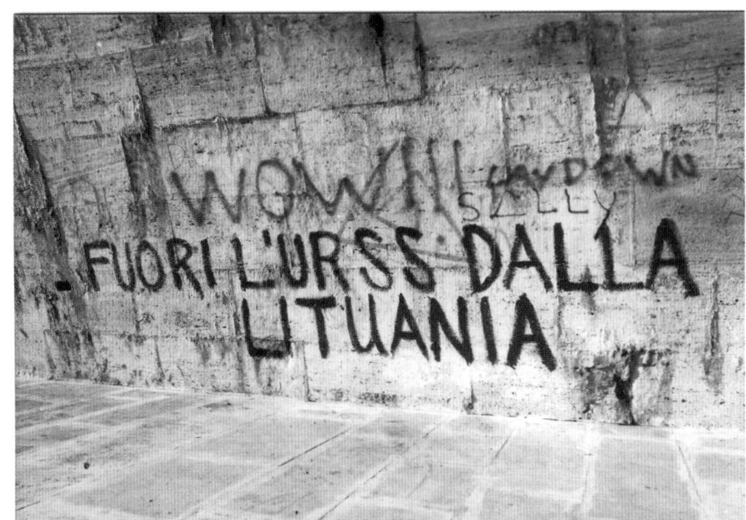

About inscriptions

I can show you where…
One was right here, and it read:
Viva la Lituania Cattolica Martire!
or in other words, "Long live the church of Lithuanian martyrs!" These inscriptions appeared shortly after Kalanta burnt himself in the seventies for freedom. There were many more such inscriptions elsewhere, at the Pantheon, closer to the Vatican. In the eighties other slogans appeared. Nearby here, close to that wall, an inscription read: *La forse de la fide lituana vincerà* ("The power of Lithuanian faith will win") There are more, near that wall, we can look from this side…

This wall had a text written in huge letters: Freedom for Lithuania! (*Libertà per la Lituania!*) And this is quite a busy place. Further on, you can see the Vatican Radio premises and the main entrance to the priests' quarters. This is next to the Vatican. Back in those days the main bus would go from the Vatican to Termini Station, through this place.

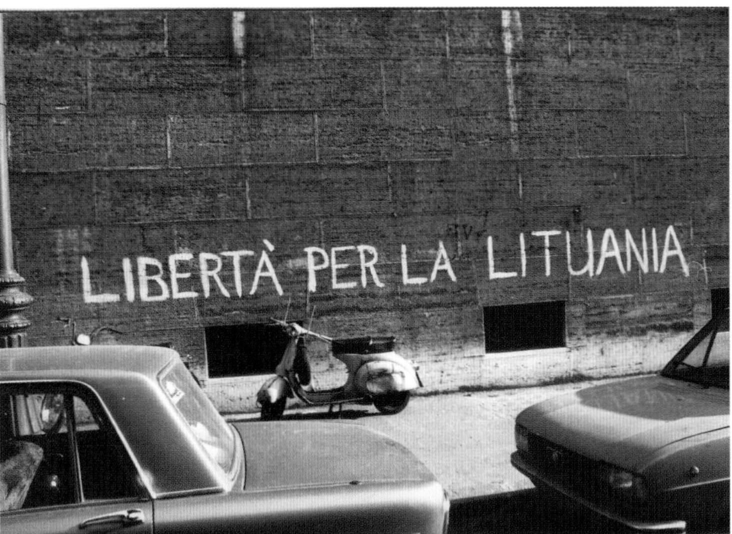

And thousands, tens of thousands of tourists passing this place, would all see these inscriptions.

It is interesting how this graffiti disappeared. On the eve of Gorbachev's visit to Rome and his meeting with the Pope, Italy's intelligence service erased it in one night.

We may proceed further on to Borgo and I'll show you another place where similar inscriptions were seen. They remained there a long time for fifteen or twenty years. They were once an important part of the city.

I think that they were mostly ignored or seen accidentally. The Vatican's officers saw them for sure. They all knew what they meant, and during Gorbachev's visit it was impossible for the inscriptions to remain. This was an historical visit by Gorbachev to the Vatican and, probably, someone didn't want to raise the issue

developing a major building in the area, known as La Nuvola (*The cloud*)—the projects would have made nice neighbours. It was through Fuksas' agency that direct contacts were made with the offices of the Mayor of Rome, Walter Veltroni, and the city's senior architect, Mario Cutuli.

Despite the advocacy of the highest offices of the city, restrictions on the accommodation and training of animals in public spaces precluded the construction of the pigeon loft on municipal property. The Animal Rights Department, in dialogue with LIPU, the Italian League for the Protection of Birds, suggested that the loft might be constructed – and pigeons kept – in the Bioparco, the Rome Zoo located in the Villa Borghese. This would, however, do away with the concept of the race as part of the loft's purpose, although an extra educational function would be ascribed to the loft – including a notice about how the loft came to be in the Zoo and the reason for its particular architecture. At this time it is still unclear whether this part of the Villa Lituania story can proceed as planned, as the process of negotiation is ongoing (at least at the moment of writing these lines).[6]

A permanent architectural presence would also be gained; in effect, a compensation for the lack of a national pavilion in the Giardini in Venice. In architectural terms it would link conceptually with the Penguin Pool in London Zoo designed by Berthold Lubetkin and the Tecton Group in 1934, which remains (along with Mendelsohn & Chermayev's De La Warr Pavilion, 1935), one of the United Kingdom's finest examples of experimental modernist pavilion architecture. Lubetkin, a Russian émigré and constructivist who had a major impact on British architecture, was associated with a number of utopian and experimental movements in architecture, and was also renowned for designing the sculptural monument to Lenin in Finsbury Park (1941).

It is unclear whether Kazys Lozoraitis, the former Ambassador-in-exile and Ambassador to the Holy See, who was an important advocate of the project – and of the restitution of Villa Lituania itself – would have seen the positive aspects of the symbolic Embassy being relocated to the confines of a zoo. This fate exemplifies Giorgio Agamben's theory of biopolitics, in which the nation-state necessarily subsumes *naked life* (zoe) under *political will* (bios). Agamben radicalises these terms to articulate the difference between the poor and the privileged, equating *zoe* with "people" and *bio* with "People" – in effect the poor suffer the fate of animals. In this case Lithuanian national imaginary has been alloyed to the Zoo and its national historical fate has been repeated – even in good will.

The production process of *Villa Lituania* is rather more organic and less controlling; interested in engaging with different groups and audiences in relation to the construction of temporal spaces, activities or communities, in connection with a desire to link different layers, orbits, trajectories and meanings that in other circumstances would not meet. The project moves freely between the fields of art, sport and "society", gathering together insights, expertise and future potentialities from different fields. Despite this fluidity, art remains the main driving force, because the "precincts of art lend themselves more readily today than other fields to the redistribution of roles and competences," as Jacques Rancière points out. Art is always both a departure point and a point of return: it is the project's "homing device".

The invitation to collective creativity bears a certain resemblance to the open source movement, which is created through a process of making its audience the agencies of the work. An audience that interacts and engages in action, debate and discussion is an audience that takes the work and uses it for its own purposes.

Having open-ended destinations in mind, *Villa Lituania* is now a route planner that operates with various points of departure: from the Russian Consulate that received

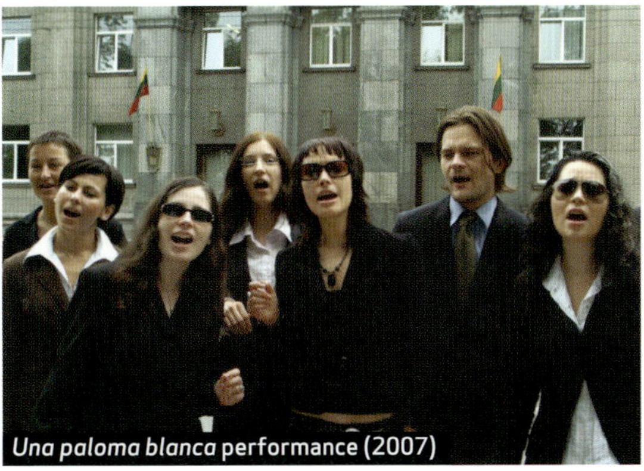

Una paloma blanca **performance (2007)**

of Lithuania's independence for fear of overshadowing discussions with the Pope. So here we are. If we go further, we can see the premises of Italy's TV company, RAI. There were other inscriptions there. Bad weather, we can't change it. Wow, that was Pope Ratzinger's secretary! It's cool we got that on film!

Here, look, you can see white traces of the old inscription, incredible! Here they are just visible... Here you can see: *Viva la Lituania cattolica!*, something like *ca-to-li-ca* is discernable, right here. This building belongs to RAI, the Italian radio and TV company, a branch office, which has to deal with the Vatican.

Such inscriptions mainly used to be near the Vatican. I hadn't seen some of them myself. I've heard people say that there were inscriptions addressed directly to the Pope. For instance, "Paul VI, what have you done to Lithuania?" And in fact someone complained that he hadn't done much good for Lithuania, but this is simply a matter of opinion.

One of the inscriptions was just under the bridge: *Fuori l'URSS dalla Italia!* In other words, "Soviet Union, get out of Lithuania!" These inscriptions were clearly visible to passers-by looking down from Lungo Tevere Road. But soon after the appearance of these inscriptions, Tiberina Island hosted a traditional festival and feast for Italian Communists, Festa dell'Unità. I was so curious about their reaction towards such a thing. My friend and I went to check it out and realised that it had already been painted over, everything was erased right away.

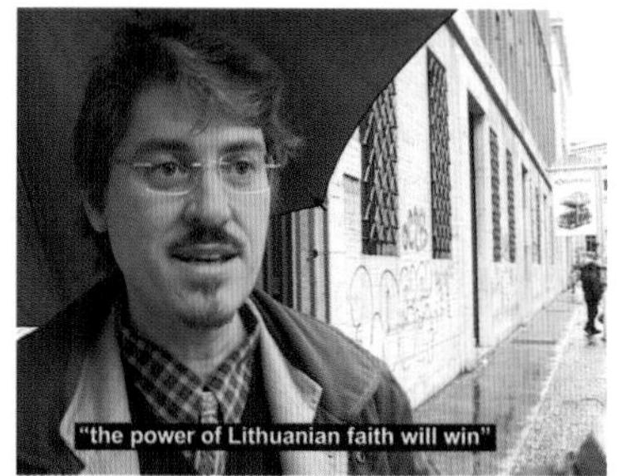

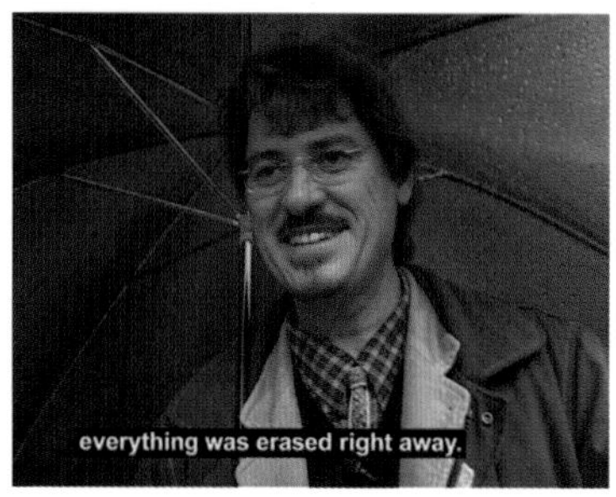

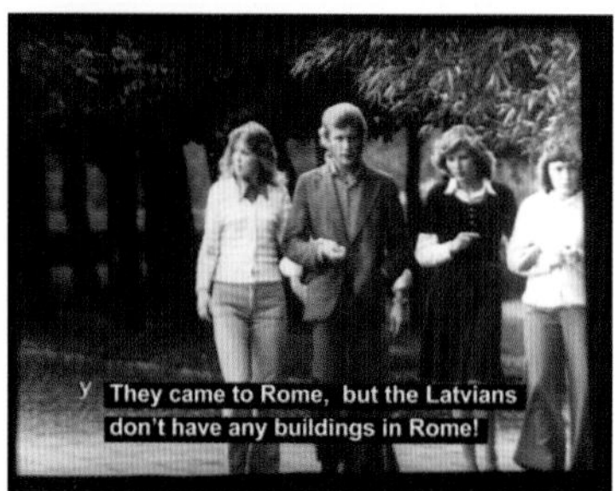

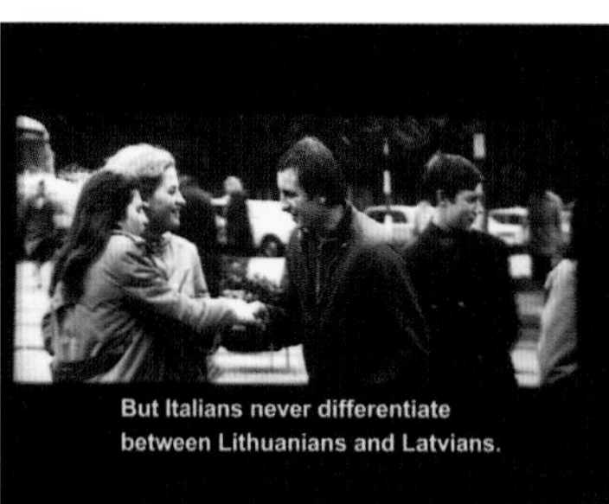

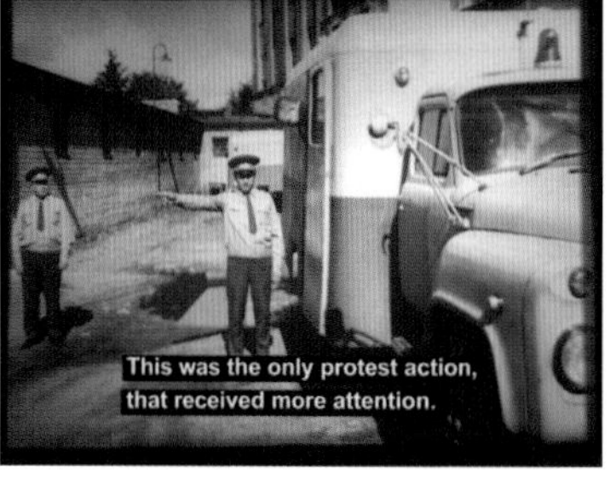

So the Italian Communists were the first to erase the inscriptions long before Gorbachev's visit...

Saulius Kubilius' story
(*Defending the Villa. Graffiti*, 2007)

About Latvians

I can only tell you one very interesting story, although it's too bad I don't remember which year it was, maybe 1988 or 1983, I don't know exactly. The Latvians were celebrating – well, mostly immigrants, the Latvian diaspora, mostly from the United States or Germany – celebrating their independence day and they decided to take more specific and braver steps. They decided to chain themselves to their occupied palace and elsewhere. They came to Rome, but the Latvians don't have any buildings in Rome!

They said the best thing would be some embassy or something Soviet. So I said, go to Via Nomentana, to Villa Lituania there... And so they did. There were three Latvians, I don't know whether they were Americans or from Germany. They chained themselves up and we notified the media and they were even photographed, a picture appeared in the local press. But Italians never differentiate between Lithuanians and Latvians. So the headline read, "Lithuanians chain themselves to their Embassy."

The Latvians were arrested, but they were prepared for that, they had proof that they had return tickets. They were expelled from Italy at once.

Saulius Kubilius' story
(*Defending the Villa. The Latvians*, 2007)

a letter requesting a land permit to build a pigeon loft;
from the Ministry of Foreign Affairs and the Lithuanian
Embassy in Rome, which were approached about building a pigeon loft; from Eros Carboni, a leading Italian
pigeon-fancier who organised the strategy for a pigeon
race; from Duke Vladimir Gorelov, owner of Viltis (Hope),
the leading pigeon club in Vilnius, who helped organise
Lithuanian and Russian pigeon-fanciers; from architect
Massimiliano Fuksas, who is negotiating the site for the
loft in Rome; from Mario Cutuli, of Rome City Council,
and Sondra Litvaityte, a student of political sciences at
La Sapienza University in Rome, who was engaged in the
planning of the construction site and activities around
the project in Rome; as well as links that connect this
project to the Vatican Radio station.

These connections cannot simply be reduced to the
auxiliary or preparatory, as the proposal is tested at each
stage of its development and has been jointly shaped
with the people involved. This process requires mutual
engagement and learning from both sides, and not just
reducing expertise into the simple execution of particular demands. The project maps the relations and trajectories of both the pigeons – bred from birds in Lithuania,
Italy and Poland – flying between buildings in Venice and
Rome, and the communities that have been involved in
the production process, including architects, pigeon-
fanciers, designers, lawyers, journalists, diplomats,
politicians and finally the viewers, who are all waiting
for a final destination and result.

The road to Kaunas: revenge of the crystal

Like every sporting contest – and the Venice Biennale
for that matter – a pigeon race needs trophies to be
awarded to the winning birds and trainers. The models
of the trophies are installed as sculptures in the pavilion
exhibition and will extend a number of themes running
through the project.

Made of crystal, they were fabricated at the Aleksotas
Glass Factory in Kaunas, a hundred kilometres from
Vilnius, the largest glass factory in the Baltic States. In
times gone by, Aleksotas specialised in the production
of stained glass. The Soviet Five-Year Plans stretched
to the applied arts as well as industrial production,

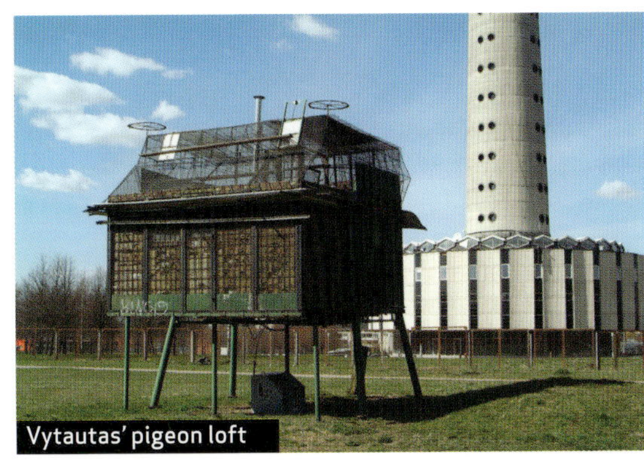

Vytautas' pigeon loft

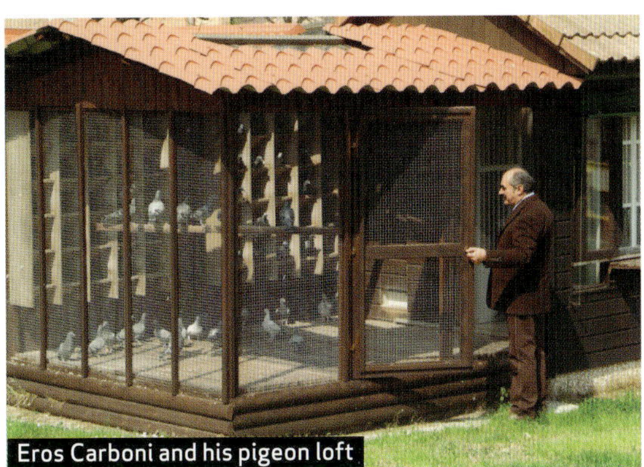

Eros Carboni and his pigeon loft

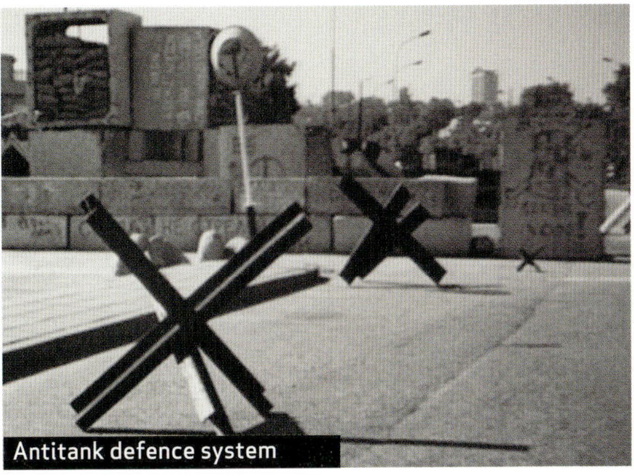

Antitank defence system

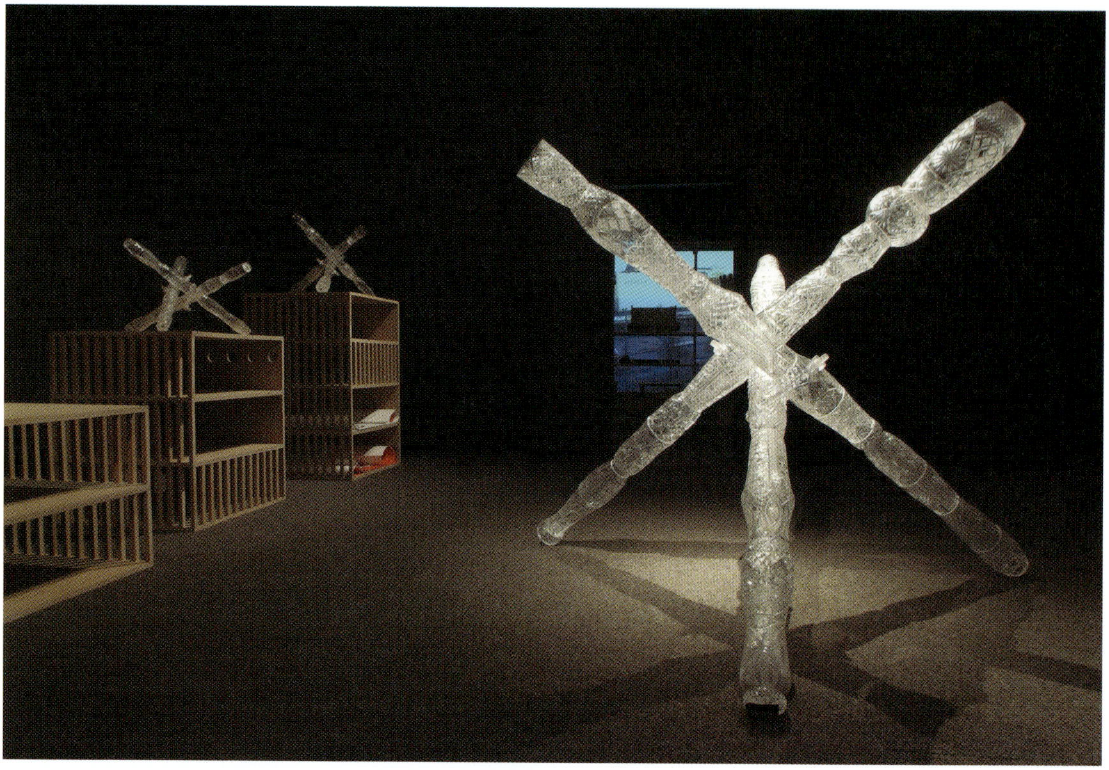

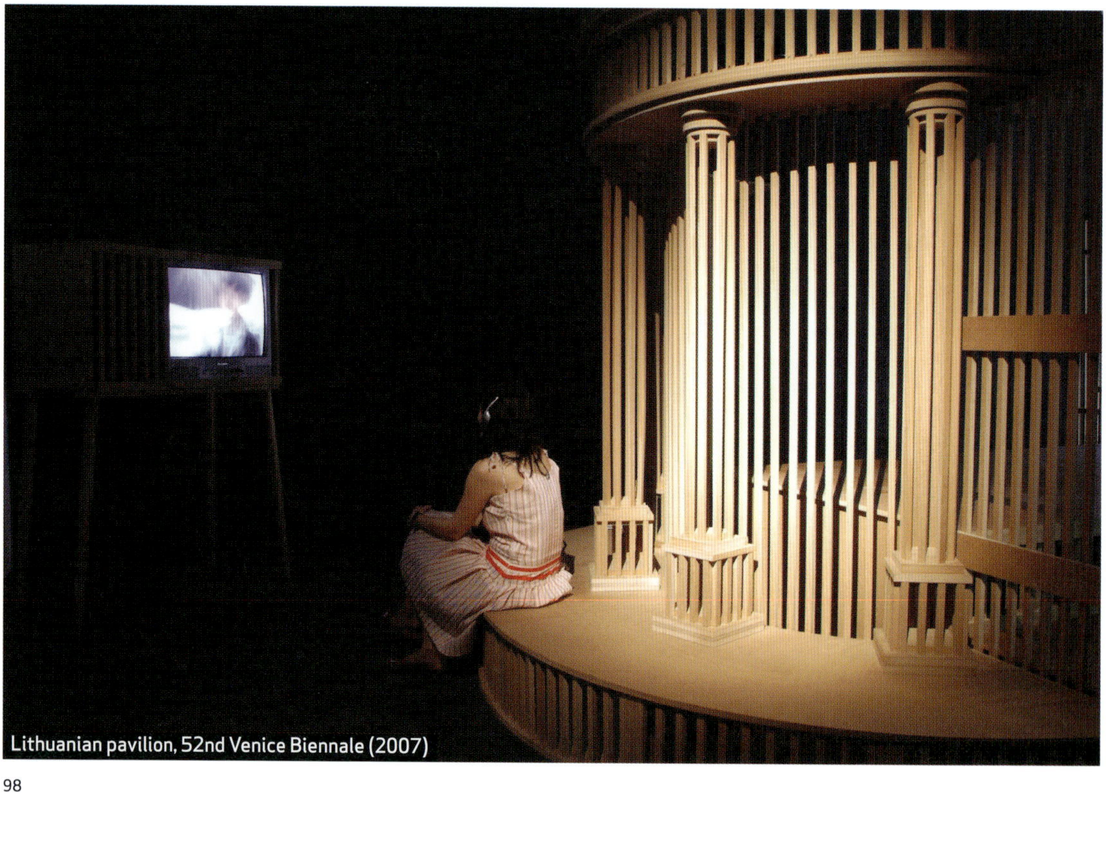

Lithuanian pavilion, 52nd Venice Biennale (2007)

and different Soviet states had different areas of expertise. As part of its five-year plan for industry, Lithuania produced specialist glass and stained glass for the entire Union. Stained glass became a feature of the embassies in Africa and Latin America, and of many official Soviet modernist buildings, where it added light and colour to the blocky, heavy, and often dark, concrete architecture. Working in the field of the applied arts was for many artists a form of escape from the socialist-realist canon, a refuge that allowed them to experiment with technologies and forms within a legitimate area.

The stained-glass industry collapsed with independence, a time when international demand dried up. Today, the factory survives by making beer bottles for breweries around the Baltic, except for one tiny department that produces experimental glass. The company's archives, which are on display, are reminiscent of earlier days, being replete with lifelike grapes, apples, dildo-like bananas, and even glass pigeons. They don't, however, produce crystal. Moreover, like industries all over Europe, Aleksotas cannot keep pace with the economics of Chinese glass production, nor the increasing fickleness and changeability of consumer taste and fashion.

Under the planned economy, crystal vases and their imitations were made in the Neman factory in Belarus and Bohemian crystal was imported from Warsaw Pact allies, Czechoslovakia. The heavy-cut objects were a popular Soviet-era domestic ornament: houses were packed with glassware and crystal. They were even a valued item of exchange (or bribery) that could serve instead of hard currency. Even if as status symbols they are no longer in fashion, they remain signifiers of the cultural values of the past.

A large selection of crystal was bought at market, begged, borrowed and stolen from friends and relatives, and drawn from the artists' collection. Each particular piece-tumblers, goblets, mugs and vases – possessed an individual history and set of relations, and involved both personal and collective memories. The pieces were cut down into tubular sections – requiring stems, bases, handles, flutes, and spouts to be removed – and fused and glued together into rods. The

rods then had screw holes drilled into them so that they could be assembled into three-pronged sculptures – in the shape known as the *Czech hedgehog*. The shape is based on a tensegrity model created in the 1920s by the Latvian constructivist Karl Ioganson and redeployed as an antitank defence system used during the Second World War – which is the immediate visual association. This subsuming of the object's artistic heritage under a prosaic military function parallels the interment of the crystal's earlier Soviet glory. And it also provides a precedent for art – Ioganson's sculpture being re-imagined politically and materially as an antitank defence.

Czech hedgehogs can be seen in the video describing the events of January 1991, when Russian tanks rolled into Vilnius to occupy the Lithuanian Radio and Television tower, and tried to halt the Lithuanian independence movement. Although the Russians took Lithuanian lives, their incursion was disastrous and failed, with the lustre of Empire fading like the lustre of the crystal.

The Venice pavilion exhibition

Spread over two halls, the exhibition collects and visually deploys the different aspects of the project. A 1:1 scale architectural model of the artists' vision for the pigeon loft in Rome is the focus of the first space: its facade is based on the neo-Classical style of Villa Lituania, designed in 1912 by the leading Roman architect of the day, Giovanni Piacentini. This design was created following an architectural competition for the design of the pavilion that resulted in a series of workshops with young Lithuanian architects held in Vilnius in spring 2007.

Generally speaking, pavilion architecture has played a crucial role within both the modernist architectural canon and the culture of national representative exhibitions (at world fairs and biennales). In effect the structure is an avatar, as Lithuania lacks both a permanent pavilion in the Giardini in Venice and an Embassy in Rome. Videos included in the space track the process of making the work, including material from the Kazys Lozoraitis family archive. Lozoraitis spent part of his childhood growing up in Villa Lituania: his father was Ambassador and later the Minister of Foreign Affairs

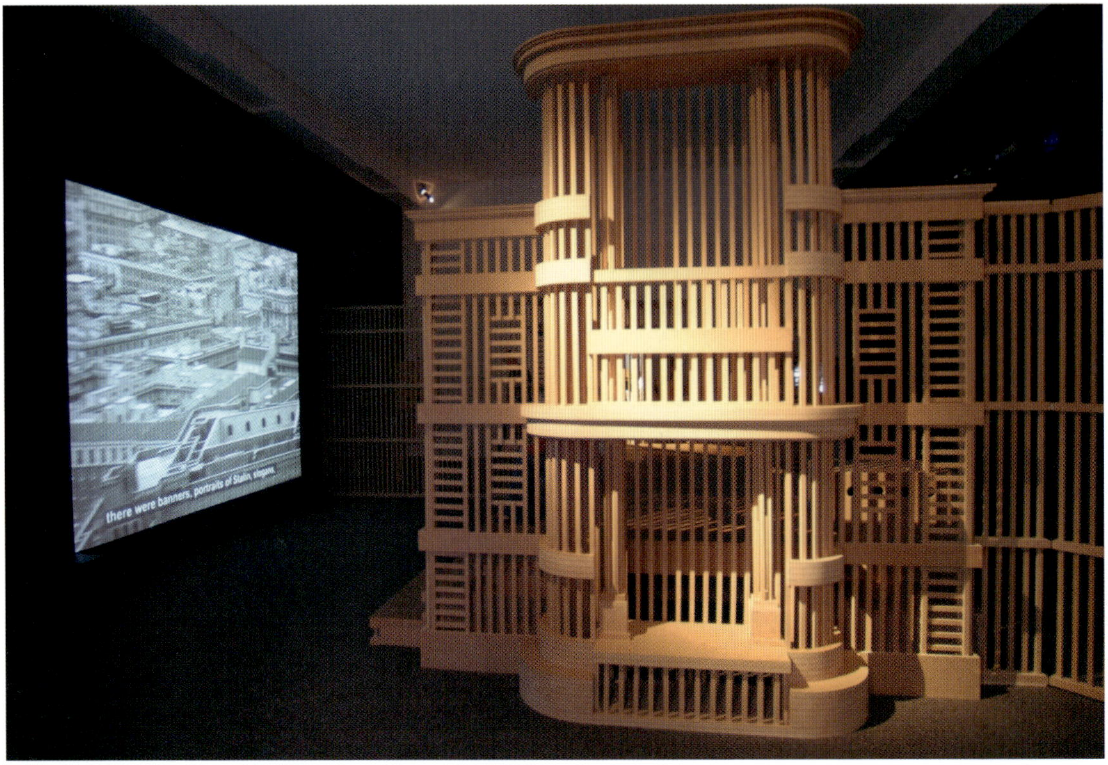

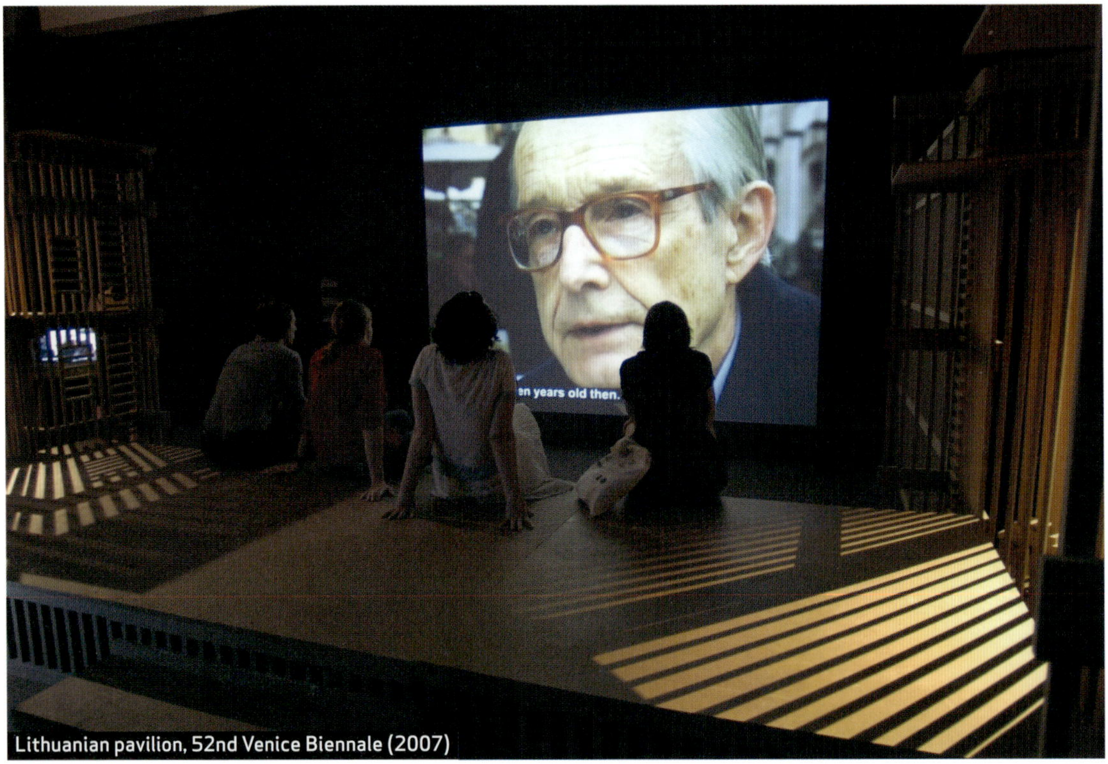

Lithuanian pavilion, 52nd Venice Biennale (2007)

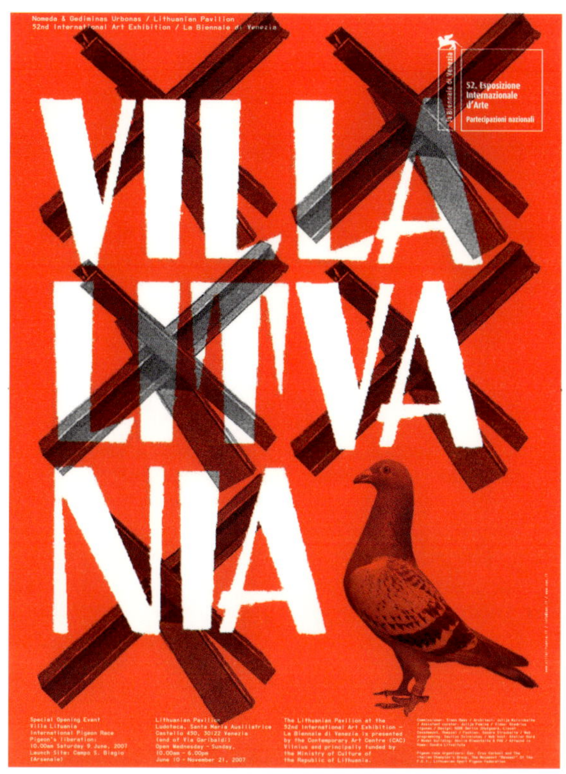

in exile. He made his life and career in Rome and became, along with his elder brother, one of the bearers of the Lithuanian torch in Italy and a campaigner on behalf of the fate of his former home. From 1992 to 2004 Kazys Lozoraitis served as the Lithuanian Ambassador to the Holy See.

The 1:1 scale model, generated in part from reconstructed film footage from Lozoraitis' childhood, integrates the neo-Classical style of Villa Lituania and the structure of the travelling boxes for racing pigeons. It is a proposal for the pigeon loft, whose construction the artists spent months negotiating in Rome. This model also provides an open architectural structure, a platform-type set for the archive of films that re-posit the territory of Villa Lituania, and from a bird's eye view peers over the security walls blocking the Villa off from the public gaze.

NOTES

1. "The Molotov-Ribbentrop Pact refers to the officially titled Treaty of Non-aggression between Germany and the Union of Soviet Socialist Republics, signed in Moscow. The Pact is known as the Nazi-Soviet Pact, Hitler-Stalin Pact and German-Soviet Non-aggression Pact. In addition to stipulations of non-aggression, the treaty included a secret protocol dividing the independent countries of Finland, Estonia, Latvia, Lithuania, Poland, and Romania into spheres of Nazi and Soviet influence, anticipating 'territorial and political rearrangements' of these countries' territories. All were subsequently invaded, occupied, or forced to cede territory by Nazi Germany, the Soviet Union, or both." (Wikipedia)

2. "Stasys Lozoraitis (1898-1983) was a Lithuanian diplomat. He served as the Foreign Minister of Lithuania from 1934 until 1938. After the Republic of Lithuania was invaded by the Soviet Union in 1940, Lozoraitis formed a Government in exile that existed from 1940 until 1991. Headquartered in Rome, he served as its head from June 15, 1940, until his death on December 24, 1983." (Wikipedia)

3. Edward W. Said: "Better to Know", *Le Monde diplomatique*, (October 2001).

4. Audrone Zukauskaite: *Performative Art and the "Invention of the Real"*, 2007.

5. Dove for Peace refers to a Pablo Picasso drawing made for the peace conference in Paris in 1949.

6. Excerpt from the *Villa Lituania* diary, September 2007. Simon Rees (ed.); Nomeda & Gediminas Urbonas: *Villa Lituania*. Berlin, New York: Sternberg Press, 2008.

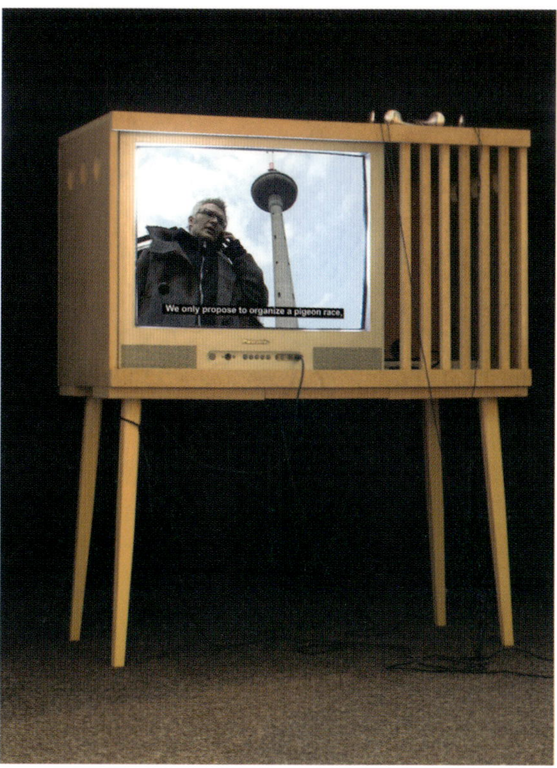

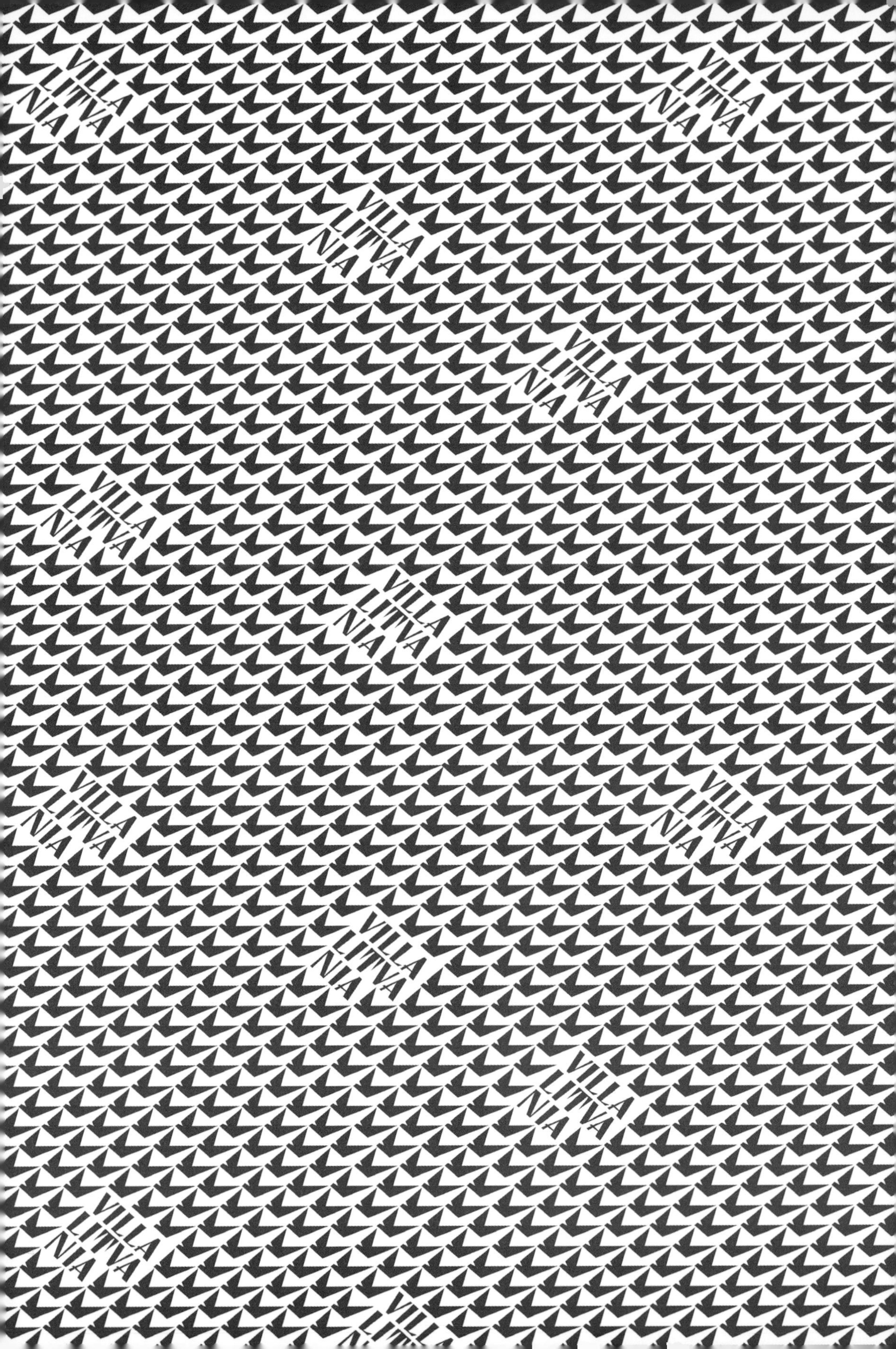

AFTER LENIN, LITTLE FRANKFURT
History and self-organised styles in the work of Nomeda and Gediminas Urbonas

Lars Bang Larsen

History and self-organised styles in the work of Nomeda and Gediminas Urbonas

Lars Bang Larsen

Nation as symptom

Since they started their collaboration in the early 1990s, the work of Nomeda and Gediminas Urbonas has revolved around meetings between art and historical space. By articulating the cultural traumas, predicaments and new possibilities that have been laid bare after Lithuania's independence from Soviet rule in 1991, their work stages collective searches for new forms of belonging. Rather than just picturing or interpreting these struggles, these investigations are implemented as self-organised processes, such as the independent exhibition space Jutempus (1993-1997) or the tvvv. plotas (1998-1999), a TV programme initiated and run by the Urbonas. As little pieces of social fabric that expand in unexpected ways, projects such as these encourage a collective response rather than an individual one.

Most sociologists and political scientists agree that there is no uniform and persistent *Leninist legacy* detectable among the numerous communist successor governments.[1] That is, there is no particular common trend between the subsequent democratic developments of the former Soviet polities and in fact they are all likely to display diverse regime properties that depend on different factors (proximity to the Western countries, for example). These volatile political trajectories have a strong resonance in Lithuania, a nation which itself has been caught up in irregular historical patterns: not counting its post-Soviet independence, the small Baltic state has only experienced 22 years of autonomy since the late 18th century.

In the work of the Urbonas the idea of the national is addressed not just on an institutional scale, but as a social symptom that pervades imaginaries on subjective and collective levels.[2] As Freud pointed out, the symptom occurs as one part of a trinity where the two other elements are fear and inhibition. In this psychic economy the symptom represents the elusive trace of an "ultimate cause" of inhibited pathology, which will remain displaced, usually because of fear of punishment if it is revealed. In psychoanalysis the symptom is a sign and surrogate for what is known of old and long familiar. This becomes a perfect analogy for the idea of the nation as a repressed sign that is compulsively revisited in disguised forms under the threat of punishment of a Soviet father figure, or associated with the post-Soviet dementia of nationalism.

The question of historical belonging being in this way couched in terms of subjectivity, the fundamental entities that make up a societal ontology – population, institutions, borders, geography – are shown to share properties with symbolic structures that hold communities together; structures of feeling that define our sense of individual and collective belonging. This was most explicit in the project *Transaction* (2000-2004), in which the notion of the victim as woman was applied to the representation of Lithuania in Lithuanian film from the Soviet era. To work with such *idea-scenarios*, to use the Urbonas' own term, amounts to establishing "a model that is never real, but true at the same time."[3] In this case a psychoanalytic working-through of the imaginary of the nation. Such an approach bypasses the nationalist model, which is an ideological causal explanation intent on fixing territories and behaviours once and for all. Instead, in the idea-scenario, belonging is a question of becoming through a desire to push existing limits of historical being. In this way the question of the national is opened up through concepts that may counteract exclusionary nostalgia as an aftermath of imperialism or globalisation.

Simulatory regimes

A chapter of Jonathan Franzen's bestseller, *The Corrections* (2001) – a saga of the disintegration of the North-American nuclear family – takes place in contemporary Vilnius. Lithuania is portrayed as a rogue state; not a threat to international peace, perhaps, but one whose role as a global player has "been fading since the death of Vytautas the Great in 1430" and which is now "rattling down the road toward anarchy." [4] Ruled by gangster entrepreneurs, drive-by shootings in the Lithuanian capital are the order of the day, while pop hits of yesteryear are heard on the radios of prostitutes through the low-hanging clouds of high-sulphur smoke that envelop the streets.

Perhaps this portrait of societal collapse is inspired by the attempted Red Army takeover of the national TV broadcast station in 1991, and employed by the author with freewheeling artistic licence; or it has grown out of hazy stereotypes called forth in the Westerner's mind when he imagines what life is like on the – as we all know – invariably crisis-driven flipside of Europe. Whatever the author's reasons, or however shoddy his research, it is significant that even though the representations of Lithuania and *homo sovieticus* skid off the actual reality of 1990s Vilnius, crime-ridden and politically unstable as it may have been, these representations are powerful enough to appear in the book's fictional economy as a distorted imaginary that mirrors the institutionalised, yet "ultimately no less brutal," capitalism of America.

The book's Lithuanian chapter – which was quoted with some resentment in newspapers here when it appeared – seems to be the author's intended challenge to the claim to "the end of history" (the well-known pseudo-philosophical backup to the New World Order declared by George Bush Sr. in 1991).[5] Ironically, by the author's use of Lithuania as a mere counter-image to life in the US, the novel repeats, and thereby itself fails to resolve, what approaches can be taken to address the relation between history and nation. One of the novel's Lithuanian characters muses how resistance to the *free* market offers no gratification similar to the Lithuanians' legendary resistance to Soviet imperialism: "What *positive* thing do I stand for? What is the *positive* definition of my country?" [6] In other words: nobody knows what Lithuania is. *The Corrections* sheds no light on the question because the novel basically repeats an imperial narrative: just as Lithuania in Soviet times was (not) the Soviet Union what defines it in the novel is that in post-Soviet times it is (not) the United States of America.

The use of Lithuania as not-America in *The Corrections* is an example of an idea-scenario that is overdetermined and articulated from the outside. The very real and urgent struggles over the imaginaries of historical space and cultural subjectivity is reflected in the Urbonas' *Pro-test Lab* (2005 – ongoing). The project consisted of a squat in the Lietuva cinema, a piece of landmark architecture built during the Soviet era and, after 1991, functioning as Vilnius' only independent cinema. In 2002 the building was privatised by a corporation, which announced that it was to be razed and an apartment block with a commercial centre built in its place. In opposition to the privatisation of public space, the *Pro-test Lab* provided an open framework, which could be used by groups and individuals as a space for civic protest, with an agenda to controvert the Lietuva's demolition. *Lietuva* means Lithuania, and hence *Pro-test Lab* metonymically involved Lithuania's entire Leninist legacy with specific reference to the redevelopment of the city of Vilnius under the aegis of an accelerated capitalism.

In order to sketch out a context for the *Pro-test Lab*, let's have a very quick look at the urban fabric of Vilnius. The historical centre, with its sturdy and well-preserved volumes of Vilnius Baroque, re-emerged during the 1990s via a kind of Disneyfied folklorism. Hence, the city council is encouraging artisans to set up shop here and sell token national arts and crafts; they are

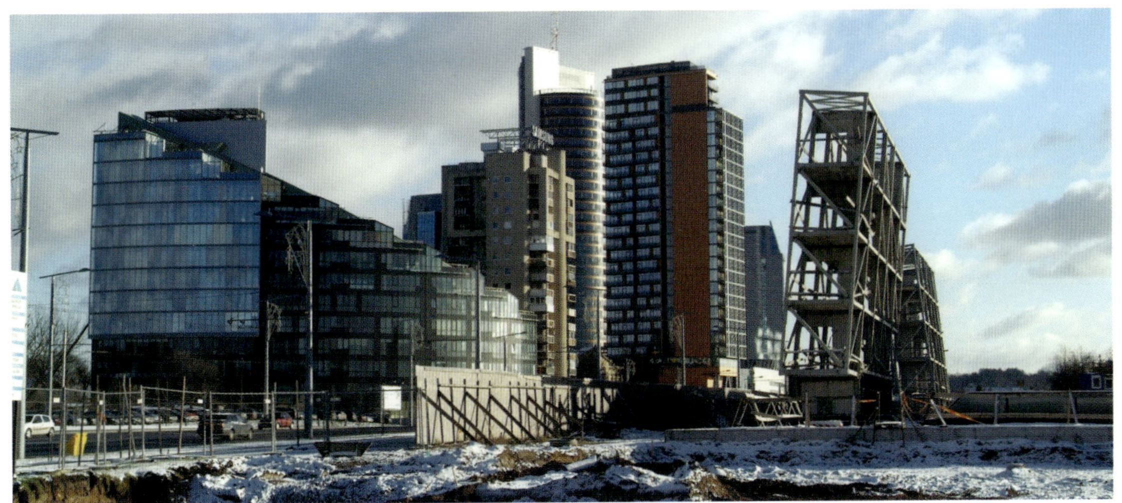

provided with a commercial space for half the rent that other professions have to pay in the district. Unsurprisingly rustic styles are dominating here, creating a strange historical glitch in their coexistence with the corporate facades of Scandinavian banks.

Adjacent to the historical centre is a large building site, where the Castle of the Lithuanian Kings is currently under construction. Expected to be finished in 2009, the Castle will be a museum and a tribute to the historical rulers and heydays of the nation when, during the Polish-Lithuanian commonwealth, it was Europe's biggest country, with an empire stretching from the Baltic to the Black Sea. Even though officially a reconstruction of a castle razed by Russian invaders in 1801, the project is based more on revisionist desire than on historical fact, as almost no documents of the original castle remain. Nobody really knows what it looked like.

The River Neris' right bank was developed immediately after 1991, most visibly in the form of the high-rises that host the city's new financial and governmental centre. These have inspired the district's nickname Little Frankfurt, after the similarly stark verticality of Germany's banking city. Exclusive condominiums in the area are home to, among others, wealthy Russians who have preferred to invest in property inside the European Union zone. Beyond Little Frankfurt, and next to the 1970s-style social housing and an area with Klondike-style old and decrepit wooden houses, are located two new shopping malls, the Acropolis and the Hermitage,

as big and sophisticated as any you will see in Europe or the US, and favourite hangouts for the city's teenagers.

To top it all off in a way that answers *The Corrections* back in a voice the city is borrowing from North America, the Guggenheim emporium is preparing its arrival on the scene. A media campaign is currently preparing public opinion for a Guggenheim Vilnius and the substantial costs such a project implies for the public budgets. However, the global museum chain has already won the art-historical battle, as it has ensured that the archives of Jonas Mekas and George Maciunas will be deposited here (rather than in the national collection).

In this way Vilnius, like so many other of the world's cities, is an assemblage shot through with social and spatial effects of calculability, control and representation. The contrasts in this newly developed city reveal the irrationality of the postulated rationality of such strategies, as it is expressed in the near-fictitious engineering of historical continuity and the ideological effects of exemplary and recognisable *local values*. Both aspects are based in hostility towards the survival of public cultures.

It was against such simulatory regimes that the Urbonas organised *Pro-test Lab*. Originally launched as a quasi-autonomous project within the framework of the international group show *Populism* at the nearby Centre for Contemporary Art (CAC), it quickly took on a life on its own that expanded beyond the temporal and spatial lim-

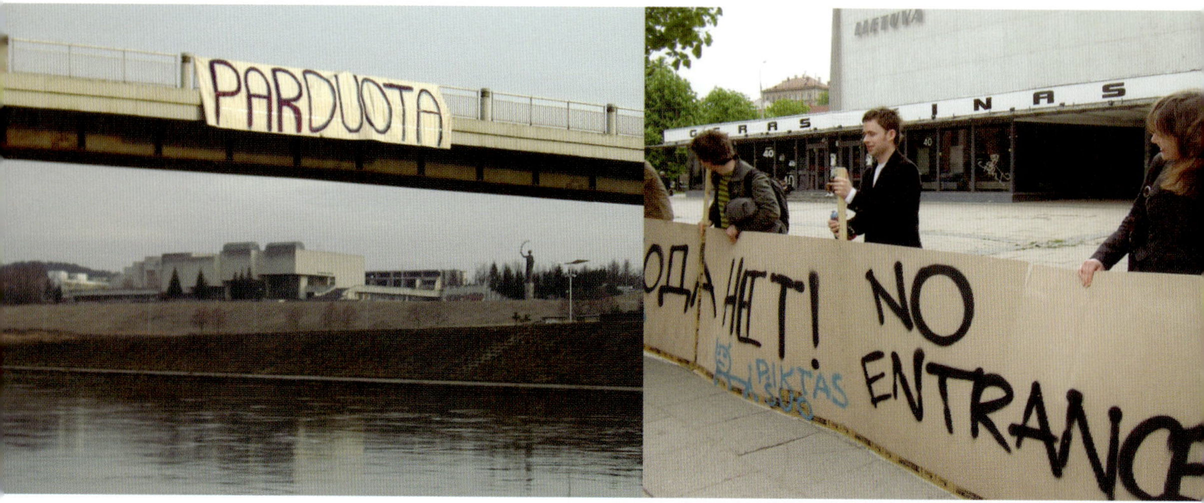

itations of the exhibition.[7] The same is true for the cultural location of the *Lab*. As Gediminas Urbonas stated in a conversation with me, "It started as an art project, but we don't know if it is one anymore." This was indicative of the project's dynamics but also of a loss of control: as things developed, and people started frequenting the *Lab*, not all groups and users of the space would be known to the artists, who had to go with the flow of events. This is significant for the ideological underpinnings of *Pro-test Lab*, and symptomatic for arguments related to art activism's location *outside* the art system, as well as to its notions of authorship. Let's take a closer look at these theoretical issues, in order to find out about *Pro-test Lab*'s status as an activist idea-scenario.

Authorship and meeting in art activism

It is a staple of art activism's self-understanding that it is predicated on the political rather than the critical. Hence its slant towards the production of space (which is so clear in *Pro-test Lab*).[8] In politics, the stakes are bigger, *for real*, unlike the more specialised vocabulary of criticality that is internal to the art system (such as institutional critique). One argument that is typically used to support art activism's claim to political agency is its collective authorship, and the claim that activism lies *at the heart* of collaborative practices is an almost conditioned response to current discussions about them.[9] While this is undoubtedly true about the intentionality of many artistic collectives, it seems like an all

too hasty coding of the premises and possibilities of the collaborative when one considers historical practitioners like, for example, Gilbert & George, Medical Hermeneutics or Art & Language.

After modernism, the issue of collective authorship was raised again in the way artists of the 1990s revisited collaborative strategies. Implicitly or explicitly, they evoked retrospective discourses about the idealised collectivism of the modern era, while at the same time producing some surprising – and perhaps inadvertent – overlaps between artistic practice and vanguard managerial ideologies. If the art market and a traditionalist understanding of authorship have often excluded collective authorship from art history, it is now important for these practices to confront their own historical exclusion *at the same time as* deconstructing such heroic collectivist referents as the Paris Commune or the October Revolution. Of course, these examples of strong collectivism – or what, with Marx, we might call free association – go some way towards explaining a genealogy of collective authorship and agency, inasmuch as they clearly have informed historical avant-gardes such as the Russian Constructivists and the Situationist International. But they also contain the germs of nostalgia and overdetermination, because the Paris Commune and the October Revolution are precisely examples from militant politics.

Militancy is a referent which flatters art activism's utilitarian presuppositions, at the same time as art activism often fails, or refuses, to articulate the difference between a socio-political community and an artistic one. Moreover, today's networked artistic collectives try to wring engagement from quite different types of oppression than those which in other eras called for insurrection: ours is a privatised, post-political, mass-mediated, de-institutionalised, and usually middle-class, existence. Inside this regime, one is often hard put to figure out what are authentic hybrid identities, and what makes for violent or oppressive hegemonies. Moreover – and hence the need for encouraging collaboration in the first place – it is *one's own problem*, because bureaucratic, spectacular capitalism has managed to dismantle the structures that held notions of solidarity in place.

Collaboration is obviously a highly important moment in the organisation of the production of art, and our reading of it. But it is its pulse, dynamics, contexts and effects that should be articulated, rather than its authorial form. That is, if we want to proceed in the question of art's proximity to activism or militancy, by collaboration we must understand self-organisation. Focusing on collaboration as such then appears to be a continuation of older discussions of authorship ('What is an author?' as Michel Foucault put it at the end of modernity), now projected onto a new authorial body that appears to have certain given qualities – almost as in modernist preoccupations with the inherent properties of artistic media.

As suggested above, I would argue that the artistic collective's authorial logic could have any number of different characteristics; it does not necessarily follow from collaboration that it is activist or political (in the sense that it manifests itself as an organised process). However, it is true that self-organised art and the political share one crucial aspect – the meeting. But the meeting in collaborative art is vastly different from the political nature of the meeting. The latter has a universal character or, in the words of Alain Badiou, it is *topologically collective*; there is no place where it is not valid.[10] The artistic collective, on the other hand, is usually self-sufficient, at least in part. The artists' group can be its own audience, something which was not uncommon for the historical avant-garde and neo-avant-garde movements, which had no or little public reach outside of their inner circle – and sometimes claimed it did not desire any. The meeting in collaborative art is hence different from the political meeting, for the simple reason that the artistic collective does not admit new members. If there was an artistic collective which ever existed that ended up with more members than it started out with, it would be the exception rather than the rule. The Situationists were decimated by Guy Debord's notorious proclivity for expulsing its members ("It was really about keeping oneself in a pure state, like a crystal," as Henri Lefebvre recalls about his brief time in the movement).[11] In this way, while the artistic collective can undermine various inherited cultural hierarchies, it is in itself not topologically inclusive. What is fascinating about artistic collectives is not their authorial transparency – because that is illusory in itself. Every authorial subject is a hypothetical subject, if we accept that authorial identity is something other than the psychosocial subject who *conveys* it. The collective author represents no less of a hypothetical subjectivity, but now in the form of a previously undeclared or non-existing singularity's agreement to proceed as a author.

Artistic collectives are characterised by a paradox, then, namely the fact that their circle can be more hermetic than the salon, while the particular kind of authority they convey can be more open and unfinished than the solitary author. Their operations thus have the potential to be both more opaque and more dynamic than the traditional artist's: where different nervous systems are hooked up to each other, art is integrated into surrounding culture. This is to say that self-organised artists' groups on one level are better equipped than the solitary author to address and discuss the foundations of art production. Where there will inevitably exist a correspondence between the individual signature and the work (if not in terms of old-fashioned, private prestige, then in terms of interest, biographical text and so on), the group literally operates at a different scale. Collective authorship is a measure of power relations, a subjectivity that is capable of sizing up institutions.

Before we return to the work of the Urbonas, just a couple of brief points to probe this hypothesis. One aspect of the idea of sizing up institutions from the outside is the politics of the alternative space, which, as in many other discussions about collective art production, harks back to the 1960s and 70s. In 1974 the North-American artist Michael Asher criticised this organisational principle in the following way:

"Another phenomenon of the early seventies, deriving from artists' anticommercialism and concern with the problem of commodification, was the development of the alternative space system for exhibition, although not necessarily for distribution. The alternative space relied for its funding on outside sources rather than the market for which the work was primarily produced. Alternative space made more works more frequently accessible than the commercial galleries, yet they falsified the work's commodity status, assuming that visibility alone would complete the reception process and that exchange value was not one of the work's features. The alternative space system provided visibility for the work regardless of specific interest, but it did not necessarily stand behind the work, with the full support necessary for reception within the culture. Paradoxically, the only way for a work to be fully received is through its initial abstraction for exchange value. To resolve these contradictions between the artist's interests and the functions and capacities of the alternative space, these institutions finally had to assume the role of being either a commercial gallery or a museum."[12]

On this note, Asher concludes that "the gallery is one essential context for the cultural reception" of his work, in which his interventionist brand of minimalist sculpture can "serve as a model of how the gallery is operating, but also "as a model for its own economic reproduction."[13] In a somewhat surprising manner this is a Marxist analysis that plays into the hands of the market by insisting on the work's essential, inescapable, commodity status. This forms the basis of the assumption that only the work's exchange in the marketplace is a real reception process (as opposed to "visibility alone"); and that this exchange process can be made transparent by the work itself. This postulate bypasses the public art institution, or any space defined as the public realm, as a legitimate destination for the work, inasmuch as *culture* is predicated on commercial transactions.

Of course, Asher may be perfectly right with regard to the shortcomings of the alternative space system; however, from a structural point of view his argument seems to support business as usual. The simple points I want to make by bringing this up are, firstly, that in the process of sizing up institutions (public and market), it is possible – for the individual but perhaps especially for the collective author, as is also demonstrated in *Pro-test Lab* – to produce a distance from the commodity status of the work.[14] Secondly, any such sizing up confronts us with the social imaginaries of the transactions and exchange processes that are considered to be real. Here, Asher is definitely right about one thing: the aim of the project, even if it originates outside the institution, should be a "reception within the culture" – whether that culture is taken to be a public or a privatised one.

Because it is typically located outside the gallery space, the studio and the museum, an art activist project is seen to belong neither to the art sphere nor to political institutions. It cannot be measured with conventional critical yardsticks because of the way its utopian gauge breaks open existing categories: the language for its evaluation does not exist yet, it is claimed, also because art activism's target groups are usually marginalised communities who don't yet have a voice in society. Hence art activism's indignation and drive to intervene, organise, educate, empower, and counteract art's potential for stagnation or reaction. As a testimony to a desire for change and experimentation, this is of course a perfectly legitimate argument (even if it may contradict the way art activists often pride themselves on working as a continuation of the historical avant-gardes).[15]

However, the argument of art activism as a free-floating category belonging neither to art nor to institutions loses its validity when it becomes a pretext for shelving discussions about the problems in equating artistic, cultural and political empowerment. Inherently hostile to art and authorship, this position erases the given limit between political and artistic representation as it tries to transcend art by re-naming it *cultural democracy* (in Lucy Lippard's term), or by evading definition altogether.[16] In other words, the claim to art activism's political instrumentality tends to remain in a theory/practice schema that evades language and conceptual work at the risk of separating politics from thought. Connections between cultural forms and social processes that interpretative, artistic agency may locate and articulate are thus bypassed.[17]

Scripting, thought, games and styles

If one wants to attempt to articulate the act of abstraction that founds the group author, it is rewarding to go through Badiou's discussion of "thought that acts through and towards a collective seized by its truth." This is of special relevance in relation the Urbonas' work, as Badiou asserts that "the collapse of the socialist States teaches us that the path of egalitarian politics do not pass through State power, that politics is a matter of immanent subjective determination, an axiom of the collective".[18] In other words, if we want to insist on the legitimacy of art and of relevant models of cultural agency other than the militant one, we will need to counter the functionalist tendency of art activism. We must ask, then, what else – which thoughts, which methods and which forms – can be produced apart from space? In the Urbonas' own words,

> "As Lithuania doesn't have a cultural history of resistance, the *Pro-test Lab* created an important space within the public sphere, the fabric of the city, the media and the existing political and cultural constellations. We were concerned with producing a new *aesthetic* language that could empower future protests."[19]

It is thus significant that the protests at the Lietuva embodied a political struggle at the same time as they made for a sort of living archive based on the instant reception of protest forms. Prompted by the historical delay of social and political repression, self-organisation became aesthetically self-aware.

A good example of this was when students from the school of architecture rigged up a giant, open-air Monopoly game outside the Lietuva, in which they played with meticulously constructed cardboard models of landmark architecture in Vilnius. The stakes were for the domination of the city's public space. This makes for an updated version of the opening scene of Öyvind Fahlström's film *Du gamla, du fria* (1971), in which a street theatre group unfold an open-air Monopoly game of life-size proportions and try to mobilise the people against capital by showing how the nation and its citizens are nothing more than pawns in a game to the large Swedish corporations. If the Lithuanian architecture students were aware of Fahlström's film, their Monopoly game is a great piece of appropriation; if they did not know it, then maybe we are dealing with something like an activist archetype! Art activist discussions aside, the point made by the students is a highly valid one: due to the absence of preservation strategies for Soviet era architecture, a significant cultural heritage in former Soviet republics is at risk of disappearing. One could argue that they were built during an era of political repression and hence are testimonies to totalitarianism, but that in itself hardly justifies neglect. After all, renowned architects like Oscar Niemeyer – to take but one example from the modern era – have participated in the realisation of no less totalitarian projects.

Pro-test Lab, like other Urbonas projects and idea-scenarios, conveys a particular vision of moving around between different plateaux; different types of vocabularies, agencies and forms of organisation, never resting in one particular register but deferring conclusions and including many new beginnings. Their work fans out in a wide range of symbolic production (including music, fashion, filmmaking, archives, and of course visual displays) to do with the production of space (which includes the distribution of information as well as concerts, fashion parades, collaborations with lobbies, interest groups and people from other professional domains).

If an idea-scenario is the production of signification and space, the Urbonas call their methodology *scripting*. This sets the stage for the redistribution of roles and competences within reproduction processes.[20] With their agenda of artistic protest in mind, we may elaborate this process of scripting with a quote from the historian Benedict Anderson,

> "[The community] is imagined because the members of even the smallest nation will never know most of their fellow-members, meet them, or even hear of them, yet in the minds of each lives the image of their communion. […] Communities are to be distinguished, not by their falsity/genuineness, but by the style in which they are imagined."[21]

In the process of scripting idea-scenarios, forms or styles are generated by or through which the community can be re-imagined. In these operations, the notion and practice of self-organisation is continuously transformed: there is obviously a big a difference between working within a self-defined framework such as *Pro-test Lab*, the Jutempus Space or the tvvv.plotas, and making a museum show or contributing to the Venice Biennial. From the point of view of the Urbonas' involvement in these various processes, self-organisation pulsates between inclusive gestures where authorship tends to be erased in participatory and even insurrectionist sequences, and periods of receding into research and production where their collaboration is reinforced.

A rare example of a collective that works with fiction is the five-member-strong Italian writer's group Wu Ming (formerly Luther Blissett). In their latest book, the Cold War thriller *54*, the pigeon-fancier Fanti appears, somewhat along the lines of the Urbonas' contribution for the Venice Biennial 2007. Fanti is:

> "…one of 3,000 [pigeon-fanciers] in Emilia Romagna [who] had become an important member of the International Federation of Homing Pigeon Fanciers, founded in 1881. At the last fair in Bologna he had gone mad and spent 300,000 lire on a slender female, with a bright-grey back tending to indigo, sgurafosso. Very elegant. Her name was Eloisa, and she had made the journey from Indochina to Italy in two months. Two hundred kilometres a day, 'a remarkable accomplishment.'"[22]

"Two hundred kilometres a day," through Asia… If we are to invent new styles and idea-scenarios through which we can re-imagine our communities across geopolitical terrains and simulatory everyday spaces, we will have to perform just as remarkably as Eloisa and cover large distances; if not geographically, then certainly in response to the challenges history poses to our thinking and doing.

Lars Bang Larsen researches the global spread of 1960s psychedelic art and culture at the University of Copenhagen. He contributes regularly to *Afterall*, *Artforum* and *Frieze*, and has co-curated exhibitions such as *Pyramids of Mars* (2001), *The Invisible Insurrection of a Million Minds* (2005), as well as *Populism* (2005), in connection with which the *Pro-test Lab* project was launched.

NOTES

1. Herbert Kitschelt: "Accounting for Postcommunist Regime Diversity. What Counts as a Good Cause?" in Grzegorz Ekiert and Stephen E. Hanson (eds.): *Capitalism and Democracy in Central and Eastern Europe. Assessing the Legacy of Communist Rule.* Cambridge: Cambridge University Press, 2003, p. 50.

2. By the term *imaginaries* the philosopher Cornelius Castoriadis understood the impact that the *magmas* of language, as well as cultural symbols and narratives, have on material social reality and subjectivity. See for example his essay "The Imaginary: Creation in the Social-Historical Domain," in *World in Fragments. Writings on Politics, Society, Psychoanalysis, and the Imagination.* Standford: Stanford University Press, 1997.

3. Interview with Jean-Charles Massera. In Lars Bang Larsen, Charlotte Brandt, Cristina Ricupero (eds.): *Fundamentalisms of the New Order* (exh. cat.). Berlin: Nifca/Lukas & Sternberg, 2003, p. 93.

4. Jonathan Franzen: *The Corrections*. London: Fourth Estate, 2001, pp. 510, 512.

5. I am, of course, referring to Francis Fukuyama's 1989 essay "The End of History," in which the author asserts that history is directional, and its endpoint is capitalist liberal democracy.

6. Jonathan Franzen: op. cit., p. 515.

7. The *Populism* exhibition was curated by Cristina Ricupero, Nicolaus Schafhausen and myself, and took place in the CAC in Vilnius from 8 April through 4 August 2005. *Pro-test Lab* existed for almost two years, and the popular mobilisation initiated by the Urbonas was finally successful in its aims of putting off the demolition of Lietuva.

8. To my knowledge, Okwui Enwezor is the first to make this point explicit, in his essay "The Production of Social Space as Artwork. Protocols of Community in the Work of Le Groupe Amos and Huit Facettes", in Blacke Stimson & Gregory Sholette (eds.): *Collectivism After Modernism: The Art of Social Imagination after 1945*. Minnesota: University Press, 2007. We should make one addition to activism's production of space. That is, there is also a modernist tradition for negotiating collaboration through medium and material. In Denmark, the neo-avant-garde group Den Eksperimenterende Kunstskole ("The Experimental Art School"), which existed from 1961 till 1965 and counted members such as Per Kirkeby and Poul Gernes, primarily worked with deconstructing painting, sculpture and graphics by reorganising artistic matter through happenings as a form of temporal involvement.

9. See for example Johanna Billing, Maria Lind & Lars Nilsson (eds.): *Taking the Matter into Common Hands: On Contemporary Art and Collaborative Practices*. London: Black Dog Publishing, 2007.

10. Alain Badiou: *Metapolitics*. London: Verso, 2005 (1998), p. 142.

11. "Henri Lefebvre on the Situationist International". A 1983 interview conducted and translated by Kristin Ross, published in *October*, no. 79 (Winter 1997).

12. Michael Asher: "September 21 – October 12, 1974. Claire Copley Gallery, Inc. Los Angeles, California", in Michael Asher & Benjamin Buchloh (eds): *Writings 1973-1983 On Works 1969-1979*. Los Angeles: The Press of the Nova Scotia College of Art and Design / The Museum of Contemporary Art, n.d., p. 100.

13. Ibid.

14. Another example of bypassing the work's commodity status is the early work of the Copenhagen-based artists' group N55 (Ingvil Aarbakke, Rikke Luther, Jon Sorvin and Cecilia Wendt), who during the late 1990s produced a sculptural vocabulary of everyday functions (chair, table, bed etc., including a Buckminster Fuller-like *Spaceframe*, a living unit). These objects were accompanied by open source information, on the internet and in the form of manuals that explained step by step how to do them yourself. www.n55dk.

15. For example, contemporary community-based art and the way this often departs from an imperative that the art work or action should heal and confirm, and not disturb, the identity and self-understanding of the beholder. As Miwon Kwon has described, the production of such "empowered" subjects is a reversal of the aesthetically politicised subjects of the historical avant-garde, because the avant-gardes didn't work on the basis of organicity but of antagonism and what is explicitly produced. In this context, the question is: can one bring about social healing and social change at the same time? (See Miwon Kwon: *One Place After Another. Site-Specific Art and Locational Identity*. Cambridge, Mass.& London: The MIT Press, 2004).

16. Nina Felshin: "[Activist artists] are creatively expanding art's boundaries and audience and are redefining the role of the artist. In the process, they seem to suggest that the proper answer to the question '…But is it Art?' is: 'But does it matter?'" Nina Felshin in her introduction to Nina Felshin (ed.): *But Is It Art? The Spirit Of Art As Activism*. Seattle: Bay Press, 1995, p.13.

17. See also my essay "True Rulers of Their Own Realm. Political Subjectivation in Palle Nielsen's *The Model – A Model for a Qualitative Society*", in: *Afterall*, no. 16. London: Central Saint Martin's College of Art and Design, London, (Autumn / Winter 2007).

18. Alain Badiou. op. cit.

19. "Flying High". Interview by Cristina Ricupero with Nomeda and Gediminas Urbonas in *CAC Interviu*, Issue nos. 7-8, Vilnius, 2007, p. 60.

20. To paraphrase Jacques Rancière, as quoted by the Urbonas: "precincts of art lend themselves more readily today than other fields to the redistribution of roles and competences." Or, as they have also put it: "What we believe in is modelling and creating organisation structures that support new modes of production as a part of artistic practice." (Interview by Jean-Charles Massera with Nomeda and Gediminas Urbonas, p. 91). Here, the collaboration with individuals and groups was articulated along linguistic lines: "The main point for us [in the work with *tvvv.plotas*] was to find out how ideas were articulated in different contexts, rather than to force any final outcome. We said: we are your syntax, you are our language. Each of the topics that were suggested for open discussion included some proposals form the collaborating participants that shaped that particular program in a different way. For instance, Modernism in contemporary art and how it was understood by a Lithuanian and by foreign experts." (Ibid.).

21. Benedict Anderson: *Imagined Communities. Reflections on the Origin and Spread of Nationalism*. London: Verso, 2003 (1983), p. 6.

22. Wu Ming: *54*. London: Arrow Books, 2006 (2002), p. 178.

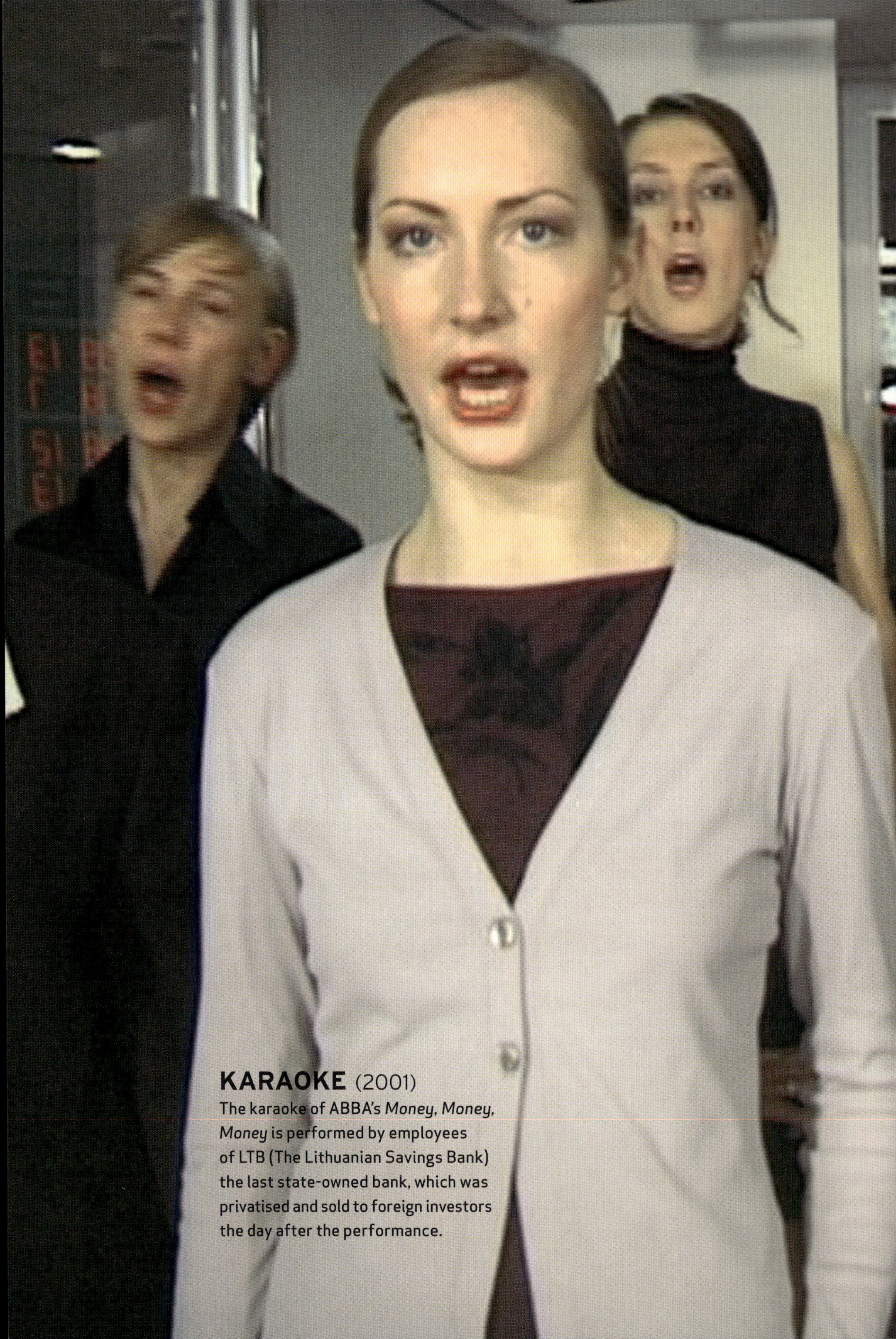

KARAOKE (2001)
The karaoke of ABBA's *Money, Money, Money* is performed by employees of LTB (The Lithuanian Savings Bank) the last state-owned bank, which was privatised and sold to foreign investors the day after the performance.

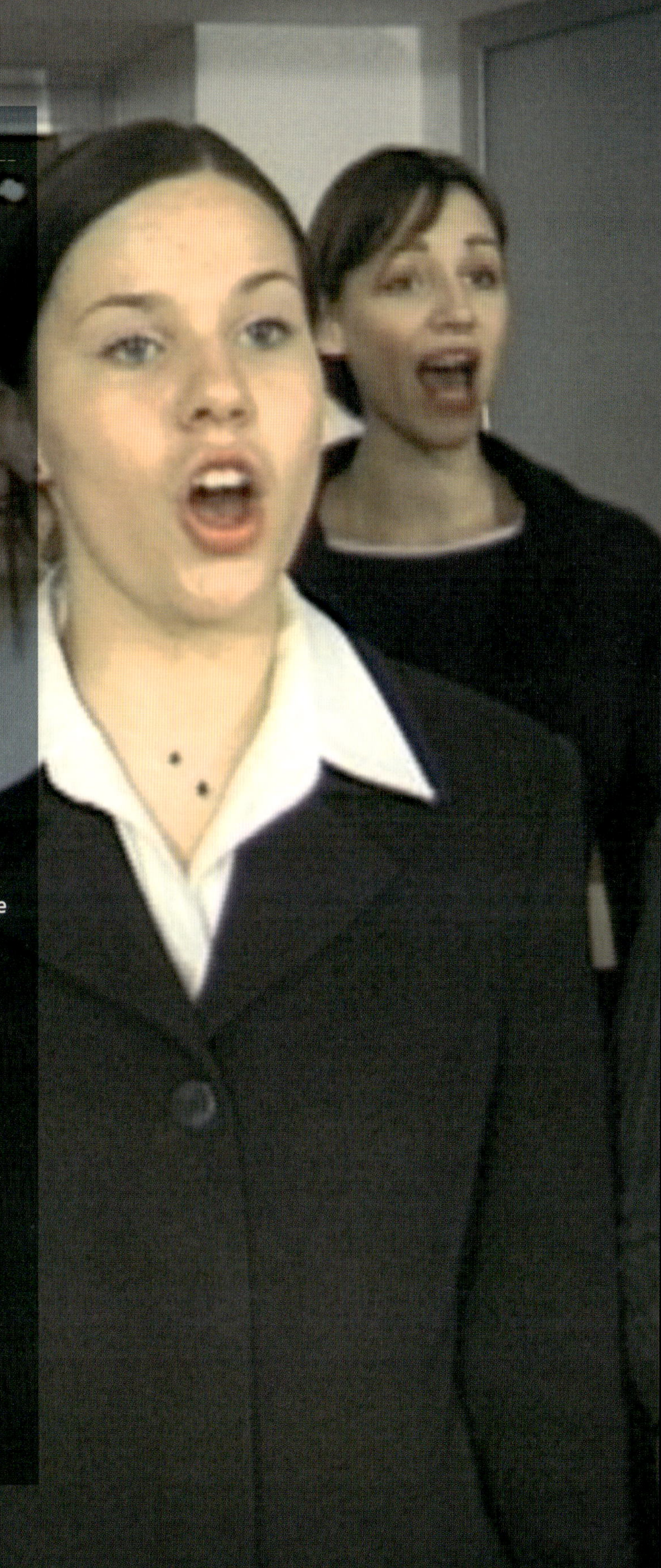

MONEY, MONEY, MONEY (ABBA, 1976)

I work all night, I work all day,
to pay the bills I have to pay
Ain't it sad
And still there never seems to be
a single penny left for me
That's too bad
In my dreams I have a plan
If I got me a wealthy man
I wouldn't have to work at all,
I'd fool around and have a ball...

Money, money, money
Must be funny
In the rich man's world
Money, money, money
Always sunny
In the rich man's world
Aha-ahaaa
All the things I could do
If I had a little money
It's a rich man's world

A man like that is hard to find but
I can't get him off my mind
Ain't it sad
And if he happens to be free I bet he
wouldn't fancy me
That's too bad
So I must leave, I'll have to go
To Las Vegas or Monaco
And win a fortune in a game,
My life will never be the same...

Money, money, money
Must be funny
In the rich man's world
Money, money, money
Always sunny
In the rich man's world
Aha-ahaaa
All the things I could do
If I had a little money
It's a rich man's world

It's a rich man's world

BIOGRAPHY

Nomeda & Gediminas Urbonas
Born in Lithuania in 1968 and 1966
respectively, the Urbonas live
and work in Vilnius
http://nugu.lt/dossier

1997: co-founders of Jutempus, an
interdisciplinary art programme
2000: co-founders of VILMA (Vilnius
Interdisciplinary Lab for Media Art)

Solo exhibitions

2008
*Nomeda & Gediminas Urbonas: Devices
for action*. Museu d'Art Contemporani
de Barcelona, Barcelona, Spain

2007
Villa Lituania, the Lithuanian
Pavilion, 52nd Venice Biennale,
Venice, Italy

2004
RR: Ruta Remake, Contemporary Art
Centre (CAC), Vilnius, Lithuania

2003
Ruta Remake. Substream,
Kunstnernes Hus, Oslo, Norway

2002
TRANSmute, Sprengel Museum,
Hanover, Germany

TRANSACTION. Translation,
Ludwig Museum, Budapest,
Hungary

2001
TRANSACTION. Unpacked, IASPIS,
Stockholm, Sweden

2000
TRANSACTION, haus.0, Künstlerhaus
Stuttgart, Germany

*TRANSACTION. Strangers
& Paradise*, Witte de With Center
for Contemporary Art, Rotterdam,
The Netherlands

Selected group exhibitions

2008
Italia, Italie, Italien, Italie, Wlochy
ARCOS - Museo di Arte
Contemporaneo del Sannio,
Benevento, Italy

*Archive Fever: Uses of the Document
in Contemporary Art*, International
Center of Photography, New York,
United States

2007
*Forms of Resistance. Artists and
the Desire For a Social Change*,
Van Abbemuseum, Eindhoven,
The Netherlands

*Fluxus East. Fluxus Networks in
Central Eastern Europe*, Künstlerhaus
Bethanien, Berlin, Germany; Ludwig
Museum, Budapest, Hungary; Bunkier
Stuky, Krakow, Polland; CAC, Vilnius,
Lithuania

*The History of a Decade That Has
Not Yet Been Named*, 9th Lyon
Biennial of Contemporary Art,
Lyon, France

*Progressive Nostalgia Contemporary
Art From the Former USSR*, Centro
per l'Arte Contemporanea Luigi Pecci,
Prato, Italy

*Monuments of Our Discontent: The
Expiration of Place*, 2nd Moscow
Biennial of Contemporary Art. Special
Projects, Winzavod Contemporary
Art Centre, Moscow, Russia

2006
*All Our Tomorrows: The Culture
of Camouflage*, Kunstraum der
Universität Lüneburg, Lüneburg,
Germany

*Fever Variations. The Last
Chapter_Trace Route: Remapping
Global Cities*, 6th Gwangju
Biennial, Gwangju, Republic
of Korea

Face the Unexpected, Museum
am Ostwall; Phoenix Halle,
Dortmund, Germany

2005
Populism, CAC, Vilnius, Lithuania;
National Museum for Art,
Architecture and Design, Oslo,
Norway; Stedelijk Museum,
Amsterdam, The Netherlands;
Frankfurter Kunstverein,
Frankfurt, Germany

Madonna, Kunsthaus Dresden,
Dresden, Germany

*Archive cultures:
Representations*, Museo de Arte
Contemporáneo Español,
Valladolid, Spain

2004
Extended Views, Centre Céramique,
Maastricht, The Netherlands

ISEA2004, Kunstihoone Tallinn Art
Hall, Tallinn, Estonia

*3rd Berlin Biennial for
Contemporary Art*, Berlin,
Germany

Auf Sendung, Galerie für
Zeitgenössische Kunst, Leipzig,
Germany

2003

VJ7/Verbindingen/Jonctions,
Constant vzw, Brussels, Belgium

Neue Freunde, Akademie Schloss
Solitude, Stuttgart, Germany

The Labyrinthine Effect, Australian
Center of Contemporary Art (ACCA),
Melbourne, Australia

The Fate of Alien Modes, Secession,
Vienna, Austria

Money for Nothing, Artspace,
Auckland, New Zealand

2002

Re-direct, haus.0, Künstlerhaus,
Stuttgart, Germany

Voice Session. Karaoke, Akademie
Schloss Solitude, Stuttgart, Germany

Fundamentalisms of a New Order,
Charlottenburg, Copenhagen,
Denmark

documenta 11, Kassel, Germany

Manifesta 4, Frankfurt, Germany

The Music In Me, GAK, Bremen,
Germany

Learning and Singing, Hansapanga
Galerii, Tallinn, Estonia; Center for
Contemporary Art, Moscow, Russia

2001

Self-esteem, CAC, Vilnius, Lithuania

Out of Money, Kulturhuset,
Stockholm, Sweden

Presence Balte, Baltic Art Center
(BAC), Visby, Sweden; Ileana Tounta
Contemporary Art Centre, Athens,
Greece; Metrònom, Barcelona, Spain

2000

Innocent Life, CAC, Vilnius, Lithuania

Duchamp's Suitcase, Arnolfini, Bristol,
United Kingdom

1999

NL-LT, Kunstcentrum Begane Grond,
Utrecht, The Netherlands

Lithuanian Art: 1989-1999, CAC,
Vilnius, Lithuania

Apartment 99, project in private
spaces, Vilnius, Lithuania

**Selected screenings, workshops
and conferences**

2008

*Lo que nos queda / What's left, what
remains?,* VI Simposio Internacional
sobre Teoría de Arte Contemporáneo
(SITAC), Mexico City, Mexico

2007

*Still Here: humour in post-communist
performative video,* Art Space, Sidney,
Australia

*Art Institutions as Catalysts or
Indicators,* Latvian Centre for
Contemporary Art (LCCA), Riga, Latvia

*Land of Human Rights - Artistic
and Activist Strategies of Making
Human Rights Visible,* Rotor,
Graz, Austria

Flux is not dead, it just smells funny,
«Fluxus – Networks Between West
and East», Art Forum Berlin Talks,
Berlin, Germany

2006

Sex and Sadness, Platform Garanti,
Istanbul, Turkey

Sex and Sadness, Exploding
Television – Satellite of Love, Witte
de With, International Film Festival,
Rotterdam, The Netherlands

2005

Femme Totale, International Film
Festival, Dortmund, Germany

Shifting Boundaries, Royal University
College of Fine Arts, Stockholm,
Sweden

Appendix. Kiss the Frog!, The National
Museum, the National Gallery, Oslo,
Norway

*Role of the museums of
contemporary art,* Museum
of Contemporary Art (MOCA),
Belgrade, Serbia

*Navigating Globalisation: Stability,
Fluidity, and Friction,* Norwegian
University of Science and Technology,
Trondheim, Norway

2004

Who If Not We, Stedelijk Museum,
Amsterdam, The Netherlands

Art. What Is It Good For?, Dartington
College of Arts, Totnes, United
Kingdom

Klangraum, Festival of Contemporary
Music, Stuttgart, Germany

Social Affairs, Den Haag, The
Netherlands

Show Unit, Riksutställningar,
Sweden

2003
It Is Hard to Touch the Real,
Kunstverein, Munich, Germany

2002
Darmstadt University of Applied
Sciences, Darmstadt, Germany

AWID's 9th International Forum,
Guadalajara, Mexico

Transmediale Salon, Podewil, Berlin,
Germany

International Festival of New Cinema
and New Media, Montreal, Canada

Transat Video, Caen, France

48th International Short Film
Festival, Oberhausen, Germany

Projects

2007
Villa Lituania: a study of the
mechanisms constructing the last
occupied territory (of Lithuania)
through a set of events featuring
pigeon racing, the development of
pavilion architecture and political
encounters.

2005 - ongoing
Pro-test Lab: a space and archive of
various protest forms against the
corporate privatisation of public
space; and a case study of the
destruction of the Lietuva cinema –
the largest pavilion-type example of
Soviet modernist architecture in
Lithuania.

2003 - ongoing
Druzba. A Friendship: a project
constructed as a device for reading

the psycho-geography of the oil
network (Druzba: the biggest oil
pipeline build by the Soviets) and for
studying the flows and energies
produced through the disintegrating
infrastructure of power.

2002-2004
Ruta Remake: a project (and
instrument) that studies the social
construction of the female voice,
weaving together layers of gender,
technology, performance
and fashion.

RAM: Re-Approaching New Media,
the intersecting networks of CRAC
(Sweden), Atelier Nord (Norway),
E-Media Centre (Estonia), Olento
(Finland), RIXC (Latvia) and VILMA
(Lithuania).

www.transaction.lt: an ongoing web
archive and tool for the *Transaction*
project, with interviews, texts, images
and films.

2000-2004
Transaction: a project that
describes the role of the victim via
the history of the media, inviting
psychiatrists, filmmakers and
female intellectuals to participate
in a three-way dialogue.

1998-1999
tvvv.plotas: a TV project developed
as a collaborative platform and
production space for institutional
critique on the national TV channel,
combining the tools of
broadcasting, net-casting and
meetings in a physical space.

1995-1997
*Ground Control: Technology
and Utopia*: book, website and

exhibition; an exchange between
British and Lithuanian artists; a
collaboration between Beaconsfield,
London and Jutempus, Vilnius.

Awards, fellowships and grants

2007
Lithuanian National Prize for the
achievements in the arts and culture

Honorable Mention for a national
pavilion at the Venice Biennale, Italy

2006
Prize for the Best International
Artist at the Gwangju Biennial,
Gwangju, Republic of Korea

2003
International Studio Programme
grant, Office for Contemporary
Art (OCA), Oslo, Norway

2002
International Residency Programme
Fellowship, Akademie Schloss
Solitude, Stuttgart, Germany

2001
IASPIS, Stockholm, Sweden

Selected bibliography

Exhibition catalogues
and books

2008
Enwezor, Okwui (ed.): *Archive Fever:
Uses of the Document in
Contemporary Art*. New York:
ICP/Steidl [exh. cat.]

Urbonas, Nomeda & Gediminas:
Devices for action.

Museu d'Art Contemporani de Barcelona, Barcelona [exh. cat.]

Urbonas, Nomeda & Gediminas; Simon Rees (ed.): *Villa Lituania*. Berlin, New York: Sternberg Press

2007
Misiano, Viktor (ed.): *Progressive Nostalgia*. Prato: Luigi Pecci Centre for Contemporary Art [exh. cat.]

Moisdon, Stephanie; Obrist, Hans Urich (eds.): ∞ – *The History of a Decade That Has Not Yet Been Named*. Lyon: 9th Lyon Biennial of Contemporary Art [exh. cat.]

Stegmann, Petra (ed.): *Fluxus East: Fluxus Networks in Central Eastern Europe*. Berlin: Künstlerhaus Bethanien [exh. cat.]

Think With the Senses – Feel with the Mind. Venice: 52nd Venice Biennale [exh. cat.]

2006
Arns, Inke; Wettengl, Kurt (eds.): *Mit Allem Rechnen / Face the Unexpected*. Frankfurt: Revolver [exh. cat.]

Bauman, Zygmunt: *Liquid Life*. Cambridge: Polity Press

Ricupero, Cristina: "The Last Chapter – Trace Route: Remapping Global Cities", *Fever Variations*. Gwangju: 6th Gwangju Biennial [exh. cat.]

2005
Blasco Gallardo, Jorge (ed.): *Culturas de archivo*, vol. 2. Valladolid: Junta de Castilla y León

Larsen, Lars Bang; Ricupero, Cristina; Schafhausen, Nicolaus (eds.): *The Populism Catalogue*. Helsinki and New York: NIFCA and Lukas & Sternberg [exh.cat.]

Mennicke, Christiane (ed.): *Madonna*. Dresden: Kunsthaus Dresden [exh. cat.]

Miles, Malcolm; Hall, Tim (eds.): *Interventions*. Bristol: Intellect Books

Steiner, Barbara; Schafer, Julia; Koralova, Ilina (eds.): *Kulturelle Territorien / Cultural Territories*. Cologne: Walter Konig [exh. cat.]

Zukauskaite, Audrone; Malasauskas, Raimundas; Blasco Gallardo, Jorge (eds.): *Emisija/ Emission*. Vilnius: CAC [exh. cat.]

2004
Balkema, Annette W.; Slager, Henk (eds.): *Artistic Research*. Amsterdam: Lier en Boog; Series of Philosophy of Art and Art Theory, vol. 18

Bauer, Ute Meta (ed.): *Komplex Berlin*. Berlin: 3rd Berlin Biennial of Contemporary Art [exh. cat.]

Lovejoy, Margot: *Digital Currents: Art in the Electronic Age*. London / New York: Routledge

Schuijren, Jan; Van Den Boom, Bart: *Extended Views*. Maastricht: Centre Céramique [exh. cat.]

Zaya, Octavio: *FILES*, Valladolid: Junta de Castilla y León and Museo de Arte Contemporáneo de Castilla y León

ISEA 2004: International Symposium on Electronic Art [exh. cat.]

2003
Engberg, Juliana (ed.): *The Labyrinthine Effect*. Melbourne: ACCA [exh. cat.]

Ruhm, Constanze (ed.): *The Fate of Alien Modes*. Vienna: Secession [exh. cat.]

Neue Freunde: Art, Science and Business. Stuttgart: Akademie Schloss Solitude

Substream. Oslo: Kunstnernes Hus [exh. cat.]

2002
Brandt, Charlotte; Larsen, Lars Bang; Ricupero, Cristina (eds.): *Fundamentalisms of the New Order*. Helsinki, Copenhagen and New York: NIFCA, Charlottenborg and Lukas & Sternberg [exh. cat.]

documenta [ed.]: *Documenta11_ Platform5*. Kassel: Documenta GmbH and Hatje Cantz [exh. cat.]

Manifesta 4. Frankfurt: Manifesta and Hatje Cantz [exh.cat.]

Money. Stockholm: CRAC [exh. cat.]

Self-esteem. Vilnius: CAC [exh. cat.]

2001
Pousette, Johan (ed.): *Presence Balte*. Stockholm: BAC, [exh. cat.]

Rosenfeld, Alla; T. Dodge, Norton: *Art of the Baltics: The Struggle for Freedom of Artistic Expression Under the Soviets*. Piscataway: New Jersey Rutgers University Press, p. 361

Strangers & Paradise, FROM #3.
Rotterdam: Witte de With Centre
for Contemporary Art

1999
Jaukkuri, Maaretta (ed.); Bauman,
Zygmunt; Blom, Ina: *Artscape
Nordland.* Kulturetaten: Nordland
Fylkeskommune

*Changing the System? Artists talk
about their practice.* Rotterdam:
Witte de With Centre for
Contemporary Art; Helsinki: NIFCA

Lietuvos Daile 1989-1999. CAC,
Vilnius [exh. cat.]

1998
Warr, Tracey (ed.): *Sutemos /
Twilight.* Vilnius: CAC [exh. cat.]

1997
*Ground Control: Technology
and Utopia.* London: Black Dog
Publishing

Reviews and articles

2007
Piccoli, Cloe: "Gediminas e Nomeda
Urbonas", *L'Uomo Vogue*, no. 381
(May-June)

Hofer, Gustav: "Free like birds.
Venise, le 52ème Biennale", *Arte TV
blog* (June)

Gabri, Renne: "Lithuania: skipping
over history", *DOMUS web* (8 June)

Heiser, Joerg: "Die Lucken zwischen
den Bildern", *Suddeutsche Zeitung*,
no. 130 (9-10 June)

Jurenaite, Raminta: "The 52nd
Venice Biennial: Art as a Mirror
of Global Conflicts and Simply Art",
Kulturos barai, no. 7 (July), pp. 35-41

Rees, Simon: "Vanagas tarp balandziu:
Nomedos ir Gedimino Urbonu *Villa
Lituania* 52-ojoje Venecijos Bienaleje",
Siaures Atenai, no. 21 (21 July)

2005
Kuzma, Marta: "On the Shoulders of
Giants", *Flash Art* (January-February)

Narusyte, Agne: «Nomeda and
Gediminas Urbonas: The Voice from
the Black Box», *Daile*, no. 1/2005

Lovink, Geert: "The Politics of
a New Media Space Inside the
Lietuva (Soviet) Cinema", *Institute
of Network Cultures* (25 June)

Harrison, Nell: "The End of the
Lietuva. The Death of Community
Culture", *The Baltic Times* (9 July)

Juodelyte, Karina: "The Modern
Renaissance of Rue", *The Baltic
Times* (3 August)

2004
Batz, Oliver; Schafer, Andre:
"Vilnius et la passion pour le centre
de l'Europe", *ARTE TV* (1 May)

Zukauskaite, Audrone;
Malasauskas, Raimundas: "Penkios
temos ir issetines variacijos",
Siaures Atenai, no. 31 (21 August)

Vanhala, Jari-Pekka: "La vida en
tiempos de transparencia", *EXIT
Express*, no. 7 (15 November)

2003
Strommen, Marit: "Interview with
N ir G Urbonai", *Klassenkampen*
(11 August)

Kreivyte, Laima: "Kam reikalinga
mediju laboratorija, interviu su
N ir G Urbonais", *7 meno dienos*
(26 September)

2002
Kreivyte, Laima: "Budapest
transakcions", *7 meno dienos*
(1 February)

Schnurr, Eva-Maria: "Nomeda und
Gediminas Urbonas: Transaction-
Projekt", *Die Tageszeitung*
(6 September)

Tan, Pelin: "Global Resistance Now",
NEID, no. 9

2000
Mclaren, Duncan: "A Mixed Bag
From the Curators' Bulging
Suitcase", *Independent*, no. 38
(27 August)

Kachelriess, Andrea: "Irgendwie
prädestiniert für die opferrolle",
Stuttgarter Nachrichten
(8 November)

1999
Kincinaitis, Virginijus: "Erotika arba
vieno termino menopauze", *Daile*,
no. 1/99

Urbonas, Nomeda & Gediminas:
"tvvv.plotas statement", *Acoustic
Space*, no. 2, E-LAB

Trilupaityte, Skaidra: "Interview
with jutempus", *7 meno dienos*
(27 August)

1998
Hogsbro Ostergaard, Cecilie:
"Twilight", *Ojebliket*, no. 35 (April)

LIST OF WORKS IN THE EXHIBITION

TRANSACTION (2000-2004)

This project was presented for the first time at Witte de With, Rotterdam. It has subsequently been developed at haus.0 Künstlerhaus, Stuttgart; IASPIS, Stockholm; the Ludwig Museum, Budapest; Manifesta 4, Frankfurt; documenta 11, Kassel; the Sprengel Museum, Hanover; GzfK, Leipzig; the Junta de Castilla y León, Valladolid; the International Center of Photography, New York.

Installation materials: filmed interviews with women and sessions with psychiatrists; film archive and voice archive material, slide collection, victim dress

Films:

> *Interviews With Women About Films*, 2000
> Mini DV transferred to DVD, colour, sound, English subtitles, 30'

> Film archive (compilation used at the psychiatrists' session), 2000
> Mini DV transferred to DVD, b/w, sound, English subtitles, 27'

> *Psychiatrists' Session*, 2000
> Psychotherapy room, Mental Health Centre, Vilnius
> Mini DV transferred to DVD, colour, sound, English subtitles, 27'

> *Interviews With Women About Voice*, 2002
> Mini DV transferred to DVD, colour, sound, English subtitles, 23'

> *Psychiatrists' Session*, 2002
> Psychotherapy room, Mental Health Centre, Vilnius
> Mini DV transferred to DVD, colour, sound, English subtitles, 27'

Film archive: collection of 60 titles from the period 1947-1997. Lithuanian Film Studios production

Slide collection, 2000: collection of 160 slides – stills from documentary and fiction films and street life

Victim dress, 2008: fictional reconstruction of a dress that partisan Maryte Melnikaite wears in the execution scene; nabuk, silk, size 38

Participants: Grazina Arlickaite, film researcher; Daiva Budraityte, musicologist; Ausrine Burneikiene, lawyer; Zita Cepaite, writer; Solveiga Daugirdaite, literary critic; Viktorija Daujotyte, philologist; Patricija Droblyte, philosopher; Karina Firkaviciute, musicologist; Jolanta Gelumbeckaite, philologist; Ruta Gostautiene, musicologist; Erika Grigoraviciene, art critic; Veronika Janatjeva, musicologist; Margarita Jankauskaite, art historian; Rasa Kalinauskaite, journalist; Zita Kelmickaite, musicologist; Laima Kreivyte, art critic; Egle Laumenskaite, sociologist; Indre Mackeviciute, student, Dalia Marcinkeviciene, historian; Marija-Ausrine Pavilioniene, philologist; Zivile Pipinyte, film critic; Rima Praspaliauskiene, historian; Birute Purvaneckaite, student; Giedre Purvaneckiene, educator; Daiva Raciunaite, musicologist; Daiva Sabaseviciene, theatre critic; Ugne Sipariene, journalist; Lolita Sutkaitiene, journalist; Marta Vosiliute, stage designer; Anele Vosiliute, sociologist; Sonata Zalneraviciute, music historian and film critic; Audrone Zukauskaite, philosopher

Translation: Angela Butterstein, Simonas Sorys

Archive images: Lithuanian Central State Archives, AB Lietuvos Kinas, Lithuanian Radio and Television

Acknowledgements: Virginija Aleksejunaite, Sara Arhenius, Fareed Armaly, Darius Bagdziunas, Jorge Blasco Gallardo, Ute Meta Bauer, Darius Ciuta, Nuria Enguita Mayo, Okwui Enwezor, Marius Gabrijolavicius, Gaumina, Saule Griciute, Dora Hegyi, Bartomeu Marí, Zivile Pipinyte, Asta Plechaviciute, Johan Pousette, Laurence Rassel, Cristina Ricupero, Constanze Ruhm, Julia Schafer, Inka Schube, Gediminas Stoskus, Lolita Sutkaitiene, Dalia and Saulius Svirmickas, Paulius Turskis, Marius Vaupsas, Aiste Zalatoriute

RUTA REMAKE (2002-2004)

This project was presented for the first time at the haus. 0 Künstlerhaus, Stuttgart, and supported by the Akademie Schloss Solitude. It has subsequently been developed at Secession, Vienna; the 3rd Berlin Biennial for Contemporary Art, Berlin; the Künsthaus, Dresden; the Kunstnernes Hus, Oslo; the CAC, Vílnius.

Installation materials: voice archive, sign system, light system, light box, curtain, Theramidi, video, CD, fashion collection

Voice archive: collection of samples of female voices from Lithuanian media sources. Sound composition: Mail Maier (Jens Neumaier and Maik Alemany). Programming: David Beltran, 2008

Voice Lab, live performance (CD): Otto Kränzler,
Laura Aurylaite, Giedre Gaizauskaite, Ugne Giedraityte,
Juste Janulyte, Laima Jedenkute, Egidija Medeiksaite,
Erika Siekstelyte, Ruta Vitkauskaite, 2004

Sign system: 9 posters, cotton, 52 x 400 cm

Performance (film): pianist Guoda Gedvilaite
playing *Ruta Remake;* mini DV transferred to DVD,
colour, sound, 2002

Camouflage pattern and fashion collection: Nomeda
& Gediminas Urbonas, with the collaboration of Sandra
Straukaite; edition of 10 unisex samples, 100% linen,
various sizes, 2004

Curtain: 100 % linen, 550 x 1,800 cm, 2002

Light box: documentary film still, acrylic glass,
medium-density fibreboard, 50 x 100 cm, 2008

Translation: Angela Butterstein, Simonas Sorys

Archive images and sounds: Lithuanian Central State
Archives, Lithuanian Radio and Television

Acknowledgements: Fareed Armaly, Atle Barcley,
Rimantas Baumilas, Roman Fronckevic, Tania Galanto,
Steven Greenwood, Jean-Baptiste Joly, Inghild Karlsen,
Gediminas Kavaliauskas, Skaiste Kerpyte, Karolis Klimka,
Edmundas Kolevaitis, Otto Kränzler, Rudolfas Levulis,
Christiane Mennicke, Linas Paulauskis, Marius Plitninkas,
Ruta Rudvalyte, Constanze Ruhm, Gediminas Stoskus,
Saulius Svirmickas, Ula Tornau, Dalius Zizys; APM
kompiuteriai, Atelier Nord, and the Klasikine tekstile,
Kaunas

DRUZBA (2003 - ongoing)

This project was presented for the first time at the *Art,
Science and Business* programme at the Schloss Solitude,
Stuttgart and has subsequently been shown at the 9th Lyon
Biennial of Contemporary Art.

Installation materials: posters, black banners, pieces
of carpeting, film archive material, performance

Translation: Angela Butterstein, Simonas Sorys

Archive images: Lithuanian Central State Archives

Poster design: NODE Berlin (Anders Hofgaard, Vladimir
Llovet Casademont, Serge Rompza)

Acknowledgements: Vytautas Bikneris, Ivan Dolozinsky,
Jean-Baptiste Joly, Arturas Jonkus, Giedrius Karsokas,
Vytautas V.Landsbergis, Natasa Petresin, Zivile Pipinyte,
Darius Silas, Kestutis Stoskus, Gediminas Stoskus,
Gabriele Urbonaite, Raimundas Variakojis, Marius Vaupsas,
Peter Zilahy, Dalius Zizys

PRO-TEST LAB (2005 - ongoing)

This project was presented for the first time at the
Populism exhibition, NIFCA. It has subsequently been
developed at the Museum am Ostwall and Phoenix Halle,
Dortmund; the 6th Gwangju Biennial, Republic of Korea;
Fluxus East exhibition at the Künstlerhaus Bethanien,
Berlin; the CAC, Vilnius; Bunkier Stuky, Krakow; the Ludwig
Museum, Budapest.

Installation materials: films and video performances,
architecture models, wallpaper, fashion collection, reader,
posters, banners

Films:

VIP Market, 2005
Mini DV transferred to DVD, colour, sound, 3′

Sold Out, 2005
Mini DV transferred to DVD, colour, sound, 14′ 20″

America Will Help Us, 2005
Mini DV transferred to DVD, colour, sound, 2′

Dogs Barking Will Not Disturb the Clouds, 2005
Mini DV transferred to DVD, colour, sound, 2′

Human Chain of Swimming Enthusiasts, 2005
Mini DV transferred to DVD, colour, sound, 3′

Cinemas That Have Disappeared, 2005
Mini DV transferred to DVD, colour, 5′

Lietuva. Sold Out, 2006
Mini DV transferred to DVD, colour, sound, 17′

Pro-test Lab Slide Show, 2007
Mini DV transferred to DVD, colour, 20′ 27″

*The Exploration of Public Space: Vertical
and Horizontal Values,* 2007; mini DV transferred to DVD,
colour, sound, 5′ 30″

Collection for work and rebellion, 2004-2006
In collaboration with Sandra Straukaite

Team Lietuva scarves, 2006
Limited edition of 100 b/w, 100 colour; wool and polyester

Camera: Giedrius Ilgunas, Nomeda & Gediminas Urbonas

Architecture models: Julija Ksivickaite and ASK, Architecture Students Club

Translation: Angela Butterstein, Catherine Hemelryk, Simon Rees, Simonas Sorys

Archive images: Lithuanian Central State Archives and *Pro-test Lab* Archive

Acknowledgements: Inke Arns and Kurt Wettengl, Lars Bang Larsen, Atle Barcley, Kristin Bergaust, Roman Fronckevic, Milda Grabauskaite, Sabina Grinceviciute, Lolita Jablonskiene, Rytis Juodeika, Skaiste Kerpyte, Agne Kreismontaite, Aurelija Maknyte, Gintautas Mazeikis, Shaheen Merali, Viktor Misiano, Renata Petrauskaite, Ruta Pileckaite, Bartos Polonski, Vida Ramaskiene, Cristina Ricupero, Akvile Rimantaite, Petra Stegmann, Gediminas Stoskus, Saulius Svirmickas, Paulius Turskis, Ruta Valiunaite, Dalius Zizys; APM kompiuteriai, Atelier Nord, and the *For Lithuania without quotation marks* community movement

VILLA LITUANIA (2007)

This project was commissioned for the Lithuanian Pavilion at the 52nd Venice Biennale.

Installation materials: film archive and video performances, architecture model, crystal trophies, posters, pins, diplomas, fashion collection, book

Film archive and video performances:

Ambassador in Exile, 2007
Mini DV transferred to DVD, colour, sound, 11' 26"

Defending the Loft, 2007
Mini DV transferred to DVD, colour, sound, 7' 48"

Rehearsal at the Palace of Culture and Sports, 2007
Mini DV transferred to DVD, colour, sound, 7' 31"

Defending the Villa. Graffiti, 2007
Mini DV transferred to DVD, colour, sound, 5' 48"

Defending the Villa. The Latvians, 2007
Mini DV transferred to DVD, B&W, sound, 1' 58"

Architecture Workshop (Heart and Hearth), 2007
Mini DV transferred to DVD, B&W, sound, 1' 18"

Calling the Russians, 2007
Mini DV transferred to DVD, colour, sound, 1' 37"

Ambassador's Song, 2007
Mini DV transferred to DVD, colour, sound, 3' 32"

Villa Lituania pigeon loft model, 2007
Medium-density fibreboard, scale 1:1, 3.5 x 5 x 4.5 m

Vitrine, 2007
Acrylic glass, medium-density fibreboard, 100 x 180 m

Villa Lituania International Pigeon Race (film), 2007
Mini DV transferred to DVD, colour, sound, 4'

Limited edition: pigeon fancier's waterproof, book bags, diplomas, pins; various materials, various sizes

Villa Lituania trophies, 2007
Series of 4 trophies, 50 x 80 cm; 1 trophy 200 x 200 cm; crystal vases

Villa Lituania posters, 2007. Offset print, 70 x 100 cm

Camera: Giedrius Ilgunas, Nomeda & Gediminas Urbonas

Architecture assistant: Julija Ksivickaite

Translation: Catherine Hemelryk, Simon Rees

Archive images: Lithuanian Central State Archives, Lozoraitis Family Archive, Saulius Kubilius Family Archive

Poster design: NODE Berlin (Anders Hofgaard, Vladimir Llovet Casademont, Serge Rompza)

Fashion collection: Nomeda & Gediminas Urbonas with the collaboration of Sandra Straukaite

Acknowledgements: Gorelov Vladimir Albertovitch, Algirdas Baniulis, Atle Barcley, Danute Butkiene, Mario Cutuli, Roman Fronckevic, Massimiliano Fuksas, Lolita Jablonskiene, Giedre Jankeviciute, Saulius Kubilius, Kestutis Kuizinas, Sondra Litvaityte, Kazys Lozoraitis, Agne Mackeviciute, Aurelija Maknyte, Gediminas Meiliunas, Regina Moller, Vytautas Narbutas, Andrea Nyiro and Eros Carboni, Cristina Ricupero, Vytautas Sabaliauskas, Algirdas Saudargas, Gediminas Stoskus, Saulius Svirmickas, Ona Volungeviciute, Dalius Zizys; APM kompiuteriai, Atelier Nord, the Italian Champion's Group, the Movement for the Renewal of the FCI Lithuanian Sport Pigeon Federation, the *For Lithuania without quotation marks* community movement, and the staff of the CAC

MACBA 2008

Founding Companies
Agrolimen
Fundació AGBAR
BBVA
"la Caixa"
Cementos Molins
Cobega
Comsa
El País
El Periódico de Catalunya
Freixenet
Fundació Abertis
Fundació Banc Sabadell
Fundació Jesús Serra
Fundació Puig
Gas Natural SDG
Grupo Planeta
La Vanguardia
Uniland Cementera

Honorary Members
Repsol YPF
Reinhard i Ute Onnasch

Major Benefactors
Daniel Cordier
Juan March Delgado
Havas Media
Jorge Oteiza
Leopoldo Rodés Castañé
José Antonio Rumeu y de Delás
Fundación Bertrán
Sara Lee Corporation

Corporate Sponsors
Caixa Penedès
Diesel
Epson Ibérica S.A.U.
ISS Facility Services

Corporate Benefactors
El Consorci de la Zona Franca
El Corte Inglés
Fundación Telefónica

Corporate Protectors
Fundación Cultural Banesto
RACC Club
Random House Mondadori

Corporate Contributors
Alpino
Basi
Banco Espírito Santo
Bodegues Sumarroca
Bowers & Wilkins

Cadena Ser
Catalunya Ràdio
Cerveses Moritz
Ernst & Young
Ferrater Campins Morales
Fundació Miguel Torres
Fundació Antoni Serra Santamans
Fundació Privada Damm
Grupo Esteve
Illycaffè
Instituto Javier de Benito
JP Morgan
KPMG
Lombard Odier Darier Hentsch & CIE.
Obrascón Huarte Laín -OHL-
Meridia Capital
Rodés & Sala, Abogados
ScannerFM.com
Screen projects – LOOP
Associació de galeristas Artbarcelona
Wonderland

Corporate Partners
Deloitte
Equipo Singular
Fundación Baruch Spinoza
Fundación Cuatrecasas
Garrigues Advocats i Assessors
  Tributaris
Gràfiques Pacífic
Grand Hotel Central
Vigilancia y Sistemas de Seguridad
  (VSS)

Individual Benefactors
María Entrecanales Franco
Lady Jinty Latymer
Enrique Ordóñez Las Heras
Alfonso Pons Soler
Maria Reig Moles
José Rodríguez-Spiteri Palazuelo

Individual Protectors
Elena Calderón de Oya
CAL CEGO. Col·lecció d'Art
  Contemporani
Bruno Figueras
Liliana Godia Guardiola
Pedro de Esteban Ferrer
Dinath de Grandi
Hubert de Wangen
José Mª Juncadella Salisachs
Pere Portabella i Ràfols
Josep Suñol Soler

Individual Contributors
M. Carmen Buqueras de Riera
Josep M. Català i Virgili

Individual Contributors
M. Carmen Buqueras de Riera
Josep M. Català i Virgili
Federico Correa
Eva de Vilallonga
Ventura Garcés Bruses
Ramón Negra
Jordi Soley i Mas
Marta Uriach i Torelló
Mercedes Vilá Recolons

Contemporary Circle
Manuel Curtichs Pérez-Villamil
Fanny de Castro
Dr. Mario Deus
Anna Esteve Cruella
Solita Mora
Javier Sagarra
Ernesto Ventós Omedes

El Taller de la Fundació MACBA
Manuel Barbié Nogaret
José Luis Blanco Ruiz
Berta Caldentey Cabré
Eulàlia Caspar
Cristina Castañer Sauras
Pilar Cortada Boada
Mª José de Esteban Ferrer
José Mª de Villalonga
María Entrecanales Franco
Josep Gaspart i Bueno
Ezequiel Giró Amigó
Teresa Guardans de Waldburg
Pilar Líbano Daurella
Juan Lladó Arburúa
Álvaro López Lamadrid
Ignacio Malet Perdigó
Jaime Malet Perdigó
Ignacio Mas de Xaxàs Faus
Mercedes Mas de Xaxàs Faus
Àngels Miquel i Vilanova
Jordi Prenafeta
Sara Puig Alsina
Jordi Pujol Ferrusola
Alfonso Rodés Vilá
Pol Rovira Mascort
Francesc Surroca Cabeza
Tomás Tarruella Esteva
Álvaro Vilá Recolons

Director
Ainhoa Grandes Massa

Fundraising Department
Isabel Crespo Martínez
Ariadna Delgado Pons

Secretariat and Administration
Marisa Avillà Plaza

This book has been published on the occasion of the exhibition *Nomeda & Gediminas Urbonas. Devices for action*, showed at the Museu d'Art Contemporani de Barcelona from 14 March to 15 June 2008.

Acknowledgements: David Beltran, Julija Ksivickaite, Maik Maier (Jens Neumaier & Maik Alemany), NODE Berlin (Anders Hofgaard, Vladimir Llovet Casademon, Serge Rompza), Simon Rees, Simonas Sorys, Gediminas Stoskus, Kestutis Stoskus, Sandra Straukaite

Sponsor

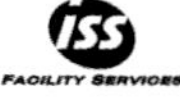

Communication Sponsor

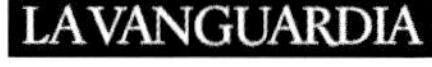

With the support of

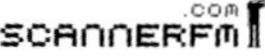

EXHIBITION

Curator
Bartomeu Marí

Head of Production
Anna Borrell

Coordination
Neus Miró

Registrar
Ariadna Robert i Casasayas
Aída Roger de la Peña

Assistant of Registrar
Patricia Quesada

Conservation
Lluís Roqué
Xavier Rossell

Architecture
Isabel Bachs
Eva Font

Audiovisual Technicians
Miquel Giner
Jordi Martínez
Albert Toda

PUBLICATION

Edition
Clara Plasencia

Coordination
Ester Capdevila

Photo Research
Dolores Acebal

Graphic Design
Lali Almonacid

Translation and Proofreading
Paul Hammond

Editorial Assistance
Pere Bramon
Neil Charlton
Simon Rees

Pre-printing
Cousins

Printing
SYL Creaciones gráficas
y publicitarias, SA

Publisher
Museu d'Art Contemporani
de Barcelona
Plaça dels Àngels, 1
08001 Barcelona (Spain)
t:+ 34 93 412 08 10
f:+ 34 93 412 46 02
www.macba.es

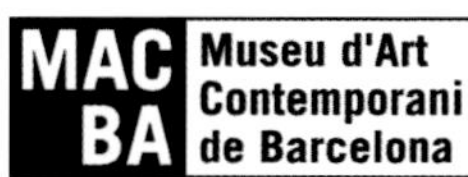

Distribution
ACTAR - D
Roca i Batlle, 2-4
08023 Barcelona (Spain)
office@actar-d.com
t:+ 34 93 418 77 59
f:+ 34 93 418 67 07
www.actar-d.com

© edition: Museu d'Art Contemporani de Barcelona, 2008
© texts: the authors, 2008
© works: Nomeda & Gediminas Urbonas, VEGAP, Barcelona, 2008
© photographs: Tony Coll, CUBBYSLOFT.COM, Lithuanian Central State Archives, Lozoraitis Family Archive, Saulius Kubilius Family Archive

ISBN: 978-84-89771-65-9
DL: 19422-08

Typography: Apex
Paper: Savile Row Plain, 300 g; Tatami White, 135 g; Savile Row Plain, 100 g (Fedrigoni)